PITTSBURGH THEOLOGICAL

Accession no   LG
        802707   01

STER COLLEGE LIBRARY

36 GEORGE STREET

EDINBURGH EH2 2LQ.
(TEL: 031 - 225 - 4703)

11

The New Testament and Structuralism

Library of Congress Cataloging in Publication Data
Main entry under title:

The New Testament and structuralism.

    (Pittsburgh theological monograph series ; 11)
   "Originally published in 1971 as number 22 (June)
issue of Langages, entitled Sémiotique narrative: récits
Bibliques."
   Bibliography: p.
   Includes index.
   1. Bible. N. T.--Criticism, Textual. 2. Struc-
turalism (Literary analysis) I. Galland, Corina.
II. Johnson, Alfred M., 1942-   III. Series.
BS2325.N48   225.6   76-25447
ISBN 0-915138-13-1

THE NEW TESTAMENT AND STRUCTURALISM

A Collection of Essays by
Corina Galland, Claude Chabrol,
Guy Vuillod, Louis Marin
and Edgar Haulotte

CHESTER COLLEGE

ACC. No.   DEPT. X

802707

CLASS No.

225.6 JOH

LIBRARY

Edited and Translated
by
Alfred M. Johnson, Jr.

THE PICKWICK PRESS
Pittsburgh, Pennsylvania
1976

Originally published in 1971 as Number 22 (June)
issue of LANGAGES, entitled: "Sémiotique Narrative: Récits Bibliques". Copyright 1971, Librairie Marcel DIDIER et Librairie LAROUSSE.

By permission of Centre Protestant d'Études de
Genève, the article by Corina Galland on "An
Introduction to the Method of A. J. Greimas"
is added to this collection of essays. This
article also appeared in *Etudes Theologiques
et Religieuses*, 48 (#1, 1973), 35-48.

Translation copyright © 1976
by The Pickwick Press
Pittsburgh, Pennsylvania 15213

CONTENTS

iii

INTRODUCTION:
THE NEW TESTAMENT AND STRUCTURALISM

This work is not intended to be an introductory work on
the subject of the relationships between those methods known
collectively and somewhat inaccurately as "structuralism" and
the New Testament. Instead these articles ·present a more
mature, coherent, and advanced program primarily by two "structuralists" (or more precisely semioticians or semiologists) who
have been described as "the most subtle, rich, and complex" of
them all. Therefore, the newcomer to this subject is advised
to read several introductory works on this subject before attempting to approach these articles. For those readers who
wish an excellent brief introduction, the absolute minimum
reading list might be composed of the translation of the
latest introduction to the *Russian* edition of Propp's *Morphology of the Folktale* by E. M. Meletinsky ("Structural-
Typological Study of the Folktale", *Genre* 4 [3, 1971], 249-
279) and of course the book which began it all, Vladimir
Propp's, *The Morphology of the Folktale*, 2nd ed., trans. by
Lawrence Scott, Austin: University of Texas Press, 1968.
For a more specific application to the Bible, the reader
may also want to read my earlier translation of R. Barthes
et al., Structural Analysis and Biblical Exegesis, Pittsburgh: Pickwick Press, 1974. The reader will find an extensive bibliography therein for further reading.

The present collection of articles was mainly taken
from the French linguistic journal *Langages* 22 (June, 1971).

But one article from that collection (E. R. Leach, "La Genèse comme mythe", 12-23) has been excised because it was originally published in English (*Discovery* 23 [May, 1962]) and has also been reprinted in E. R. Leach, *Genesis as Myth*, London: Jonathan Cape, 1969, 7-24. The present collection has been edited to reflect this omission without, however, omitting anything of value (see pp. 43-44, n. 15 below).

In order to increase the usefulness of this collection, I have added to the *Langages* 22 collection the best introduction to the method of A. J. Greimas (by Corina Galland) I could find. This was done because much of the work of Chabrol and Marin, in particular, is based on the work of Greimas and unfortunately none of the major works by Greimas are now available in English, e.g. especially his *Sémantique structurale* and *Du sens*. It is hoped that this introduction will help fill this void until these two books appear in translation.

It should also be noted that only two years after it appeared, the *Langages* 22 collection was translated and published in German with the title: *Erzählende Semiotik nach Berichten der Bibel*, eds. C. Chabrol and L. Marin, trans. K. H. Neufeld, Munich: Kösel, 1973. Likewise the original title of the *Langages* 22 collection was "Sémiotique Narrative: Récits Bibliques", but because of the changes noted above and the desire to use a more widely recognizable title, I have taken the liberty of entitling this collection: *The New Testament and Structuralism*.

A few remarks should be made about some translation problems which appeared in this collection. Unlike my first translation in this field (i.e. *Structural Analysis and*

Biblical Exegesis), when there were very few English precedents for the French structuralist terms, a flood of books
and articles have now appeared which have greatly assisted
me in the task at hand. In particular I should mention the
appearance of the SBL journal *Semeia* which has been most
helpful. Thus although I have minor misgivings at several
points in the choices made, I have accepted these precedents
because (according to Saussure and the structuralists) one
must use the accepted usage or risk being misunderstood.
The reader should note, however, that two French terms in
particular in this collection, *écriture* and *ouverture* still
created some problems. I have sometimes translated the first
term by "writing" and sometimes by "scripture", but the
reader should note that although these terms possess quite
distinct and different significations in English, they are
synonymous in French. This is important because much of the
logic in these articles is based on an equivalence between
these two terms. A similar problem existed with respect to
the French word *ouverture* which has sometimes been translated "opening" (when it was contrasted with the French word
clôture meaning "closure" or "closing") and sometimes "overture" (when it possessed the musical or literary meaning of
an overture or introduction). Again the reader must remember
that despite the differences which exist in English between
an "opening" and "overture" that these terms are synonymous
in French. There were other similar problems, as there always are in translation when two language "nets" have to be
matched as closely as possible. However, this problem is
exacerbated here because of the subtlety of the wordplays
here. Finally, as in all my other translation, I have included the original pagination of the French articles in

the text by brackets, e.g. [p. 10]. Moreover, a number of errors have been detected and corrected in the original *Langages* 22 collection (especially in the page references back and forth between the different articles).

As my contribution to this collection, I have compiled a glossary of Formalist and Structuralist technical terms for use by the reader. To my knowledge this is the first attempt to present such a list and like all pioneering attempts it also suffers from a lack of guidance that the existence of precedents would produce.

In conclusion, I should add that this work has been sent to Prof. Louis Marin at Johns Hopkins University for his comments and corrections. He informs me that he is generally pleased with these translations, but his busy schedule may prevent him from making the specific changes he would like before this work goes to press. We will try, however, to include as many of the changes and additions he desires before publication. I would like to thank him, however, for reading over his own articles and as many of the others as his time permitted.

I must also thank those others who have assisted me in preparing this collection of articles for publication. First and foremost, I must express my gratitude to Mrs. Eunice M. Paul whom I consulted whenever I became totally frustrated with some difficult phrase or sentence. Secondly, I must thank Mr. Dikran Y. Hadidian, the general editor of this series, whose constant advice, guidance, and help I most appreciate. Likewise my typist, Ms. Kathy Herrin, deserves much credit for her careful work. (The reader might also like to know that the covers of this book were created by Ms. JoAnne D. Sieger, a fellow-student with me

here at the University of Pittsburgh.) It has been a
pleasure working with all these scholars and I hope the
work will favorably reflect their efforts. I, of course,
remain responsible for its imperfections.

Alfred M. Johnson, Jr.

University of Pittsburgh
March 29, 1976

AN INTRODUCTION TO THE METHOD OF A. J. GREIMAS

by

Corina Galland

The biblical text is today the object of new readings which are applied to it in order to examine the networks of its meanings. What we are concerned with is inscribed in a research ensemble which one groups under the name of *Structuralism*, which has been used to such an extent that it has become hackneyed--or at least faded and deformed. Some experts on the structural analysis of the narrative and some non-theologians have examined the biblical text--or examined their method by it--jumping with more or less tact into this well-protected domain, at the risk of smearing traditional criticism or spiritual meditation. I am thinking in particular of the works of Claude Chabrol and Louis Marin.[1]

Although a definitive balance-sheet of the results obtained may not be possible at this time, it is necessary to take note of this enterprise because it will no doubt become more important. And by being interested--or following its progress--one may fulfill the twofold need to discover a method which can improve and test one's own reading of the Bible in order to renew it.

I will not repeat here the history of structuralism in detail, from the linguistic research of Saussure (who drew up the program for a science of its expansion, and gave it the name of semiology) to the study of phonology by Troubetskoy and Jakobson. Nor will I discuss the application of their phonological model to anthropology by Lévi-Strauss and to the human sciences in general, one of which is literature, by the Russian school of Formalists and its continuators, Barthes and Greimas in France.

I am not going to take a look at the present state of research in the different fields of structuralist investigation (e.g. linguistics, semantics, history, psychoanalysis, and anthropology). Instead I will place myself within one of these areas, that of the analysis of the narrative, and more particularly, I will devote myself to presenting the method of one of its experts, A. J. Greimas.

This is a personal choice. Of course, one could also talk about Barthes, Genette, Todorov, and others. Their investigations would easily fit well into a single project, but neither their analytical practices (and the theory which supports them) nor their ideological choices are the same. It is not useful, nor even possible to present a synthesis of them at a stage where the research is still being worked out and each investigator is occupied with clearing a patch of ground in order to make his own path.

Moreover, my restriction to Greimas is arbitrary: the descriptive models which I will present are inconceivable without the support of works which are earlier and parallel to his. And the same thing is true here of one of the characteristics of his research. He works from results or hypotheses already formulated by other researchers in different areas, in order to compare, re-examine, develop, modify them, and produce some models.

Throughout his writings, which are, moreover, not very numerous and are collected in two volumes (to which one must add his completely new preface to a collection of analyses of poetic texts), the research of Greimas follows an evolution. From his works in lexicology, which ended in failure, he passed in 1966 to semantics with his *Sémantique structurale*; and then in order to broaden the framework of semantics, which was too restricted, he offered some semiotic essays in 1970 in his *Du sens*.

I will situate myself at the practical level, and not at a philosophical level where there would be a question of determining the theory of meaning assumed by the method, in order to present and to illustrate, or, let us say, propose the general principles of a structural reading. Before defining some points, I will very briefly give three quotations:

The first is from Rimbaud on the subject of *A Season in Hades*: "I have attempted to say what that says, literally and in all its meanings."[2] Then from Barthes: "A work is 'eternal' not because it imposes a single meaning to many different men, but because it suggests many different meanings to a single man."[3] And finally from Todorov: "The inaugural action of every reading is a certain disruption of the apparent order of the text."[4]

Thus unlike a method based on history (a history of words, their meaning, or their use; a history of the social, political, and religious milieus which have presided over the redaction of the text; a history of [p. 37] borrowings and influences[5]), there is no question in structural analysis of finding the genesis of a text and its sources or of going back to the original text, because attempting to go back to the origin of the text (i.e. to its author, its era, or more generally to the human spirit and its non-temporal properties) will lead one to project another kind of discourse on the text. This discourse will be biographical or psychoanalytical if one attempts to find the author. It will be sociological if one explains the text by the era of its redaction. It will be philosophical (or anthropological) if one goes back to its human spirit.[6] Such an approach uses the text then in order to arrive (through it) at a reality which is external to the text and would explain its production. It is precisely this projection which structural analysis rejects. Structural analysis places itself on another level of observation and proposes an immanent approach to the text in order to demonstrate the text's coherence. Structural analysis does not attempt to follow the meaning by commenting upon the text word by word (in order to say finally what is the meaning of the whole work?), but it seeks the relationships behind the words which unite them. It attempts to determine a textual grammar, the internal organization of its system and its structure, by drawing up an inventory of textual terms which are not considered individually but in their relationships and an inventory of the operations which transform them.

Joseph Bya writes negatively with respect to traditional criticism: "For what is a text, namely, a *Fabric, plot, braid,* or *interlacing* of which criticism keeps only one thread. What is *broken off* is often the best and the most fragile. At the same time, it reveals its falsehood to us (without knowing it) by assuring us that this is the *conducting* thread and the deep meaning, while neglecting to tell us what it has done with the other threads."[7] Thus it is a matter of escaping from the trap of linearity by testing all the threads which weave the text, and by playing with the patterns of its meaning without excluding any.

That being said very briefly, I now come to Greimas' method by presenting some models of a narrative grammar which are in the process of being worked out and are therefore still fragmentary and sometimes hypothetical. Greimas' method attempts to be deductive and inductive at the same time. The models have to be tested beginning with particular texts in order to arrive at an always greater degree of generality which could permit one to take account of the largest number of possible texts.

First it is necessary for me to say a few words about the work of a Russian folklorist, Vladimir Propp,[8] to which Greimas' work is greatly indebted. Both Propp as well as Saussure have only very recently been read in France. If Saussure's work marks the beginning of structural linguistics, Propp's work is the origin of the structural analysis of the narrative. Propp's *Morphology of the Folktale*, which appeared in 1928, was only translated into French in 1965. [p. 38]

Propp stated that every object can be studied from three points of view: that of its structure, that of its origin, and that of its transformations. Choosing the Russian fairy tale as his object of study, he thought that before one could say what its origin may have been, one must know what it is. In other words, one must give a description of it. But a description of the fairy tale genre will only be possible within a classification of the genres. Now what is it that determines this classification? It is the *structure* of the folktale. Formal structural study precedes and conditions genetic, historical study. Therefore one must discover the laws of the structure. Referring to Goethe's botany, Propp chose to study the *morphology* of the folktale, in other words, to describe the folktales according to their constitutive parts and the relationship of these parts between one another and with the whole. Discovering that the same actions are found in several folktales but these actions are attributed to different characters, Propp decided to begin with these actions, or to use the technical term, with the *functions* of

the characters. The function--and this is essential for
every structural analysis--is the action of a character defined from the viewpoint of its signification in the unfolding of the plot. Starting with one hundred fairy tales,
Propp isolated a matrix, a measurement unit of 31 functions,
which should permit one to define every fairy tale. Therefore the set of folktales can be considered to be a chain
of variants produced from a single model.

This analysis permits Propp to formulate his four
theses:

1. The constant elements of the folktale
   are the functions of the characters.
   Some of them may be these characters
   and some may be the way in which the
   functions are filled. The functions
   are the fundamental constitutive parts
   of the folktale;

2. Their number is limited;

3. Their succession is always the same;

4. All fairy tales belong to the same
   type as far as their structure is
   concerned.

Therefore a fairy tale is a sequence which begins from
a villainy or a lack and passes through some intermediary
functions in order to end in the denouement, that is to say
in the reparation of the lack. Each new villainy or lack
gives rise to a new sequence. A single folktale can be made
of several sequences which follow or are entwined with one
another. If there is no freedom in the order of the succession of the functions, there is freedom in the choice of the
functions used. Certain functions can be missing in a narrative, or on the other hand, they can be repeated.

A second definition of the folktale is proposed by Propp. In all the tales, the functions are divided among 7 types of characters: (1) the princess or the father, (2) the hero, (3) the mandator, (4) the villain, (5) the donor, [p. 39] (6) the helper, (7) the false-hero. Therefore the folktale is a narrative with 7 characters who share the functions.

Propp's discovery opened a large number of new perspectives into the analysis of folkloric texts, and moreover into the analysis of the narrative in general. But its importance was only perceived when the methods of structural analysis were introduced into linguistics and anthropology. The two definitions of the folktale by Propp--beginning with the functions and the characters--attracted Greimas' attention at the time when he was attempting to find a model capable of organizing the semantic universe. He had examined linguistics and especially the sentence. According to traditional syntax, the functions in the sentence are only the roles played by the words--the subject is only someone who does the action; the object is someone who undergoes the action. Greimas had the idea of passing from this sentence to a higher unit, the narrative, and of finding at this level the larger functions of the sentence. He began by isolating two axes (to which a third would soon be added): (1) the axis of *desire* and a *quest*, which links a *subject* (Sub) and an *object* (O): the subject desires the object and begins a quest for this object; and (2) the axis of *communication*: a sender (S) transmits the object to a receiver (R). Greimas will still add a *helper* (H) and an *opponent* (OPP) to these four poles. The helper and opponent confront one another on the plane of the struggle, and they correspond on the narrative plane to the circum-

stantial complements of the sentence. While the helper comes
to the assistance of the subject in his quest for the object,
the opponent creates some obstacles for the subject by being
opposed to the realization of this quest.

Such an extrapolation of the syntactic structure from
the natural language permits Greimas to produce his actantial
model with six terms:

Sender (S) ————→ Object (O) ————→ Receiver (R)
                              ↑
Helper (H) ————→ Subject (Sub) ←———— Opponent (OPP)

Now by modifying them slightly, he also succeeded in repeating the structural model of Propp's characters: the
mandator and the father of the princess are combined into
the sender; the hero is divided into the subject and the receiver; the princess is the object; the villain and the
false-hero are combined into the opponent; and the donor
and the helper are combined into the helper.

This schema divides the innumerable characters of the
narrative into some formal classes which Greimas calls
actants. Unlike the *actor*, who is the character as he
appears in the narrative, the *actant* is a semantic unit
and it is situated on a more abstract level. Several explicit actors or characters can form a single actant in a
narrative. If a little girl departs on a search for her
little brother and is helped by a stove, a river, and an
apple-tree, the stove, river, and apple-tree are actors who
form only one actant, the helper. On the other hand, one
[p. 40] single actor can occupy one or several actantial
positions. A hero can decide to depart on a quest by himself, and he will then be the subject and his own sender at
the same time. Moreover, it is necessary to state pre-

cisely that the actants are not necessarily anthropomorphous.
They can also be abstract ideas, such as a desire to be
healed, trust, or faith operating as a helper.

Greimas then improved the second structural model
established by Propp, that of the functions. He compared
it with the research on the theater by E. Souriau, who had
drawn up an inventory of dramatic functions. Propp's discovery that several functions are articulated in pairs was
then exploited:

> lack/reparation of the lack
> interdiction/transgression of the interdiction
> combat/victory

By improving and pushing these binary articulations
further, Greimas proposed reducing and structuring Propp's
inventory, which with its 31 functions was much too large,
in order to make it more manageable. He sought to obtain
a simple structure which could take account of a large
number of narratives. This modification freed the functions
from the compulsory order of succession which Propp had
postulated. Greimas would not study these functions in their
syntagmatic order, that is to say in their linear sequence,
but according to a paradigmatic dimension, that is to say,
in their achronic relationship of association.

First he would study the somewhat indistinct functions
at the beginning and end of the narrative, i.e. the initial
and final sequences. He took Propp's first coupling, inter-
diction/transgression of this interdiction, and gave it the
name of *Contract*. The contract can be formulated in a positive form: mandate *vs.* acceptance, or in a negative form:
prohibition *vs.* violation. This contract is established by

10

a sender and receiver between whom communication is thereby
insured. The notion of a contract is essential to the narrative. The whole narrative is set in motion by the *breaking
of the contract* which will have to be reestablished at the
end of the narrative.

Analyzing a corpus of Lithuanian folktales in this way,
Greimas defined the initial situation, which is a constant in
all these folktales and which is more widely a constant in a
large number of narratives: the initial situation is characterized by the existence of a social order. But a breaking
of this order takes place because of the disobedience of one
group which has as its consequence the appearance of a mis-
fortune, an alienation of the society, or a lack. The role
of the hero, who is an individual separated from the social
group, consists then of undertaking a mission with the twofold purpose of abolishing the alienation and reestablishing
the communication. All narratives of a restitution of the
social order have this structure. One then has a narrative
whose initial and final sequences can be formalized in this
way: [p. 41]

initial sequence: $\overline{A} + \overline{C}$----------final sequence: $C + A$
(social order disturbed)   (social order reestablished)

where: A = contract; C = communication; $\overline{A}$ = breaking of
the contract; $\overline{C}$ = non-communication; vs. = versus, against

The narrative comes to be unfolded between these two
poles, by having the function of organizing the transformation from one to another, and by inverting the signs of the
contents.

Thus the mythical narrative, the folktale, and all narratives which have a dramatic form have this common struc-

tural property. Their unfolding is situated in a temporal
dimension which is articulated in a *before* vs. an *after*.
And this before vs. after corresponds to a reversal of the
situation or to an inversion of the signs of the content.
One can organize the narrative with a schematic diagram of
the structure of the mythical narrative:

	BEFORE		AFTER	
contents	Inversed Content		Posited Content	
narrative	Correlated	Topical	Topical	Correlated
sequences	content	content	content	content

(The correlated contents represent the initial and final
sequences, which are situated on different planes than the
body of the narrative.) This schema is useful for narratives other than myths. We have used it in particular for
the story of Paul on the road to Damascus with his conversion
being the passage between a *before* and an *after.*[9]

Another essential component in the narrative, which is
not contractual but factual and not at the level of communication but at the level of the *action* [*faire*], is situated
within the contract relationship which is broken at the beginning and reestablished at the end. This component will
be the *Tests* which have the role of annulling the negative
effects of the alienation. While the contract and the communication were found in a negative form at the beginning of
the narrative and in a positive form at the end, the test is
a solitary, asymmetrical sequence, and it is unfolded in
time. The test is composed of a series of functions which
has a *struggle* (confrontation vs. victory) at its center.

This struggle is preceded by a *contract* (mandate vs. acceptance)--a small or new contract within the contract which brackets the whole narrative--and it will be followed by a *consequence*. The contract is established by a sender who entrusts the hero with a certain mission. This contract forms the axis of the *quest* which manifests the *desire* of the subject to obtain the object. This desire constitutes the *raison d'être* of the struggle on the plane of the external comportment. The consequence after the struggle (a communication which sanctions the accomplishment of the contract) corresponds to the contract.

The test is repeated three times in the narrative. Each consequence implies a partial reestablishment of the broken, global contract. The tests, which are to a certain extent progressive, must lead to a victory which will have as its consequence the total liquidation of the lack. These tests are only differentiated from the point of view of their consequence. They are presented in this way, according to the order of the narrative:

    I. *Qualifying test:* The hero is qualified as the subject of the quest. In the terms of this test, he receives the helper who will help him accomplish the following test.

    II. *Principal test:* This leads to the reception of an object, the possession of which assures the liquidation of the lack.

    III. *Glorifying test:* This corresponds to the recognition by the social body of the subject who is the victor in the tests.

An example: "The Healing of Blind Bartimaeus"
Mark 10:46-52[10]

Qualifying: The confession of Jesus as the Son
of David qualifies Bartimaeus to
be the subject of the principal
test.

Principal: contract: What would you like me
to do for you? Lord, let me re-
cover my sight!
Liquidation of the lack: healing;

Glorifying: "He began to follow Jesus":
Bartimaeus is recognized as a
disciple.   [p. 43]

The schema of the test maintains a parallelism with that
of the actants. The six actants are implied by the text. The
contract is established between the sender and receiver. The
struggle confronts the helper and the opponent. The consequence is the acquisition of the object by the subject. It is
necessary to add to this form an inventory of the *displacements*
which have a great importance for the unfolding of the narrative because the departures and returns conceal some conjunctions and disjunctions.

The use of these actantial and functional models places
the analyst on a more formal level than that of the text so
that one apprehends the text revealed in the first reading.
It is a matter then of clarifying the existence and status of
the levels of the narrative grammar a little bit. This is a
delicate point. In order to be well done, structural analysis
must work at every moment on these three different levels by
carefully distinguishing them and establishing the correlations of one to another. But the procedures for passing from
one level to another are not precisely defined. This is a
disputed point in the actual research. How does one pass

from a particular text, so that one can read it, to the
narrativity itself and its structures and vice versa (i.e.
from the structures and narrativity to the particular text)
because the latter preexist in the text just as the meaning
preexists in it? In reality, when one leaves the performance
of a play, one first has a general impression of its meaning;
and this impression is expressed, in the first place, by a
confused recollection of some event in it which summons
another, etc. It is only after that that one is in a position
to retell it in a coherent narrative or in the ordinate,
temporal succession in which one has seen it.

The proof that the narrative structures or the structures of signification are found in languages other than
those of the natural *langues* (e.g. the cinema, painting,
music, and comic strips) leads one to differentiate between
the *deep level* (where the narrativity is situated and organized prior to its manifestation and where the structures are
the same, whatever may be the kind of language in which they
are later manifested) and the *surface* [or superficial] *level*
(which depends on the laws characteristic of each kind of
language: the linguistic laws for the narrative).

I. The *deep* level is an abstract, conceptual level
which has its own grammar. This is the elementary structural
level of the signification—the latter being defined by the
presence of two terms and the relationship articulated between
them. This elementary structure can be developed into a model,
that of a *semiotic square*. Beginning with it, one poses the
existence of two terms S' and S'' which are in a contrary relationship. Each of these two terms can project a new term
which is its contradictory, $\overline{S}'$ and $\overline{S}''$. The semiotic square,
which is taken from Aristotle's logical square, has been

developed into a logical hexagon by Blanché.[11] [p. 44]
Blanché preferred a triad of contraries to the schema of
binary opposition and thus he produced two new positions:
the *compound* and the *neutral*. These two new positions have
great importance for the signification of the narrative because they are precisely those which offer a synthesis between terms of the opposition.[12]

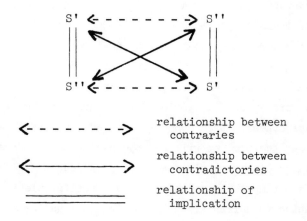

← - - - - - →	relationship between contraries
←————→	relationship between contradictories
═════════	relationship of implication

EXAMPLE:

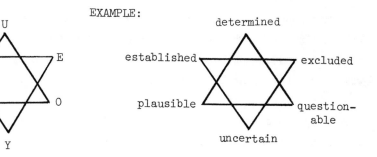

U: compound term (and...and; or...or)
Y: neutral term (neither...nor)

In order to construct a semiotic square starting from a clear text, in other words, in order to pass from the personified actors in the narrative to the abstract terms (S', S'', S̄', S̄''), one proceeds by noting the semantic units, i.e. the semes and especially those which are privileged by their redundancy. Each seme corresponds to a thread of the textual fabric. When one pulls a thread, it is not one seme which appears but an opposition, i.e. an elementary structure. One constructs the square beginning with this opposition. This square articulates the meaning and produces the signification. Each of its terms are capable of being invested with diverse contents. Each of its terms, which may or may not be present in the text itself, is therefore present behind every narrative; the presence of a single term presupposes the existence of all the others. Each opposition noted can produce a square, but the problem will be to organize the different squares according to their degree of pertinence. The squares must be superimposable on and finally substitutable into one square which is universal enough to take account of the entire narrative which is being studied.

This deep level has its own grammar: to state the terms is to define the morphology. Now every grammar, compared with a morphology, has a syntax. The terms which have only been defined thus far by their opposition (contrariety or contradiction) can be handled by a set of logical operations which form this syntax. For example, the contradiction on the level of the relationship (therefore on the level of the morphology) has its correlation on the level of the syntax in the operation of negation and affirmation. There is a contradiction when to deny one of the terms is to affirm the other.

But if there is an operation, there is an operator; and that forces us to pass to the second level. [p. 46]

II. The *superficial* level (superficial is not meant to be taken in a pejorative sense, but in order to denote a level which is closer to level III, that of the manifestation)[13] is a level which is not logical but anthropomorphous because the negation and the affirmation, which were noted in the deep level, imply an *action* [*faire*] (to deny or affirm) and this action implies a *subject* (it may be a person or not; to say "the pencil writes badly" is to personify the pencil). For example, if one of the terms of the square, S', is invested with the content "LIFE" (S'' being "DEATH"), and one notes a logical operation of the negation of LIFE at this deep level, one will have at the superficial level an *action* of the order of destruction which implies a *subject* of the destruction (an enemy and an object, the town). The action can be transcribed into a canonical form: EN = F(A), where EN = Narrative statement; F = Function; A = Actant.

In order to illustrate this work on the three levels, let us take an example from the book of Revelation (12:7ff.) which offers at the level of its manifestation:

> There was a battle in heaven.
> Michael and his angels were fighting
>   against the dragon
> And the dragon also fought them
>   with his angels,
> But he did not have the upper hand;
> There was no longer a place for them
>   in heaven.
> The dragon was thrown down....

This text can be formalized on the superficial level by these narrative statements:

$$EN' = F: \quad \text{confrontation} \quad (S' \leftarrow \rightarrow S'')$$
$$EN'' = F: \quad \text{domination} \quad (S' \rightarrow S'')$$
$$EN''' = F: \quad \text{attribution} \quad (S \leftarrow O)$$

This is the schema of the *performance* which is the unit most characteristic of the narrative syntax. There is a relationship of implication among these three statements which is so close that in order to reconstruct the entire unit (which is so often elliptical in the narrative) it is only necessary to have the third narrative statement (the attribution of the object) revealed in the text.

At the deep level, there will be some relationships and some logical operations which will take account of the opposition revealed in Rev. 12 as a struggle which unfolds itself in time. The relationship of contradiction will correspond to the confrontation. The setting into motion of the negation of one of the terms will correspond to the domination, and the affirmation of the other will correspond to the attribution.

After this example it is necessary to return to the superficial level in order to see other kinds of narrative statements. If the performance is situated at the level of the action, the subject [p. 47] of this action must have the *competence* to accomplish this *performance* [Galland is referring here to Noam Chomsky's linguistic competence/performance dichotomy.]. And the competence is situated at the level of the modalities: willing, knowing, being able. Before acting, one must *will to act*, but that is not enough, one must *know how to act* (and then the subject acts by trickery) or *be able to act* (and then the subject acts by power). There is therefore a "development" in the narrative:

willing $\longrightarrow$ knowing $\longrightarrow$ being able $\Rightarrow$ action

$$\underbrace{\hspace{5cm}}\qquad\underbrace{\hspace{3cm}}$$

virtuality   actualization
competence   performance

This development is set in motion by the contract.
A sender communicates the will to the subject; and this will
makes the subject able to accomplish the first performance
which will win him the attribution of the helper. The helper
will communicate a knowledge and/or a power to him which will
permit him to arrive at the action.

Therefore one has some modal statements in
addition to some narrative statements:

EM (for Modal Statements) = F: willing

                                       knowing $\Big\}$ (subject;
                                                        object)
                                        being able

A third type of statement exists, the attributive statements, i.e. statements which are neither about an action nor
a modality, but a *being* or *having*: EA (for Attributive Statements) = F: attribution (subject; object). In reality, when
the narrative has a structure of exchange, the attribution of
an object to someone, this signifies the loss of this object
by someone else. The attributive statement, therefore, becomes a statement of transference (ET).

The transcription of the text into statements puts it
into a very useful form, to the extent that it permits one
to eliminate the narrative elements which are not relevant
to the signification and to reestablish other indispensable
elements which are presupposed by the narrative. This transcription permits one to present in detail the objects or

values which are transmitted from one actant to another. The
actants are not so much conceived then as some operators as
some positions where the values are situated, i.e. where they
are led and from whence they are withdrawn. The rules of
these transfers organize the narrative, and they contribute
to the production of its meaning. But the transcription of
the text into statements has relevance only if the statements
are organized and reduced.

Once achieved, Greimas says, such a narrative grammar
would depict a set path for the manifestation of the meaning.
Beginning with the logical operations of the deep grammar
and through their surface anthropomorphic representations,
the contents are invested, in order to arrive at the signification revealed in a narrative. [p. 48]

One point remains which it is necessary to say something
about. The statements which we have discussed belong to the
narrative. But this narrative can be considered in its totality as the object of a statement which would have *storytelling*
as its function and the *author* as its subject. If structural
analysis places the historical person of the author and reader
into parenthesis, it is because it does not (yet) have the
means to study them. But in reality every statement presupposes an enunciation and a subject of this enunciation:
"He is cold" presupposes "I am saying that he is cold". The
problem of the enunciation has a very great importance. And,
like linguistics, semiotics is beginning to reflect on it in
order to be in a position to propose a structural description
of the situation of the discourse and the act of *parole* in
addition to a structural description of the statement. The
enunciation will therefore be studied as a component which
is implicitly contained in the text. But sometimes it is
explicit because the text often carries some marks of its

enunciation. It is by beginning with these marks that the study will be made, with the requirement that it limit itself to a linguistic subject in order not to fall back into biography and psychologism.

(Translated from *Études Théologiques et Religieuses* 48 [1, 1973], pp. 35-48.)

NOTES

1. See the articles by Chabrol and Marin which follow
in chapters III, V-VII, IX of this work. Louis Marin has
also published a *Sémiotique de la Passion*. [The editor of
this work, i.e. *The New Testament and Structuralism* will
publish a translation of this latter work under the title:
The Semiotic of the Passion Narratives in this same series.]

2. A. Rimbaud, quoted by Roland Barthes in his
Critique et vérité, Paris: Seuil, 1966, 41.

3. *Ibid.*, 51.

4. T. Todorov, *Poétique de la prose*, Paris: Seuil,
1971, 247.

5. Cf. Paul Ricoeur in *Exégèse et herméneutique*, ed.
X. Leon-Dufour, Paris: Seuil, 1971, 36.

6. Cf. T. Todorov, *op. cit.*, 241ff.

7. J. Bya in "Littérature et Idéologiques," *La Nouvelle
Critique*, special vol. 31a (Colloque de Cluny II, April,
1970), 114.

8. V. Propp, *Morphologie du conte*, Paris: Seuil, 1970.
[Eng. ed.: *The Morphology of the Folktale*, trans. L. Scott,
2nd ed. Austin: University of Texas Press, 1968.]

9. The distinction between topical and correlated contents is established by Greimas in his article, "Élements
pour une théorie de l'interpretation du récit mythique,"
Communications 8 (1966), 125-151. It has been reprinted in
his *Du sens*, Paris: Seuil, 1970, 185ff. and W. A. Koch,
Strukturelle Textanalyse, Hildesheim, N.Y.: Olms, 1972, 115-
146. An English translation is also available: "The Interpretation of Myth: Theory and Practice," in *Structural
Analysis of Oral Tradition*, eds. P. and E. K. Maranda, Philadelphia: University of Pennsylvania Press, 1971, 81-121.
   Greimas does not define these terms. However, here
is how he introduces them (Ed. note: The quote begins with
section (2) of the discussion.):

2. A sub-class of *dramatic narratives* (myths, folktales, plays, etc.) is defined by a common structural property, the temporal dimension, on which they are found situated and which is dichotomized into a *before* vs. an *after*.

A 'reversal of the situation' corresponds to this discursive *before* vs. *after* which, on the plane of the implicit structure, is nothing else than an inversion of the signs of the content. Thus a correlation exists between the two planes:

$$\frac{\text{before}}{\text{after}} \simeq \frac{\text{inversed content}}{\text{posed content}}$$

3. Let us reduce the inventory of the narrative once more. A large number of them (the Russian folktale, but also our reference myth) possess another property. They include an initial and final sequence situated on some planes of mythical "reality" which are different than the body of the narrative itself.

A new articulation of the content corresponds to this particularity of the narration: two other *correlated contents* are found united to the two *topical contents*-- one of which is posed and the other inversed--which have, as a rule, the same transformational relationship between them as the topical contents (*op. cit.*, 187-188) [cf. Eng. trans., p. 83].

Thus the *correlated contents* only appear to be some particular cases of the *topical contents*. They have the characteristic of being situated at the beginning and end of the narrative. The topical contents are the dramatic places, the sequences, and the fragments of the narrative syntagm which are opposed to one another in order to form the plot of the narrative. [This note was added by the editors of *E.T.R.*]

10. Cf. *Foi et Vie*, Cahiers bibliques, May-June, 1970, 80ff.

24

11. R. Blanché, *Structures intellectuelles*, Paris: Vrin, 1966.

12. Aristotle constructed his *logical square* starting from systems of opposition (*antikeimena*) and oppositions (*enantia*) such as: high vs. low, heavy vs. light, hot vs. cold, white vs. black, etc. (See Aristotle, "Categories," 6:6-17, etc.):

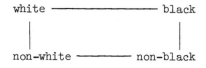

It is by perfecting the Aristotelian distinction between *contraries* and *contradictories* that Greimas presented his semiotic square (cf. Greimas, *Du sens*, 136ff.).

If we transform the semiotic square according to Blanché's instructions, we obtain the following schema:

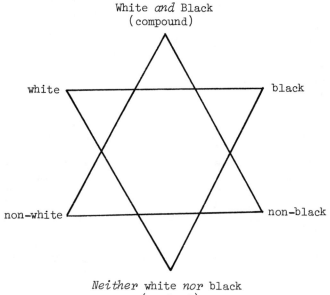

One must note that the advantage of the *logical square* for Aristotle is that it subsequently permits one to unravel the incompatibilities which one will find in the *judgment* (cf. Aristotle, "Analytics"). A single thing cannot be said to be white and black *at the same time* and *in the same way*. Either it is *said* to be white, and it is not black; or it is *said* to be black and it is not white. Although, if it is white, it may be at the same time non-black and vice versa.

That precludes the possibility of a semiotic square becoming a *hexagon*, in the manner of Blanché (and Claude Chabrol).

On the other hand, the compound and neutral terms are both possible in a narrative without any contradiction because, on the one hand, it is not a question of normative exclusions, while, on the other hand, one actant can fill two functions or any function at the same time.

Thus here are some relationships between Helpers (H) and Opponents (OPP):

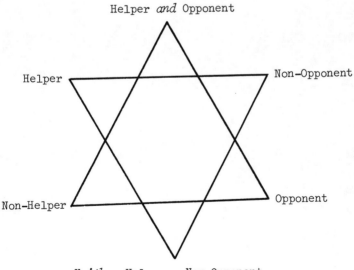

Helper *and* Opponent

Helper

Non-Opponent

Non-Helper

Opponent

Neither Helper - *Nor* Opponent

Thus in the Parable of the Good Samaritan, the priest and the Levite are neither helpers nor opponents (position Y: neutral), while the "lawyer" (Lk. 10:25) is, in certain ways, a helper and opponent (position U: compound) at the same time. [This note added by the editors of *E.T.R.*]

13. One should understand that level III, that of the *manifestation*, is the *surface* level of the text. [This note also added by the editors of *E.T.R.*] [Ed. note: See the discussion of these "levels" in the glossary of this work.]

III

PROBLEMS OF THE NARRATIVE SEMIOLOGY
OF THE BIBLICAL TEXTS[1]

by

Claude Chabrol

...One can see that I was formerly interested in astronomy. I do not wish to deny
it. Then it was geology which whiled away
a little bit of my time. Next it was anthropology which briefly made me sick....What I
liked about anthropology was its power of
denial, its tenacity to define man in the
image of God, in terms of what he is not....
Oh, I have tried everything. I finally got
interested in magic, and even today, when I
read about it, I find some traces of it
again. But most often, it is a place without any plan or limit and it is not only its
content which is incomprehensible to me, not
to mention their arrangement....

Samuel Beckett, *Molloy*

1. The Reading Experience.

Reading a text and that of the Bible in particular produces in us what some people ascribe to the profession of the
psychoanalyst, in other words, "the suspension of certainties
about the subject until the last illusions waste away".[2]

The reader will prove in every sense of the word that
this experience creates "some eyes for not seeing (reading)
at all, and for detecting what must be seen (read) in agreement with the Gospel" down to [p. 4] the important proof where
"knowledge comes instead of the truth to cover up the loss of
the object so much as to make one forget its existence".

The desire--This reference to psychoanalytic discourse in no way attempts to be decorative. We believe the reading situation has to examine in the field of enunciation a field punctuated with a premonitory preciseness.

In what follows, to read is always to forget the text and its meaning and to do this once and for all. Instead of this forgotten text and meaning, a "subject desiring knowledge" is constituted whose quest is not an object but a desire or more precisely a desire to know which creates this particular relationship of interlocution from which its reading is taken. It is established in no way external to the text, which would make it the instrument of a real "author-reader" relationship, but on the contrary inside the text which articulates the fundamental relationship of a "textual" narrator and reader.

Note 1--We have suggested that this first relationship on the plane of the enunciation could be observed on the plane of the statement in that which connects the Sender and Receiver. This assumes the existence of a duplicate function of the statement which "reflects" some relationships of the enunciation.

Recent investigations of narrativity have shown that the modal values (such as Willing, Knowing, Being Able) which modify the basic narrative statements imply some pre-supposed terms.[3] This is what Greimas points out when he says that the operator-actant who sets the syntactic development into motion *can be found* in the contract which establishes the subject of the desire by the attribution of the modality of willing, which is a "probable" actualization of a "will to act" of the original sender,[4] which calls for us to consider a "willing of the willing" of the receiver.

Thus the actantial Sender-Receiver relationship beyond the transmission of an object of communication or knowledge and an object of desire can be organized:

From a presupposed
$$\left\{ \begin{array}{l} \text{Willing} \\ \text{Knowing} \\ \text{Being Able} \end{array} \right\}$$
there ought to correspond

a
$$\left\{ \begin{array}{l} \text{Willing of the Will} \\ \text{Knowing of the Knowledge} \\ \text{Being Able of the Power} \end{array} \right\}$$
equally presupposed in the receiver

In all these cases, the terms of this relationship of one subject with Another shows their basis beyond the action or the object of the syntactic development in the *desire* (one can see on this subject our notes on the "non-knowledge of the knowledge" by the Jews in the Passion and those of Edgar Haulotte on desire as a "mediator of the communication" in the discourse of the *reader*).

Note 2--The study of enunciation in the biblical text also leads Louis Marin and Edgar Haulotte to a study of the "illocutionary" and "perlocutionary" (Austin's terms) dimension of language in this volume. This consists of describing the act of *parole* which not only makes a statement but an action of the language. The imperative [p. 5] or (negative or positive) assertive interrogative rule of the sentence has a decisive importance for the text of the Passion, as the distinction between statements of predictions or facts. One can hope to clarify by these analyses the definition and use of narrative modes of "being and appearing" whose complexity reveals an inadequate elaboration of what belongs to them from the plane of the statement and the plane of the enunciation.

Marin's notes apply here on the indicial elements (spatial-temporal index in the episode of the "Women at the Tomb") of the biblical discourse.

The meaning--There is another point of agreement between the psychoanalytic reading and our own which illustrates quite well the question of "interpretation". This loss of the text is never done for us for the benefit of the production of a second *meta-* or *infra-* text. Our reader does not seek the hidden text under the exposed text or the signified meaning beyond the anecdotal unfolding of the signifiers. Instead he should pursue the "hidden signifier which signifies it",[5] provided that one precisely states that it is not a hidden signifier which he attempts to bring out of its "hiding place" but a network of correlations where this signifier and its "family relations" come to be caught in its meaning as in a net.

The meaning is not behind the text, it is the system of rules which permits one to generate the differential interplay of oppositions which controls my reading throughout a "never-ending" text. The text which I read is only an accidentally (or, in other words, historically) restricted actualization. That is to say, it will be impossible to stop the reference of some signifiers to other signifiers and thereby that of the signifieds. In this way, the enumeration of the order producing this reflection is substituted for the "suturing" illusion of an ultimate signified ("the basic events" of the Old Testament which Paul Ricoeur alludes to[6] or even God).

At first glance, this trait would explain the opposition with hermeneutics defined by Ricoeur[7] as:

> The interpretation of a transmitted meaning consisting:
> 1. of the conscious recovery
> 2. of an overdetermined symbolic substratum
> 3. by an interpreter who places himself in the same semantic field as the one which he is understanding and he enters in this way into the hermeneutical circle.

This "interpretative" attitude would be characteristic of those who "internalize their own myths"[8] or constitute a "true tradition, that is, a series of interpreting recoveries".[9] (It would be characteristic) "of a community which speaks to itself and uses the narrative not in order to make some analyses of the text but in order to restore it in the *parole*".[10]

In this way, one would easily oppose those who are still "spoken by the text and from inside of this text", by including their actual variations, to those which analyze it from the "outside": in short the "natives" to the "scholars".

The accompanying exoticism of this position does not satisfy us. This entire work which is developed here attempts to question this pseudo-division of the work--between hermeneutics or exegesis and semiotic analysis--we think instead that if there is a gap, it is between a non-semiotic analysis of the texts, [p. 6] of which the *Formgeschichte* and *Redaktionsgeschichte* commentaries give one example among others, and a semiotic analysis.

This means that the sacred text *vs.* profane text opposition, from the point of view of the reader's community, is not at first relevant for the analysis. This is not the place to show the agreements between non-structural analysis of the sacred text and classical literary criticism, historical linguistics, functionalism (and even French or German phenomenology). We would simply like to suggest that the problem of these agreements is not secondary but fundamental. In other words, every reader is subjected to a certain scientific inter-textuality, which implies (explicitly or not) a position on the meaning.

Formgeschichte belongs to a scientific area which develops a historicist, realist, and univocal conception of meaning. It cannot avoid some first determinations which are also those of historical linguistics, literary criticism, or functionalism.

Semiotic analysis, like psychoanalysis (with Lacan) or philosophy (with Derrida), constitutes a scientific area which poses a suspension or a deconstruction of meaning. This position leads to a repudiation of the classical categories of inside-outside, subject-object, text-reality, history-writing; as Louis Marin and Edgar Haulotte illustrate here in their analysis of the discourse position of the reader of the biblical text.

In short, we should make this formula of Todorov[11] our own: "Science does not speak of its object but is spoken with the help of its object", provided that one extends this proposition to every *reading* and also accepts the idea that the object is not described by the reading but is re-written thanks to it.

One should also state that this re-writing is not the same because it is produced by a new development from the same matrix.[12]

2. The Semiotic Practice of the "Construction".

This volume has for the most part put some semiotic models to the test which have already been worked out. It is their experimentation and their verification. The theoretical elaboration of new categories can be developed from the insufficiencies revealed by their application.

Corpus and text--This application raises a major question: the constitution of the text in the biblical corpus. The latter raises in its turn some prior questions:

1) Can one begin an analysis without a precise knowledge of the Semitic ethnographic context?

2) Or, shouldn't the analyst first make an inventory of the ancient mythological sources of the biblical literature?

3) Or, can one analyze the biblical text with its French translation?

One could respond to the first objection that we do not [p. 7] properly speaking lack historical knowledge of the Semitic (or even proto-Semitic) milieu. But the problem doesn't seem to us to be precisely posed. In fact, it first resides in the relationship to be established between the semiotic analysis of texts and the context.

The context which interests the analyst is not (at first at least) the whole sociological context but the mythological or more general textual context which is present as Greimas notes[13] in the form of contents which are bestowed independently of the narrative itself and controlled *a posteriori* by the narrative model. These invested contents are already formed when the "mythical affabulation" or the textual process form the actors. These actors are provided with conceptual contents. The widespread knowledge of these contents is common to the narrator and his society. It is this wide-spread knowledge of the contents which forms this semantic substance that is the context and which it is a matter of organizing into a code. But this substance never lacks forms which control it in the text themselves.

It would be useless to attempt to arrange this context by constructing a dictionary (which moreover exists) from some lexemes revealed in the text (what is a patriarch or publican from the functional or qualitative point of view?).

These lexemes can play many different roles according to their position in a text or from one text to another. It would therefore be necessary to isolate their semic content at the level of the code, which is a formal structure producing the ensemble of invested contents from which the text draws. This step assumes therefore that one begins with the analysis of texts, which will be enough for us at first.

The second objection calls for a much shorter response. Semiotic analysis favors the study of the synchrony, not because it neglects the sources or the prior states of its texts but because it subordinates them to the elaboration of synchronic models which give a hypothetical model of the state of the *langue* or the discourse.

That does not mean that the mythologies of the Mesopotamian basin must be neglected by the analyst of the Bible. But there is an order to respect in the analytical method.

It is by beginning with the fundamental models, which are based on the New Testament or Old Testament for example, that some more precise questions could be posed, and that the transformations which operate from these mythologies in the biblical literature will be describable.

Finally we will attempt to justify the use of the French text (Father P. Benoit's translation). We should

remember a fact which is sometimes overlooked. For the
majority of French readers, the Bible, and the New Testament
in particular, only exists in its French version. Thus the
text belongs to its culture. Certainly a translation, as
good as it may be, always introduces some changes which can
sometimes affect the semantic or narrative structure. Moreover, it can only give a pale idea of the stylistic interplay
of the original signifiers, metaphors, ellipses, and double
meanings which are characteristic of the interplay of a text
in its original *langue*. Nevertheless, to the extent to which
the semiotician can isolate himself from every "fetishism"
of the *first, original,* or *first edition* of the text, he will
not see any disadvantage in considering the study of the
French text of the Bible in and of itself. [p. 8]

Secondly, he could very well compare the results of this
analysis with those which were revealed from the "original"
text. This will be the object of a second question, for the
one who never favors the *prior* text: "What do these displacements signify?" Could they serve as the guideline for
a differential sketch of the cultures from a sociolinguistic
point of view?

Finally, doesn't the biblical tradition which has constituted our "object" give us the example of an unbroken
series of cultural reinterpretations well-marked by the
diachrony and of a veritable "patchwork" in the synchrony,
where Egyptian mysticism and Greek philosophy among others,
come to resound in Hebraic research.

It would be less paradoxical (than it would at first
seem) to maintain that of some texts (as moreover of every
text) we have never had the original and to add that even if
such an "original" text were assumed, it would *always* and *already* be a translation.

The Biblical Corpus and the Choice of a Reference Text

It is unnecessary to emphasize its "probable" importance
even if we limit ourselves (and for what reason besides?) to
the Canon alone.[14]

It goes without saying that the analyst confronting this
gigantic collection is seized with bewilderment. The question
"how does one begin?" will never have seemed more formidable
to him. He will therefore first attempt to separate an area,
for example the New Testament. But this arbitrary segmentation will soon appear to be too large and too small. On the
one hand, it will be shown to be inadequate for establishing
the narrative and semantic structure of certain passages from
the New Testament which of necessity *recalls* some developments
in the "Acts of the Apostles". On the other hand, it will be
shown to be too large because at first glance the New Testament is composed of a series of "narratives" which are not
very well co-ordinated (see the infancy narratives in comparison with the narratives of Jesus as an adult) and moreover it is made of a succession of "texts" belonging to some
very diverse genres (parabolic, apologetic, prophetic, etc.).

Even if these first insights assume many theoretical
bases which are still not yet established (a theory of genres
among others), the analyst will prefer to begin with a "text"
whose stylistic and narrative unity impresses him, like the
Passion narrative.

That assumes that one can extract a passage from the
ensemble of the New Testament (the one which concerns the
narration of the Passion) which one sets up as the reference
text. The problem of limits (beginning/end) will never have
been more obvious. Paradoxically, far from being a disadvantage, the capriciousness obvious from the initial and final
marks of every text, which is naïvely given, appears to be

emphasized in this case. This will force the analyst to re-
define the true initial and final stages by his theoretical
construction. Once the isotopy (or the hierarchy of several
isotopies) is established, it will attempt to construct *its*
text in the New Testament.

The latter will have the appearance of broken and dis-
continuous signs that he will attempt to restore to a continuity which is for once significant.

The method--The fact which creates the methodological
unity of the analyses presented here, even for those who
work on another part of the biblical corpus [p. 9] other
than the text of the Passion, is the primacy given to a
deductive procedure.

This deductive procedure is pushed to its limit in
those analyses by Guy Vuillod of a series of narratives
from the Old and New Testaments.[15] Vuillod does this in
order to attempt to explain more than anything else the
formative rules of a semiotic faculty of the narrative structure. Vuillod's contribution is not situated at the level
of a "fundamental semantic" but of a "fundamental grammar".
He seeks to define (or to formulate) through a series of
very short narratives, which are taken from the Old and New
Testaments, the rules of a general model of narrative competence which could permit one to generate the formal narrative structure of a large number of texts which would neither
be specifically some "narratives" (in the strict sense of the
word) nor some "biblical" texts. [p. 10]

The analyses which have the Passion narrative as their
focal point require some additional remarks.

1) If they mark the obvious agreements, as that was
foreseeable, they do not lead to an identical construction

of their object. This result must not be considered to be an implicit refutation of the method or of its use. Semiotic analysis in effect is far from being a unified "science" which is composed and recognized by all and whose theory would make use of a method of which it would only be a matter of making a correct use. Semiotic analysis pursues the constitution of its theory through some multiple and distinct investigations, even if they are quite similar. Plurality is a necessity for it, and its reading of the texts is always in "several voices".

But this plurality will only be enlarged by being thought. This reflection on the differences, beyond the polemic, is hardly sketched out today. This volume could at the very least produce the basic materials which are needed by it.

2) That posed, the analyses of the Passion (and its "extensions" into Acts) pursue the same goals: they attempt to construct an operational model which must be ulteriorly well-adapted to represent the functioning of this "text" at the semantic and narrative level.

At the semantic level, this semiotic model appears to be the formal articulation of a substance, made up of values of well-defined contents (characteristic of this particular corpus).

This specific substance, which is still scarcely recognized, has been organized and produced from the general hypothesis of a significant form.[16] The statements have been analyzed into classes of paradigmatic contents by the inversion of the same text and then by permutation and commutation from texts to texts.

It is those classes of contents, which are in opposition and are most often antonymic, that the narrativity displays in its chronological and syntagmatic space. Consequently, does the "writing down" of the narrative structure consist of isolating the narrative units (functions and sequences) by distinguishing the actants from the predicates, which develop the formal syntactical frame in which the contents have been "well-versed" and analyzed more precisely.

Conclusion-- One could be disappointed (and with good reason) by the first hypothetical results of this work. Some will find them not very specific, regretting that the grammar or the ungrammaticality characteristic of this text is not better defined. Others, on the contrary, will denounce the lack of generality of the models elaborated maintaining that it is useless to attempt to construct some particular *langues* without a precise theory of the *langue*. While a chorus will secretly whisper with all its voices that it recognizes here some interpretations of naïve theologians in scholarly disguise.

None of these criticisms appear to be unjustified to us. But at the present stage of the constitution of the semiotic, it seems to us that the questions which they designate remain "undecidable". Only future practice will say if these imperfections were false problems or not.

As a conclusion, we would like to propose some points [p. 11] of reflection on a movement which is characteristic of these lines alone, as well as the ensemble of ideas maintained in this presentation.

1) The semiotic pratique must distinguish in its method the philosophical epistemology which attempts to establish it, from the theory which constitutes it step by step. One must therefore articulate and not mix semiotic theory and semiotic meta-theory. In this sense, the works of Marx,

Foucault, Derrida, or Lacan open some perspectives directed to research on the epistemological level but not to that of the practice where they require the implementation of a systematic and verifiable procedure of application, which is yet to be worked out, in order to become operants (but isn't that their function?).

2) Like every science, semiology must construct its object of knowledge (for example, some narrative or discursive structures, etc.) and not attempt to take account of the best possible, really un-knowable object (like some "narratives", "folktales", "myths", "religious texts", etc.).

It will therefore always prefer the simplest, most general, and most systematic model possible (in the technical sense that these terms have acquired in modern linguistic research).

Ambiguity arises here from the fact that semiotics is still "a scientific project" which attempts to define some general rules by the study of particular objects.

3) Semiotics must distinguish the models of competence from the models of performance, to repeat Chomsky's terms, and elaborate the second models as hierarchically subject to the first. That means that the notion of "production" (or of productivity), which is so often proposed for it, will be twofold:

a) "Production" from the point of view of the competence, in the sense of the generation or enumeration of a system of rules which are necessary to take account of the semiotic faculty or general aptitude which permits one to produce an infinite ensemble of texts.

b) "Production" from the point of view of the performance, as a work which is necessarily situated historically where some new models should take account of the intervention

of historical subjects who learn, use, interpret, and transform the models of competence according to their position in
the global social process.

NOTES

1. I am obliged here to thank all the members of the team of biblical researchers who for two years have successfully performed a remarkable experiment, that of a collective intellectual work. More than ever the arbitrary use of the proper name is apparent, and this produces the delusion of a single ownership of the methods of intellectual production. A number of the contributions in this volume could be attributed just as well to the names of Michel de Certeau, Jean-Louis Tristani, G. Buchet, or J. Courtès *et al.*
--That being made quite clear, at least as far as the analyses of the gospel texts and Acts were concerned, we were more often the *compilators* and less often the *commentators* of the ideas of the group. Some exegetes, like X. Leon-Dufour or Dreyfus, contributed their vast knowledge and benevolent criticism to the semioticians during the joint meetings.

2. J. Lacan, *Écrits*, Paris: Seuil, 1968, 251.

3. O. Ducrot, "La description sémantique des énoncés français et la notion de présupposition", *L'Homme* 8 (1968).

4. A. J. Greimas, "Éléments d'une grammaire narrative," *L'Homme* 9 (1969), 89.

5. O. Mannoni, *Clefs pour l'imaginaire*, Paris: Seuil, 1969, 202-203.

6. P. Ricoeur, "Structure et herméneutique," *Esprit* 31 (1963), 611 and *idem*, "Reponses à quelques questions," *ibid.*, 628-653. [There is an Eng. trans. of the former in Ricoeur, *The Conflict of Interpretations*, ed. Don Ihde. Evanston: Northwestern University Press, 1974, 27-61 and the latter in *idem.*, "A Confrontation," *New Left Review* 62 (1970), 57-74.

7. Ricoeur, "Structure et herméneutique," 621. [Eng. p. 55.]

8. Ricoeur, "Reponses à quelques questions," 634. [Eng. p. 62.]

9. Ricoeur, "Structure et herméneutique," 599. [Eng. p. 32.]

10. Editor's note: The source of this quotation was attributed to p. 14 of the articles by Ricoeur in n. 6 above which is clearly erroneous.

11. T. Todorov, "La poétique" in *Qu'est-ce que le structuralisme?*, Paris: Seuil, 1969.

12. By developing the instructions of E. Haulotte (cf. p. 188), one could say that the Koran is not a re-writing of the biblical tradition but a scripture pɪ ducing a new matrix.

13. A. J. Greimas, "Éléments pour une théorie de l'interprétation du récit mythique," *Communications* 8 (1966), 33.

14. One should see on this point the contribution by E. Haulotte in this collection (p. 189).

15. Editor's note: At this point in the text, the editor has excised two paragraphs entirely devoted to the contribution by Edmund Leach which has been omitted because it was originally published in English (see the "Introduction", p. vi above). In addition, two notes have also been omitted which were only relevant to Prof. J ᵓach's article, "Genesis as Myth". Otherwise Chabrol's texᵤ remains intact. However, to satisfy the reader who might be interested in these comments, the excised material reads as follows:

> This deductive procedure is pushed to its limit in the analyses of Edmund Leach in his "Genesis as Myth" and in [those of Guy Vuillod]....
> The first [i.e. Leach] does this in order to determine the semantic structure (or content)....E. Leach states at the very beginning that 'the binary oppositions are intrinsically a part of the processes through which human thought passes', it is therefore on a binary model that he attempts to articulate the structure of the myth. He assumes, moreover, that 'all the mythical systems present the same series of binary discriminations between human/superhuman, mortal/immortal, male/female, etc., which are immediately followed by a *"mediation"* of the categories distinguished in this way'. This produces a

tension in the binary structure, which is
shown by the character of 'abnormality' attributed to this median category. This hypothetical model is projected by him as an
example on the narratives of Genesis, the
story of Cain and Abel, the saga of Noah,
the deeds of Abraham, etc. Myths for
Leach have the function of 'mediating'
these antinomic categories.[3] [n. 3: Cf.
on this point the remarks by Dan Sperber
in *Cahiers internationaux de Sociologie*
43 (1967), 136.]

One can contest the complete adequacy of
this model to the given 'reality' which
serves as the point of application. But it
seems that what is exemplary in the method
of this anthropologist is precisely that it
clearly displays, almost in the manner of a
'parable', the necessarily 'arbitrary'
character of every theory (Hjelmslev).[4]
[n. 4: That does not mean that one accepts,
as a matter of course, the hypothesis that
mythical systems must refer to the same
series of binary differentiations which the
systems have the function of reconciling.
In effect, one can: (1) question the universal validity of these semantic categories; and (2) wonder if the antinomic
categories are indeed identical for all
the levels of the social reality of a
society (e.g. economic relationships, kin-
ship systems, rituals, and the universe of
mythical representations).

But above all, one will want to note
that recent research on the narrative (to
which this volume will attempt to contribute) insists on the internal and systematic
coherence of the textual models. On the
one hand, this leads researchers to construct some simulacra of the text which
better take into account the (assumed)
structure, characteristic of their object
and, on the other hand, to develop a
grammar *a priori* from the truly general
elementary structure of the signification
because it is formal (that is to say without a specific content). In this perspective, Edmund Leach's instructions seem to

be valuable to us provided that one replaces the ternary interaction (i.e. the
opposing categories and their mediation)
of the structure that they trace inside
of the *langue* of the myths necessary for
the production of the text.]

16. See C. Chabrol, "Structures intellectuelles," *In-
formations des Sciences sociales* 6 (Oct., 1967), 205-207
and A. J. Greimas, "Éléments pour une théorie de l'interprétation du récit mythique," *Communications* 8 (1966), 28-
59.

IV

EXERCISES ON SOME SHORT STORIES

by

Guy Vuillod (Paris)

The study which we propose is based on a series of
complete stories, at least one could say after reading
them: "This story is ended." They are taken from the
New Testament and sometimes from the Old Testament.[1]
These stories are short, a few lines or a page at most.
It is this characteristic which has led us to prefer them
to others. We do not attach a particular value to their
brevity, but one must recognize that this is an element
which is favorable to an exhuastive analysis, because it
makes the comparisons between these stories much easier
and, in short, because it permits one to handle these objects more easily (all the recent investigations of narrativity confirm them). In choosing these texts, we placed
the criteria of manageableness foremost.

These stories belong to some literary genres which are
traditionally considered to be different, namely: miracle,
parable, prophetic proclamation. We will not retain these
names, even if it is not always possible to avoid them.
Each story is as good as another for us. Perhaps some rules
will appear at the end of the analysis on which the similarity or the differences of these stories are based.

1. The Healing of Two Blind Men: Analysis of a Story.

1.1. *Segmentation into sequences and functions.*

In order to show the steps of this work, we will begin
with the analysis of a story, an analysis which is articulated in five sequences. It is a question here of micro-
sequences or elementary sequences following the terms of
Claude Bremond. The functions are cardinal functions or
kernels, and a sequence is a logical series of kernels which
are connected to one another by a relationship of interde-
pendence.[2] We will show [p. 25] one or more corresponding
actants opposite each function. This separation between
functions and actants is necessary for the progress of the
analysis, that is to say for the passage from the anthropomorphic to the logical level.

Here is the text and its segmentation (Mtt. 9:27-31):

I. *Conjunction*

  --Situation (time-space) D1 And as Jesus passed
                                on from there

  --Entrance on stage D2 two blind men followed
                           him;

II. *Contract*

  --Request D2 crying and saying:
                 "Have pity on us,
                 Son of David."

  --Conditional Response D1 And when he arrived
                              at the house, the
                              blind men approached
                              him and Jesus said to
                              them: "Do you believe
                              that I can do this?"

--Acceptance	D2	They said to him: "Yes, Lord."
--Consequence: Establishment of the contract	D1 D2	

III. *Realization*

--Implementation of the means: + gesture + speech	D1	Then he touched their eyes, saying, "Let it be done to you according to your faith."
--Result (realization of the contract by D1)		and their eyes were opened.

IV. *Retribution*

--Warning	D1	And Jesus sternly ordered them saying: "Do not tell anyone."
--Glorification (realization of the contract by D2)	D2	But they (having departed) told it in all the countryside there.

V. *Disjunction*		(having departed).

Notes:

1. This story is one of the most simple. It makes use of the [p. 26] narrative structure in its essential elements. One cardinal function corresponds to each sentence and sometimes to each segment. The expansions are not very numerous. For example, the *conjunction* sequence includes several terms belonging to the receiver: to follow--to arrive at the house--to approach; and this act is continued in the following sequence.

2. We have pointed out only one pair of actants: the sender (D1) and the receiver (D2). We will study their relationships later. We could have written down another pair: the sender is at the same time the subject who transfers an object (the vision) to the receiver. This pair of actants, which is certainly interesting, is not directly used in our analysis. In other respects, as long as the analysis of the whole text is not advanced, we can only draw up an inventory of object-actants.

3. The segmentation of the *retribution* sequence may be surprising. Why did we make the glorification belonging to the receiver a retribution? As we see it, it is the regularity of this function which forces us to do this. We ought to state clearly here that the first function is a denial of the retribution; the second is an affirmation.

4. We think that it is necessary to separate two sequences in a particular way: the *conjunction* to which the *disjunction* is opposed. Both of these sequences are necessary in order that the story exist and come to a conclusion before beginning again. But these are sequences which accompany other forms of discourse. For example, "Seeing the crowds, he climbed the mountain. He seated himself and his disciples approached him. And opening his mouth, he taught them saying" (Mtt. 5:1).

We will not consider the sequences at the beginning and end of the story to be essential for the analysis of the body of the story.

1.2 *The narrative grammar.*

The three central sequences can be compared to the schema of the test which A. J. Greimas has isolated from the Russian folktale.[3] This schema is expressed as an algorithm of the functions:

$$A \;+\; F \;+\; c$$

where: A designates the contract with its two functions: mandate *vs.* acceptance,

F designates the confrontation or the struggle with two functions: confrontation *vs.* success,

c designates the consequence.

In the narrative-*occurrence* we have:

1. A contract: the final acceptance corresponds to the demand, which, if it is not explicitly expressed, is contained in the transition to the realization. The position of a *condition* between the two dramatizes the contract. We will consider it to be an expansion of the principal functions (cf. Mtt. 15:21-28 [and Mk. 7:24-30] where the contract is even more developed).

2. A confrontation: it is not difficult first of all to recognize [p. 27] two connected functions here: one which we will willingly call "manipulation" and another which is the result. (This is confirmed by the other stories: the manipulation fails, therefore the function which follows it is a failure, cf. the disciples' attempt to exorcize an illness in Mtt. 17:14-20; Mk. 9:14-29; Lk. 9:37-43). In other respects, many stories of the same type are explicitly constructed around a battle: Jesus heals a demoniac. "Then he rebuked him saying, 'Be silent! and come out of him!,' and the unclean spirit, convulsing him and crying with a loud voice, came out of him" (Mk. 1:23-28). The difference between stories of struggle and manipulation is only one of degree. The greater the powers of the hero, the more indistinct the effort or the difficulty of the enterprise appears. A. J. Greimas has noted that in the qualifying test, the

struggle was often symbolic or simulated.[4] In any case, the
main point, the comparison of which may be valuable, is that
this function of manipulation may take the place of that of
confrontation in the schema of the test.

3. The consequence is twofold. The outcome of the
operation obtains the benefit anticipated. Therefore it is
a question of a liquidation of a lack (in contra-distinction
to the stories where the initial situation is one of equilibrium, the story *ends* with a villainy, cf. e.g. Ex. 7:14-
25). However, as we have noted, another function appears:
the glorification or the revelation of the hero. That is
to say, the isotopy of the text is twofold: it must be
read on the level of the sequence itself, from the standpoint of the beneficiary as the transfer of an object-good,
and at the level of the gospel text, from the standpoint of
the hero, as the transfer of an object-message.[5]

1.3 *Conclusion.*

As remote as these stories may be from the Russian folktale, the organization of the functions is identical and the
narrativity is the same. It is the putting into parenthesis
of the actants which makes this similarity visible. The two
analyses which we have successively performed on the same
story are encased in one another. The first appears to be a
superficial recovery of the story, the second seems to go
further and it would be tempting to speak of a deep structure
in its theme. We hesitate to use the concepts of surface and
deep structures, and we restrain ourselves with this warning
from A. Culioli: "One cannot decide *a priori* that only two
levels exist, superficial and deep, except by posing a rudi-
mentary distinction...."[6] We will simply say that the levels
of abstraction where these structures are situated are differ-

ent, the second being more abstract than the first, although
this formulation is still not very satisfactory.

2. The Logic of the Contracts.

   This structuration being established, it is obvious
that a great many biblical stories are closely related to it.
It seems interesting to us from now on to see how different
or opposing stories are produced from the same structure.
The logical possibilities of the contractual relationship
[p. 28] permit us to foresee it. We will follow the instructions already given to us by A. J. Greimas on the
Russian folktale,[7] by distinguishing two kinds of contract
which correspond to the level of the actants, the first
from the perspective of the sender, the second from that
of the receiver.

2.1 *The contract in mandate/prohibition.*
   The perspective of the sender is twofold: either he
gives an order, or he forbids one to act:

2.1.1. If he gives an order, we would have:

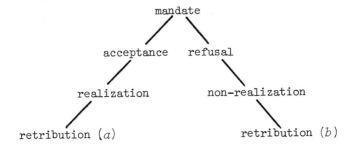

Retribution (*a*) consists of a recompense; retribution
(*b*) of a punishment.

Example (*a*):

>...He said to Simon, 'Move into deeper
>water, and cast your nets for the fish.'
>And answering, Simon said, 'Master we have
>labored all night, we have taken nothing,
>but on your word, I will go cast the nets'
>(Lk. 5:4-11).

Example (*b*):

>The word of Yahweh was addressed to
>Jonah, the son of Amittai: 'Arise,' he
>said to him, 'go to Nineveh, the great
>city, and proclaim to them that their
>evil has ascended to me.' Jonah departed,
>but to flee to Tarshish far from Yahweh...
>(Jonah 1:1ff.).

Here, as is often the case, the refusal is implicitly
contained in the act opposed to the mandate (the opposite
is also found, cf. Mtt. 9:27-31).

In the first example, before complying with the mandate,
Simon makes an objection which he immediately withdraws.
This process is the opposite to that we encountered in Mtt.
9:27-31: the objection occupies the same place as the conditional response. There is another example of this dramati-
zation: Moses presents no less than four objections before
making a decision (Ex. 3-4:17). But in another version, only
one objection is necessary (Ex. 6:2-13). Between the two,
the catalyst has done its job.

2.1.2. If the sender orders the receiver not to act, we
would have: [p. 29]

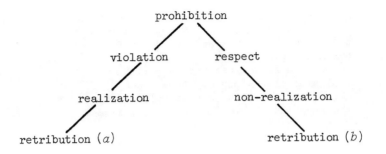

We have constructed this schema parallel to the preceding
one; it requires some explanation. If a "realization" occurs
after the violation, it is in order to enhance a positive aspect of the violation which was isolated by A. J. Greimas.
In reality, it is a kind of injunction from the point of
view of the receiver, the latter substituting his own will
(and his own act) for that of the sender. The respect of
the interdiction corresponds to the acceptance in 1.1. The
retribution (a) is a punishment which we will illustrate by
a story below.

The retribution is a recompense: it is all one part of
the biblical literature which it would be appropriate to
quote here, praising the just who do not break the divine
commandments, and for whom everything prospers:

> He is like a tree planted
> near streams of water,
> which gives its fruit in its season
> and its foliage never withers;
> in all that he does, he prospers:
> there is nothing of the kind for the wicked,
> nothing of the kind! (Ps. 1:3-4)

Example (a):

> The city and everything found in it will
> be devoted to Yahweh as accursed....Do not

go, influenced by lust, to steal something
which is accursed, because this will expose
the whole camp of Israel to the curse and
bring trouble on it....
But the Israelites became guilty of a
violation of the curse: Achan, son of
Carmi...took something that fell under
the curse and Yahweh's anger was inflamed
against the Israelites (Josh. 5:13-7:26).

2.1.3. These different possibilities allow us to articulate
the preceding contracts.

So, as A. J. Greimas has set it up:

1. $\dfrac{\text{mandate}}{\text{acceptance}}$ = establishment of the contract

2. $\dfrac{\text{prohibition}}{\text{violation}}$ = breaking of the contract

which is equivalent to the articulation of a category:
A $vs.$ $\bar{\text{A}}$ (establishment of the contract $vs.$ breaking of the
contract) or in a semic system: [p. 30]

$$\dfrac{a}{\text{non-a}} \quad vs. \quad \dfrac{\bar{a}}{\underset{\text{non-a}}{.....}} \qquad \left(\dfrac{\text{mandate}}{\text{acceptance}} \quad vs. \quad \dfrac{\text{prohibition}}{\text{violation}} \right)$$

We could introduce another establishment of a contract, and
another breaking of a contract (or, more precisely, a $refusal$),
such as:

3. $\dfrac{\text{mandate}}{\text{refusal}}$ = refusal of the contract, or $\dfrac{a}{\underset{\text{non-a}}{.....}}$

and

4. $\dfrac{\text{prohibition}}{\text{respect}}$ = establishment of the contract, or

$$\dfrac{a}{\overset{\textstyle :::::}{\text{non-a}}}$$

The refusal of an order (non-A) is equivalent to the violation of an interdiction: in the two cases, the will of the receiver is substituted for that of the sender. Likewise, the acceptance of the mandate is equivalent to the respect of the prohibition, a double negation is equal to an acceptance:

$$\dfrac{:::::}{\text{non-a}} \quad = \quad \text{non-a}$$

In fact, in our stories, it is not no. 1 which is opposed to no. 2, but 1 to 3 and 2 to 4:

$$\dfrac{a}{\text{non-a } vs. \ \text{non-a}}$$

and $\qquad \dfrac{\bar{a}}{\text{non- } vs. \ \text{non-}}$

therefore: $\quad \dfrac{a}{\text{non-a } vs. \ \text{non-a}} \qquad vs. \qquad \dfrac{\bar{a}}{\text{non-a } vs. \ \text{non-a}}$

The biblical narratives reveal more complex oppositions compared with the Russian folktale.

2.2 *The contract in question/X.*

2.2.1. Let us begin with a theoretical construction by building on the preceding basic principles. Other stories begin with a contract where it is the receiver who expresses a request. There is a symmetry between this request and the injunction, the first being the opposite of the second. Moreover, these two forms are present in the Exodus: the liberation from Egypt is *sometimes* a request on the part of the Hebrews: "The sons of Israel complained because of their slavery. God heard their complaint. God remembered his covenant with Abraham, Isaac, and Jacob. God saw the sons of Israel; God realized..." (Ex. 2:23-25). And *sometimes* it is a mission given to Moses by Yahweh (Ex. 3-6).

Thanks to the results obtained above, and considering that the demand is the expression of a negativity, or "non-a'", we obtain: [p. 31]

$$\frac{demand}{acceptance} = \frac{non\text{-}a'}{a'} \quad \text{and consequently:} \quad \frac{demand}{refusal} = \frac{non\text{-}a'}{\bar{a}}$$

It is customary to think of a negative transformation of this system, let us say:

$$\frac{\overset{\cdots\cdots}{non\text{-}a'}}{\bar{a}'} \quad \text{and} \quad \frac{\overset{\cdots\cdots}{non\text{-}a'}}{\bar{\bar{a}}'}$$

This is a theoretical construction, to be sure, which can perhaps be verified in the sacrificial ritual where the gift or the attempt to give (from man to the deity) would

correspond to the demand of the preceding contract (non-a'),
and either the refusal of God (a') or his acceptance (a')
would correspond to this gift.

2.2.2. Let us keep, for the miracle stories, the first
system whose tree is:

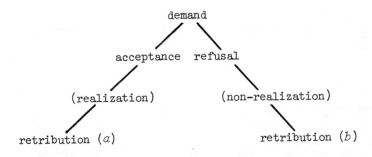

The story of the healing of two blind men (Mtt. 9:27-31)
is a typical story of (a). We will cite here an example of
the refusal of a miracle (b):

> And the Pharisees came and they began to
> argue with him seeking to obtain a heavenly
> sign from him, in order to test him. And
> sighing deeply in his spirit, he said: 'Why
> does this generation seek a sign? Truly, I
> say to you: there will be no sign given to
> this generation' (Mk. 8:11-12).

Elsewhere, confronting the same demand from the Pharisees,
Jesus refuses to perform a miracle, but responds by evoking the
enigmatic sign of the prophet Jonah:

> 'There will be no sign given except the
> sign of the prophet Jonah. For as Jonah
> was three days and three nights in the

belly of the whale, so will the Son of Man
be three days and three nights in the heart
of the earth' (Mtt. 12:38-40).

2.3 The regularity of the system appears in this completely
mechanical exposition. Freedom is only an illusion in these
contracts. It is a game within a inexorable structure.
All that the sender commands is realized; everything which
is transgressed is punished. Retribution always has the
last word. [p. 32]

3. Structures in Series.

We will now show some of the possible options in the
structure of this kind of story. On each branch of the
different trees, a narrative could take a form which is
different from the adjacent story. Moreover, all the
branches do not succeed in forming a story, properly
speaking. Thus we have chosen a poem or chant in order
to illustrate the observance of these laws. The whole
story of one just man could signify the same thing. The
same basic structure (we are not giving a technical meaning
to this term; it is simply the structure which we shall use
as a hypothesis) of departure can be varied to produce some
multiple branches which can lead to some different texts
after a certain number of relays, which it is difficult to
put in order. However, we will attempt to systematize the
story branches or the texts grafted on a common trunk.

This systematization will be formulated in Chomsky's
grammatical categories, in particular in his rules of transformation.[8] Let us briefly recall what a transformation is

in a generative grammar, retaining only what we will use for
what follows.

The transformation rules in generative grammar follow
the rules of formation. These latter rules generate a
structure or series of elements for each sentence,[9] which
we will call the syntagmatic indicator or structural index
(we are only interested in the results here). For the
sentence S, *Peter hit the ball*, the syntagmatic indicator
will be written, after the application of the formation
rules:[10]

$$\text{NP} \;\text{---}\; \text{Aux} \;\text{---}\; \text{V} \;\text{---}\; \text{NP}$$
$$1 \;\text{---}\; 2 \;\text{---}\; 3 \;\text{---}\; 4$$

This sentence is analyzed: Peter-present--hit--the ball.
The first row represents the sequence of the grammatical
categories from which the sentence is formed. On the second
row, the numbers indicate the rank which they occupy in this
indicator. The rank is not a simple transposition of the
order of the sentence. It is based on a structural analysis,
and it is a series whose order is specific.

It is this structure which the transformation rules
control and modify. They convert it to a new syntagmatic
indicator. The passive transformation (written as T passive
and symbolized [p. 33] by $\Rightarrow$), if we keep the preceding
example, will consist of switching elements 1 and 4, and
adding in their respective positions: to be + past participle (PP) and "by". The rule will be given in the following way:

T passive: *a*) structural analysis:

$$\text{NP} \;\text{------}\; \text{Aux} \;\text{------}\; \text{V} \;\text{------}\; \text{NP}$$
$$1 \;\text{------}\; 2 \;\text{------}\; 3 \;\text{------}\; 4$$

b) structural change:

1 -------- 2 -------- 3 -------- 4 ⇒

4 --- 2 + to be + PP -------- 3 -------- by + 1

The last line gives the new structural index, or:

the ball--present + to be + PP --- hit --- by + Peter.

One must still apply other rules (some transformation and phonological rules) in order to obtain the correct sentence: *The ball is hit by Peter.*

It is important to remember that a transformation is unfolded in two stages: "It will have a structural analysis (or a structural schema) of the sequence to which it can be applied for the first step. In the second place, it will be submitted to certain changes in the sequence analyzed. This second step can be said to be a structural change."[11]

In other words, a transformation is a rule which is applied to a series of elements possessing a structure determined by the analysis and which makes it undergo a change so that another sequence of elements is given.

The structure of the text (cf. 1.2 above) is comparable to the sequence of elements obtained by the application of the rules of formation. Considering this sequence of functions as a syntagmatic indicator appears to be justified to us to the extent to which, in the second case, we have a series of elements which result from a structural analysis. Therefore we propose to use these transformation rules to convert this structure into other structures.

There are theoretically several kinds of transformations. We will examine some of them one after another:

--the suppression and the addition of elements

--the permutation or movement of elements

--the arrangement of sequences.

3.1 *The suppression of elements.*

$$A \;\;\nleftrightarrow\;\; F \;\;\nleftrightarrow\;\; c$$
$$1 \;\;\nleftrightarrow\;\; 2 \;\;\nleftrightarrow\;\; 3$$
$$1 \;\;\nleftrightarrow\;\; \emptyset \;\;\nleftrightarrow\;\; 3$$

The opposition or the manipulation is suppressed. Only a contract and its consequence remains in this structure. Is it still [p. 34] a story? It does not seem to be. At best this will be the structure of juridical texts, or strictly speaking of some sentences of this genre:

> 'Blessed are the pure in heart;
> they will see God' (Mtt. 5:8).

A "parable" however may come close to this structure, if it deals almost exclusively with the contractual relationships. Here is an example:

> 'Now what do you think? A man had two sons.
> Approaching the first son, he said: "Child,
> go to work today in the vineyard." But
> responding, he said: "I will not go."
> Later, feeling guilty, he went. Approaching
> the second son, the father said the same
> thing. But the son responding said: "Of
> course, Lord" and did not go.
>   Which of the two has done the will of the
> Father? They said: "The first."' (Mtt. 21:
> 28-31).

It is apparent that the suppression of F is not complete, but the interest of the story rests on the contract where a

new dimension is introduced, that of being and appearing.
The refusal or acceptance in the first case is situated at
the level of appearance, while the execution (and the decision which underlies it) is situated on the level of being
or rather of doing.

This story perfectly illustrates the contractual alternative:

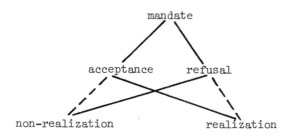

The suppression of A can be considered. Now it is difficult to find some stories in this literature which correspond
to the total obliteration of the contract. This story will
make that clear:

> As he arrived at the threshing-floor of
> Chidon, Uzzah put his hand on the ark of God
> and held it in place, because the oxen had
> almost overturned it. Then the wrath of
> Yahweh was inflamed against Uzzah; God struck
> him on the spot for this mistake, and he died
> there, beside the ark of God (1 Chron. 13:9-
> 11 and 2 Sam. 6:6-8).

Apparently there is no contract in this story. But if it
was a mistake for Uzzah to do what he did, there was a transgression of a law (it is clearly given elsewhere: "When Aaron
and his sons have finished covering the sacred things and all

their utensils, at the time of breaking camp, the sons of
Kōhăth will come to carry them. But if they touch what is
consecrated, they will die" (Num. 4:15). The contract
exists, although it is not known by one of the two protagon-
ists. As in other cases, rather than a suppression of the
contract, there is a disclosure of the contract after the
event, and the transformation which rules this structure
will be a permutation of the contract. [p. 35]

3.2 *The permutation.*

If we reintroduce the conjunction and the disjunction
(which is an addition to the transformation terms), we can
make their positions change and produce different structures.
The conjunction and disjunction frame the narrative unit;
this is the case with story no. 1 (i.e. Matt. 9:27-31).
They only bracket the contract; the realization is made
elsewhere (in time and space). We then find a story, among
others, like that of the announcement of the Angel to Mary
(Lk. 1:26-38, 46-55 and 2:1-7). Here is the text:

I. *Conjunction*

--Appearance	D1	"The sixth month, the angel Gabriel was sent by God into the village of Galilee named Nazareth,
--Situation	D2	to a virgin betrothed to a man named Joseph, of the house of David; and the virgin's name was Mary.
--Consequence: conjunction		He came to her

II. *Contract*

--Salutation	D1	and said to her: 'Greetings to you Mary filled with grace. The Lord is with you.'
--Trouble	D2	With these words, she was bewildered and she wondered what this greeting meant.
--Communication of the message	D1	But the angel said to her: 'Do not be afraid, because you have been found filled with God's grace. Behold, you will conceive and give birth to a son, and you will give him the name of Jesus. He will be great, and will be called the Son of the Most High. The Lord God will give him the throne of David his father; he will reign over the house of Jacob forever; and his kingdom will have no end.'
--Objection	D2	But Mary said to the Angel: 'How can that be since I know no man?'
--Response	D1	The angel answered her: 'The Holy Spirit will come upon you, and the power of the Most-High you will take into your womb; that is why the child will be holy and [p. 36] will be called the Son of God. And behold Elizabeth your relative also has a

			son in her old age, and this is her sixth month, she who was called barren. For with God nothing is impossible.'
--Acceptance		D2	Mary then said: 'I am the handmaiden of the Lord, let it be to me according to your word.'
--Consequence: establishment of the contract	D1	D2	

III. *Disjunction*

And the Angel left her.

IV. *Realization*

    --Being pregnant and   D2   ...Mary, his betrothed
        giving birth   was pregnant. Now
while they were there, the time came for her to be delivered. And she gave birth to her first-born son....

    --Consequence:
      realization of the
      contract on the
      part of D1

V. *Retribution*

    --Praise   D2   Mary then said: 'My
soul exalts the Lord, and my spirit rejoices in God my saviour....'"

    --Consequence:
      realization of the
      contract on the
      part of D2

By simplifying the structure of this story somewhat, one
cannot fail to compare it with that of Mtt. 9:27-31. A transformation brings about a permutation, which permits one to
pass from one to the other. It will be written:

T announcement:

Conj. --- Contract --- Realization --- Retribution --- Disj.

1 --- 2 --- 3 --- 4 --- 5 =>

1 --- 2 + 5 --- 3 --- 4 --- $\emptyset$

The structure of Lk. 1:26-38, 46-55 and 2:1-7, which is traditionally classified among prophetic announcements, will be:

Cj --- A --- Dj --- F --- C

[p. 37]

3.3 *The combination of structures.*

It is possible to harmonize the structure of Mtt. 9:27-31
and that which we have called an "announcement". The realization is indicated by a structure of this latter type and executed in a structure similar to the first structure. Some
stories like the grasshopper plague (Ex. 10:1-20) and the
miracle of the meal and oil (1 K. 17:7-15) verify this construction very well. The transformation will consist of substituting in the "realization" sequence of the second structure the whole sequence no. 1:

T combination:

$$
\begin{array}{ccccc}
C \text{------} A \text{------} D \text{------} F \text{------} C \\
1 \text{------} 2 \text{------} 5 \text{------} 3 \text{------} 4 \\
C \text{------} A \text{------} F \text{------} C \text{------} D \\
1 \text{------} 2 \text{------} 3 \text{------} 4 \text{------} 5
\end{array} \Bigg\} \Rightarrow
$$

1 -------- 2 ------ 5 + 1 + 2 + 3 + 4 + 5 -------- 4

Or   Cj --- A --- Dj --- Cj --- A --- F --- C --- Dj --- C

One must not expect that a story may be completely structured
in this way. In spite of everything, this is only a good
approximation. One will note that all the elements, except
for the realization, are doubled, which assumes, if one attempts to avoid what is pure and simple repetition, the
presence of four sender-receiver actants. The ones playing
two roles are reduced to three:

$$
\begin{array}{ccc}
D1 & \text{------} & D2 \\
(D2) = D1 & \text{------} & D2'
\end{array}
$$

3.4 *Conclusion.*

To what extent are these transformation rules general-
izable? We respond by showing how the enclave or framework
originating from the story[12] is similar to that last transformation, with one small difference: the latter produces a
suppression of an element, which is not true for the enclave.
[p. 38]

By adopting a symbolic notation,

if X —— Y —— Z were the sequence of the story in
Mtt. 9:27-31 or "R1"

and X —— Y —— Z that of the story in Mtt. 15:21-28
(and Mk. 7:24-30) or "R2"

--the enclave would be:

R1 X —— Y —— Z ⎫
                 ⎬ ⇒ X —— X —— Y —— Z—— Y —— Z
R2 X —— Y —— Z ⎭

T combination would be:

R1 X —— Y —— Z ⎫
                 ⎬ ⇒ X —— ∅ —— X —— Y —— Z —— Z
R2 X —— Y —— Z ⎭

We hope that this comparison is valid. Nevertheless,
many problems remain unsolved: among other things, at what
level do the suppressions and additions of elements occur?
Are some relays necessary in order to lead to a particular
end of the story...? But the primary question concerns a
prior one which we have considered to be known: what is a
story?

NOTES

1. Although these stories could be taken by themselves, we think that this extraction does violence to the text, considered as a whole. This is a violence which it is not good to pass over in silence.

2. Claude Bremond, "Le message narratif," *Communications* 4 (1964), 4-32 and *idem*, "La logique des possibles narratifs," *Communications* 8 (1966), 60-76. [The editor of this work has translated the first of these two articles and it will be published in a future issue of *Semeia*.] Cf. also, Roland Barthes, "Introduction à l'analyse structurale du récit," *Communications* 8 (1966), 13. [Cf. the Eng. trans. of this article in *New Literary History* 6 (1975), 238-272.] We think that this terminology is comparable to that of A. J. Greimas in his "Éléments pour une théorie de l'interprétation du récit mythique," *Communications* 8 (1966), 37. [Cf. the Eng. trans. of this article by Greimas in P. and E. K. Marandas (eds.), *Structural Analysis of Oral Tradition*, Philadelphia: Univ. of Penn. Press, 1971, 81-124, which speaks about narrative statements each including their own functions and which are followed by one or several actants and an organization of statements in narrative syntagms.]

3. A. J. Greimas, *Sémantique structurale*, Paris: Larousse, 1966, 192ff.

4. *Art. cit., Communications* 8 (1966), 39.

5. On the isotopy of a text, cf. *art. cit., Communications* 8 (1966), 30-31.

6. "La formalisation en linguistique," in *Cahiers pour l'analyse*, no. 9 (1968), 109.

7. Greimas, *Sémantique structurale*, 195-196 and 209-210.

8. Cf. esp. Noam Chomsky, *Syntactic Structures*, The Hague: Mouton, 1957; *idem, Aspects of the Theory of Syntax*, Cambridge, Mass.: M.I.T. Press, 1965; Nicolas Ruwet, *Intro-*

duction à la grammaire générative, Paris: Plon, 1968. [Eng. trans.: *An Introduction to Generative Grammar*, trans. Norval Smith, Amsterdam: North Holland Publishing Co., 1973.]

9. To follow the evolution of generative grammar in characterizing these elements would take us too far afield, and it is not completely necessary for this work (cf. "Tendances nouvelles en syntaxe générative," *Langages* 14 [June, 1969]).

10. We generally use the following symbols: --S: sentence; --NP: noun sentence (nominal syntagm, here: Peter, the ball); --Aux: auxiliary (here: present); --V: verb (verbal root, which one gives, for facility, in the infinitive form in French, e.g. *frapper* [= to hit]); --the sign "──" is not only used here in order to separate the elements, it also indicates the logical bond which unites them.

11. N. Ruwet, *op. cit.*, 192.

12. Claude Bremond, *art. cit.*, *Communications* 8 (1966), 61; T. Todorov, "Les hommes-récits," *Tel Quel* 31 (Fall, 1967), 67-69.

V

THE WOMEN AT THE TOMB:
A STRUCTURAL ANALYSIS ESSAY
OF A GOSPEL TEXT

by

Louis Marin

Our subject is limited. It consists of analyzing a
short story which we have read in Matthew (28:1-8), Mark
(16:1-8), and Luke (24:1-11) which reports the arrival of
the women at the tomb of Jesus which they found empty. This
analysis will be neither complete nor exhaustive. It will
remain at what A. J. Greimas calls the superficial structures of the narrative, while throwing out some hypotheses
for the elaboration of the codes implemented by the texts
examined. Moreover, this study of the surface structures
could only assume its full value beyond the arbitrary limits
of the texts envisaged by the integration of the narrative
in the global narrative of the Passion and Resurrection of
Jesus which should also be submitted to an analysis of the
same kind.

One of the working hypotheses which could be given for
an analysis of this kind and which ought to be tested and
verified would be the application of the functional and
mythical actantial model which was worked out by A. J.
Greimas from the works of Lévi-Strauss, Dumézil, and especially Propp. At first glance and in a general way, one
can construct the following actantial model of this whole
narrative:

Sender: *God* ————————→ Object = the Good ————→ Receiver: *man*
                            ↑   News:
                                   eternal
                                   life

Opponents: *the Chief* → Subject: *Jesus Christ* ← Helper: *the*
Priests, the Elders,   *disciples,*
Judas...   *the women*

On the other hand, the functions of the global narrative could be developed according to the following schema:

I. Contract: mandate   The Son of Man goes to be delivered
              acceptance   in order to be crucified.

II. Succession of three tests:
    1. qualifying   The anointing at Bethany
    2. principal   All the crucifixion sequences
    3. glorifying   Revelation of Jesus.   [p. 40]

This last test is characterized in the gospel narrative by the multiplication of partial tests (the meeting of the women and the angel at the tomb, of Mary and Jesus [who mistook him for the gardener], of the Emmaus pilgrims and Jesus, the recognition by the touch of Thomas, etc., and finally the recognition by the community of the disciples). However, one should note one remarkable trait in this redundancy of glorifying tests: only the recognition of the resurrected Jesus by the community is effective and genuine. *All the other recognitions made by individuals fail.*

Nevertheless, we will emphasize in order to take direct aim at the specificity of the texts considered, the process

of displacement that *these* particular texts have undergone
in the general model applied to the global text. In effect,
the narrative of the women at the tomb can be characterized
from this point of view in the following way:

1. As far as the general actantial model defined above
is concerned, the women who belong to the *helper* actant in
the global narrative, are found here in the *subject* position.
The angel, on the other hand, possesses the helper status,
but he is also a *mediator* between the sender, God, and the
receiver, who is basically formed here by the disciples as
a society or community. Therefore our narrative defines the
general receiver, humanity, as a religious community.

The *opponent* actant is perfectly represented: a) by the
sealed and rolled stone which refers to the general actant
which is defined in the global narrative as the priests and
elders of the people (these are the ones who have positioned
the stone in front of the tomb so as to prevent a possible
fraud by the apostles intending to give support to the prophetic discourse of Jesus: "I will rise from the dead in
three days"); and b) by the soldiers.

As for the *object* actant, which is defined as the Good
News announcing eternal life, the narrative makes us see a
displacement of its content.

The intervention of the angel, who is an object of
communication, and the message "that Jesus has risen" comes
to be substituted for the object which, at the beginning of
the narrative, is the object of the "quest" of the women and
the object of desire which is defined as the dead body of
Jesus. We will return later to this most important point.

2. *As far as the functions are concerned*, our narrative
is well organized as a "micro-test", which is defined at the

beginning as an established state of a lack or an absence and at the end by a liquidation of the lack. However, this liquidation is not effective but only *virtual* since it only takes place in the verbal form of a message which is either not transmitted or not believed. In short, it is not completed by recognition (= negative micro-test), or if one prefers, considering the end of the global narrative, it is virtually positive.

ANALYSIS OF THE TEXT

We have arbitrarily chosen Matthew's narrative as the guideline for this analysis, and we will use the other parallel narratives as variants. This narrative is divided into four main parts: [p. 41]

1. The arrival of the women at the sepulchre.
2. The arrival of the angel.
3. The angel's discourse or the delivery of the message.
4. The departure of the women and the transmission of the message.

Part I. *The arrival of the women at the sepulchre.*

This sequence includes three elements: (1) the spatial-temporal index; (2) the subject actant (or helper in the position of the subject): the women or the woman; (3) the object actant: the tomb.

(a) The spatial-temporal index gives us the beginning of an especially interesting code. There are two temporal indexes in Matthew. There is the index of a *religious or liturgical ritual time*: "After the day of the Sabbath"; and there is an index of a *profane cosmic time*: "as the first day of the week began to dawn". The opposition of the religious and profane marks, therefore, the determination of the moment. This is an opposition which is also found in Mark but not in Luke. However, between Matthew and Mark, on the one hand, and Luke (and especially John) on the other, a new opposition takes form within the profane or cosmic time, i.e. that of light and darkness. On the one hand, there is "the dawn" and "as the sun was rising"; and, on the other hand, there is "very early" and "as it was still dark". Thus a double interplay of oppositions—light/darkness, profane/sacred—emphasizes the initial moment of the text. There is an opposition whose common characteristic is a beginning or a commencement. It is a question of a new sacred week (after the Sabbath), a new day, and a new profane week. Therefore the profane and the sacred coincide on the temporal plane, and in this sense they are respectively beginnings or commencements. But they are also opposed to one another in that the sacred week is characterized as *past*, and the profane week is characterized as *beginning*: "after the Sabbath"/"the first day of the week"/"the first moment of the day".

This new opposition is correlated with the light/darkness opposition. The last hour of darkness is the first hour of the day; the end of the last day of the Jewish holy week is the beginning of the first day of the "Christian" week. In other words, we have a stage of a *passage* through a *threshold*, that is to say, to a *reversal* of the old/new and Jewish/Christian times (cf. the threshold rites of passage), and to the creative, initiatory moment of a new cycle.

This spatial threshold (the opening of the entrance to the tomb) which constitutes the preoccupation of the women corresponds to this temporal threshold according to the triple dimension of profane/sacred, nocturnal/diurnal, and Judaic/Christian. A space is *closed*, i.e. the tomb by the stone. One must replace this closed space with an *open* space, i.e. the stone must be rolled away. Matthew presents a truly cosmic "production" of the opening of this space, i.e. an earthquake, which, by upsetting the natural world order (a closed cosmic space) has the effect of opening the tomb.

The emptiness of this space corresponds to the opening of the sacred space of the tomb. At the same time, the crossing of the threshold [i.e. door] of the tomb has revealed its emptiness. Therefore there is a twofold interplay of spatial oppositions: opening/closing, fullness/emptiness (of the space). [p. 42]

Finally on the plane of the global narrative, this spatial opening and this temporal passage refer to another beginning, to the overture (in the musical or dramatic sense of the word) of the third glorifying test. This is the overture of a new sequence of the narrative.

One will note that one can see the same phenomenon of overture which is like an echo (Mtt. 27:51-53) at the time of the death of Christ (which marks the end of the principal test when the disqualification of the hero takes place): the temple curtain (which closes the holy of holies) is torn in two. The rocks and the earth are split; other tombs are opened. Thus there is a double opening of holy, religious space (the temple and the tombs) and cosmic space (the earth and the earthquake).

It is notable that this spatial overture, which is at the same time an initiation of a new temporal cycle, is connected to the resurrection which is also defined as an *exit* into an open space. The tomb is a holy closure like the temple, time, and death. To rise from the dead is to leave the tomb; it is to open the sacred space to the dimensions of the cosmos; and it is to open death's door which may be conceived as closed.

(b) The subject actant: the women. Neither their proper names nor their number appear to be pertinent traits. There is a question here of a *"female" class*. No doubt, it would be interesting to examine thoroughly the status of this particular actant in the global narrative and especially to define precisely the feminine inflexion of the global "helper" actant and the nature of its relationship to the "hero" actant. We will return to this point in the functional analysis of this narrative, but let us note as a hypothesis that the women are a modality of the function of *desire* or the quest. More precisely, they appear in this particular narrative as the *initiators of the final test*. In the hierarchy of the receivers of the message, they are the first ones to receive the good news, but at the same time, they are the "weakest" intermediaries.

(c) The object actant is the tomb, but it is the tomb in so far as it contains the dead body, i.e. the tomb as symbolic of a corpse. This relationship clearly appears in Mark. It is implicitly present in Luke in the sequence which interests us, but it is explicit in sequence 3. The angel says: "I know that you seek Jesus Christ who was crucified." The object of the quest is Jesus Christ in so far as he is the one who was crucified. It is the dead body which *fills* the tomb, hence the body puts a system of correlations into action:

(1) *Dead body* (= cadaver) which one can *touch* (unction)

(2) *Living body* as an object which one can *touch*, with which one can enter into contact, either directly or by the mediation of this container which is the clothing (cf. the miracles which have contact with the body, e.g. Mk. 5:25-34).

(3) *Living body* as an object which one cannot touch (cf. the *Noli me tangere* [= "Do not touch me." Jn. 20:17]).

(4) *Living body* as an object which one can *touch* (cf. the skeptical Thomas).

Contact appears here as a taking possession of the living or dead body, but always as a phenomenon of passivity. The body [p. 43] is offered or offers itself as an *object* unlike the active contacts which are produced, for example, in the miraculous healings. Hence there is a system of oppositions here.

In this sense, the episode of Thomas, who is skeptical of Jesus' resurrection, is similar to and the opposite of the episode of Mary Magdalene in John's gospel, just as the anointing at Bethany is similar to and the opposite of the arrival of the women at the tomb.

(d) The general function of sequence 1 is that of the desire or the quest of the object. The desire and the object of desire are put in the religious and ritual context of the Law.

See the Gospel of Peter 50-57:

> Now early in the morning of the (day) of
> the Lord, Mary Magdalene, a disciple of
> the Lord..., taking her friends with her,
> went to the tomb where he had been laid.
> And they were afraid that the Jews would
> see them and they said: 'Ever since the
> day when he was crucified, we have not
> been able to weep and lament, let us now
> at least approach his tomb. But who will
> roll away the stone for us, which has
> been placed against the entrance to the
> tomb, so that, being admitted, we can be
> near him and do what we must? For the
> stone was great and we are afraid that
> someone will see us....'

The accent is put on the notion of ritual and religious
duty: "to mourn", "to lament" / "to anoint the corpse",
"to do what one ought to do".

It is important to define precisely the place and meaning of this ritual of unction or embalming of the cadaver in
Judaism. But in any case, it is probable that this ritual
was intended to preserve the cadaver. In this sense, this
funeral ritual is a symbolic form of the accomplishment of
the desire for the preservation of the corpse which mimes
the possession of the body.

This is the reason for the interest in and the importance of the anointing at Bethany which constitutes a sequence opposed to sequence 1 of our narrative (Mark 14:3-9
[8], Matthew 26:6-13 [12], John 12:1-8 [7]). A woman qualified the body of Jesus to be a corpse by anointing it at
Bethany. The women qualify the corpse to be a body by
anointing it at the tomb. In the first case, the gesture
of the woman at Bethany is a stage in the qualifying test
of the hero. She qualifies it for the test of death or for
this negative principal test which is the crucifixion. In
the second case, the gestures of the women constitute a

kind of symbolic qualification for the glorifying test, i.e. for the return and recognition of the hero as living beyond death. But this qualification is symbolic because the body of Christ has risen from the dead and will be recognized as a living body, while the anointing by the women at the tomb *was intended to preserve the body* as a dead body.

The whole meaning of the narrative will consist of the frustration of the immediate (but also symbolic) accomplishment of the desire. However, its accomplishment is delayed; it is mediate but real ("he has risen from the dead").

This analysis permits us to return to the status of the woman:

1. She has a relationship with death (the weeping, burial of the dead, their embalming). The desire is realized symbolically (but perfectly, that is to say, immediately) in death.

2. She has a relationship with the hero, but it is an individual and emotional relationship of possessive passivity: hence the anointing contact, the passive touching of the object. [p. 44]

This double relationship is opposed to: (1) the affirmation or recognition of the hero as alive, but with a "difference", in other words it is a postponed but truly realized desire; (2) the affirmation or recognition of the hero by the community of the disciples in a relationship which is no longer individual but communal.

This double opposition is an inflexion of two very deep semic categories: life/death; individual/society.

Part II. *The arrival of the angel.*

a) *The index of the arrival of the angel.* We will not
return to the earthquake which is the spatial index of the
irruption of the sacred into nature and the opening of profane space. On the other hand, it is necessary to investigate thoroughly the second index of the arrival of the angel
which is his clothing. The angel's clothing is characterized
by its absence of color (white) and its brightness. It is
resplendant and as dazzling as lightning. It would be interesting to investigate white clothing--which dazzles and
blinds one and in some way annuls the real, carnal, solid
presence of the angel, while affirming it at the same time.
In any case, one can establish a relationship between the
brilliant white clothing of the angel and the substitution
of the presence of the angel for the missing body of Christ.
This substitution is more remarkable in Mark and Luke than
in Matthew. The women appear in order to see, touch, and
anoint the corpse in order to preserve it. They find one
angel or two angels in dazzling whiteness.

The angel, by its brilliant presence, annuls the dull
presence of the corpse which was sought and desired. There
is an annulment of the object of desire here. That is the
reason for this hypothesis: the brilliant whiteness of his
clothing is at the same time an index of the irruption of
the sacred, but it is also an index of the absence of the
real, human object of desire. At this point of the discourse, we could define the double opposition in this way:
presence/absence and supernatural/human (or sacred/natural)
but with this characteristic: the sacred is negatively defined as the annulment or obliteration of the real object
of desire.

b) *The actants:* The angel is presented as a helper but equally as a designation of the sender actant. It is the angel of the Lord who descends and comes from heaven. The angel is a mediator in the position of a helper of the subject (the women) because he repudiates the opponents, which are the stone and the guards. He rolls the stone away and makes the guards tremble from fear or strikes them dead. On the whole, the angel is an operator who opens the sacred space of the tomb which is closed and guarded by the stone and the soldiers.

Note 1: In a way, sequence 2 is parallel to sequence 1. The conjunction between sequence 1 and sequence 2 will take place in sequence 3. Sequence 1 is positive: the subject is in quest of the object which is the object of the desire. Sequence 2 is negative: the helper repudiates the opponent, but at the same time the helper erases the object of desire, the walk of the women to the tomb ends without the object.

Note 2: The narrative contains a blank or empty space which is, properly speaking, the resurrection sequence, i.e. the sequence of Christ's exit out of the tomb which the Gospel of Peter (35-44) restores. One can describe this blank space as an ellipsis in the linguistic manifestation which only gives us [p. 45] the consequences. The height of omission is reached in Mark and Luke where the angel does not roll back the stone but where the women find it rolled away or displaced (cf. Mk. 16:4; Lk. 24:2).

Moreover, this lack signifies to us that the subject of the statement is identical to the subject of the enunciation in the three Synoptics. In other words, the redactor or the narrator of the narrative described the scene as the women would have described or related it. There is, however, an

infringement of that rule in Matthew where the arrival of
the angel and the earthquake are described. Have we also
read this description of the angel, less in its referential
aspect than in its stereotypical, indicative aspect?

Part III. *The discourse of the angel.*

The discourse of the angel can be analyzed in three
segments which are framed by two instructions which open
and close the discourse. These instructions are the modal-
isators: first of attitude, "Do not be afraid", or even of
the opening of the discourse; second of closing or the
closure of the message: "Lo, I have told you!".

The three segments are defined as:

1) the recognition of the quest and the absence
   of its object,
2) the recalling of the message of Christ,
3) the deliverance of the angel's message which
   is to be transmitted.

1st segment: "I know that you seek Jesus Christ, who
was crucified; he is not here." This is an affirmation which
is accompanied by its counter-proof: "See the place where he
lay", which one can symbolically transcribe in the following
way:

If q = quest, and p = presence, then we have q $\neq$ p here.

2nd segment: "He has risen from the dead as he said."
This is a discourse here in the second degree which is re-

called from the discourse of Christ which announced his resurrection or = $\overline{\text{non p}}$.

The *3rd segment* repeats the discourse in the second degree, but it is not in the form of a quotation but is like an order or an imperative. The discourse in the second degree here becomes a message, properly speaking. It can be transcribed: $\overline{\text{non p}}$ $+$ $\overline{\text{q}}$. "He has risen from the dead; he goes before you to Galilee; you will see him." = the quest is repudiated by its satisfaction.

If one agrees to transcribe the opening of the discourse as a, the opening of the discourse to the second degree as α, the opening of the message as α', and the indicator of closure as b, this sequence can be written:

$$a \, (\, q + \overline{p} \quad + \quad \alpha \, (\text{non } \overline{p}) \,) \quad + \quad \alpha' \, (\text{non } \overline{p} \quad + \quad \overline{q}) \, b$$

1st degree discourse (1)	2nd degree discourse (2)	Message

The advantage of this "symbolic" transcription is to make one see that the message is a negation of discourse (1) and a repetition developed from discourse (2).

One can draw some conclusions from this analysis. The first is of a general nature. One sees here--and the definition of this *actor* "angel" as a substitute annuler of the object of desire prepares one for it--the substitution of the message for the desired object. More precisely, the absence of the object of desire is filled by the presence of a message which: (1) affirms [p. 46] the absence of the object of desire *here* and *now* but gives this absence as a positive modality of this object; and (2) affirms the presence of the object as *already* and *elsewhere*, but in the form of a message to be transmitted (the message is *present*). That is the reason for the *substitute* equation: absence of the real object here and now = presence of the message whose referent is always present and already elsewhere. One could say in Hegelian language that one sees here in the passage (by the negativity) from the reality "*here, now*" of the object, to the discourse of the "*always -- already -- there*" and to the discourse of omnipresence or rather the transformation from desire of the object to communication of the message. The desire is like a mediator of communication.

The second conclusion concerns the content itself of the angel's discourse and especially the symbolic terms α and α' which are transcribed respectively as: "he has said" (or according to the translations: "as he has said") and "Tell" (or "Go, tell").

"I know that you seek Jesus who was crucified" is an assertion of the quest whose constative aspect is strongly marked by: "I know that...."

"He is not here, because he has risen as he said." "He has said" clearly states, in a kind of equivalency, a negation and an affirmation which are not on the same level and do not belong to the same act of discourse. "He is not here" is an empirical proof which flows, as a consequence, from the preceding proof of the quest: "you seek Jesus.... He is not here." (One will note a reinforcement of the proof in Mark: "Behold the place where he was laid.") On the other hand, the affirmation, "he has risen", is the repetition in an indirect style of a word of Jesus said *long ago* or *previously*. But this repetition has the effect of making it contemporary with the enunciation of the proof: "he is not here". At the same time, this simultaneity establishes an equivalence between the proof that he is not

here and the affirmation pronounced *long ago* by Jesus: "I
will rise from the dead." In other words, the proof is a
realization of a prophetic word and it is only that. The
prophetic word, which is recalled and established in the
form of a quotation by the angel, makes the body of the
crucified one disappear, if one can say that. He *makes
himself disappear now*, by having said long ago....

"Go, tell his disciples, 'he has risen, he is in Galilee, you will see him'." The third part of the angel's
discourse modifies the internal perspectives anew. Benvéniste's definition of the performative is "a declarative
jussive verb construed with a *dictum*". But this *dictum*
(which is the prophetic word cited in the preceding segment)
is also at this precise moment of the discourse a *factum*,
a proof which it is only a question--but it is essential--of
making known. Likewise, the angel's order does not rest on
the presence of Jesus in Galilee, his resurrection, or his
visibility, but on the proclamation, the disclosure of
this presence and visibility. Perhaps this is a fundamental
function of the prophetic word which transforms the *dictum*
into a *factum* which gives the full consistence of a fact
and an existing event to what is said. It is twice said
in the angel's discourse that Jesus has risen from the dead.
But the first time, in reference to Jesus' word, a *factum*--
the absence of the dead body--is a *dictum*: "I tell you, I
will rise from the dead." The second time [p. 47], this
dictum is a *factum* by the speech act of the angel, a proclamatory order: "Jesus has risen from the dead; he goes
before you into Galilee; you will see him there."

Thus, on the one hand, a discourse in the second degree appears in the heart of part (3) of the narrative,
which opens with the expression, "the angel said". It be-

longs to the order of the narrative in general and is opened
by an expression such as: "Christ has said". And, on the
other hand, there is a message which (insofar as it still
belongs to the narrative in the form of a linguistic object)
is substituted for the object of desire, but which displays,
moreover, a non-narrative dimension, since it is of a proclamatory type: "He has awakened from death; he is somewhere else and already present."

Third conclusion: the women seek Jesus Christ as a
cadaver and a mute object. They find the angel who is a
speaking messenger delivering a message. The angel by himself is, in a way, a message since he is substituted for the
object of desire. But at the same time he delivers the
message. The angel affirms the negation (if one can say
that). He shows the absence of the object of desire to be
a presence which is somewhere else and living, that is to
say, a message (i.e. a linguistic object present here and
now). There is the mark here of a passage to what one could
call the universality of the message or the index of the substitution of the discourse *for the referent to be verified*
and of a message as a *sign to be believed*, which does not
designate the absence of the referent, but signifies, in
the absence of a referent, the presence of the word.

Part IV. *The departure of the women from the tomb.*

One must distinguish two segments here: the departure
of the women from the tomb and the transmission of the message to the community of disciples. These two segments are
modalized in a complex way, on the one hand, by what one
could call a dynamic spatial modalisator, i.e. the speed,

"they ran, they departed quickly..."; on the other hand, by
an effective or emotional modalisator which is twofold: the
fear, indicative of the angel's message and more generally
of the irruption of the sacred into the profane; and the joy,
indicative of the content itself of the message.

On this point, one will note the disagreements (which
are perhaps significant) between the text of Matthew (which
is our guideline) and the texts of Mark and Luke which function as arbitrary variants in our reading. In effect, we
note the disappearance of the notations of fear and joy in
Luke and that of joy in Mark.

Moreover, one should note the variants of Mark and Luke,
concerning the second segment of this part. The message in
Mark is not transmitted: "they said nothing to anyone".
The message in Luke is indeed transmitted materially and
physically, but a fifth part is added to the four parts of
the story which defines a failure of the denotative, cogni-
tive, or referential function of the communication: "Their
words seemed to be nonsense (to the apostles), and they did
not believe them."

In a more general way, one can say that part 4 of the
story is that of the transmission of a message by the women,
but it is a message which is not or only partially received.
From this point of view (and the dynamic and spatial point
of view), part 4 is indeed the opposite of part 1. In the
first part, the women come to the tomb, if not with haste,
at least with eagerness (i.e. early at daybreak). In the
[p. 48] fourth part, the women leave the tomb quickly, in
haste. In the first, they come in order to anoint the dead
body; in the fourth, they transmit (positively, negatively,
or partially) the message which structurally signified--and
one should weigh the "ideological" importance of this con-

clusion--that *the message has repudiated the dead body and the transmission has repudiated the unction.*

There could be an unction only if there is a dead body. Now the dead body is missing and in its place there is a message. Thus does the non-transmission of the message in Mark, which is itself physical, signify that the women in this "variant" are left with everything which the ritual of unction includes and which we have tried to define? In other words, the closing in relation to the dead body which is an individual relationship to the object of desire, while the transmission of the message reveals the substitution of the message for the object of desire and the substitution of the communal relationship for the individual relationship. One would then understand the disappearance in Mark (which is a "variant" of the non-transmission of the message) of the emotional modalisator of the sequence: the joy, which one finds, on the other hand, contradictorily combined with fear in Matthew.

In conclusion, from this partial and incomplete analysis of many of the planes, one could reconstruct this characteristic trait which is revealed from an implication, which is perhaps universal, concerning the Christian religious text and which the short story of the women at the tomb could illustrate: namely, that there is an apparent narrative in which another story is secretly told, that of the passage from a discursive figure focused on the natural human or supernatural event. It is a discourse *which says something* to another discursive figure. The former is not focused on the context as Roman Jakobson said, but on itself and its texture, on its elaboration, or even more precisely, on its own communication and its own transmission. This is the unusual stage in the narrative where the things, the referent, or the bodies fade away and are missing and where the *paroles* and the messages appear in their place like bodies and things, in short, where the words become things (cf. Michael Foucault, *The Order of Things*).

CRITICAL NOTE I: ON THE MODEL

The methodological questions, which we pose concerning the application of this semiotic model to the analysis of this text are twofold:

The first is that the constant utilization of this narrative structural model does not lead to a loss of some semantic "substance", which the specific character of the narratives examined equally lose, rendering the formation of the underlying codes in this particular narrative discourse all the more difficult. Now it is indeed *this* discourse which interests me, and not the general abstract model whose emergence will be selective and combinative.

Second, in possession of the model, we are not in danger (at the level of the methodological practice) of making the text (considered in its manifestation) undergo some distortions, simplifications, etc. so as to make it more [p. 49] manipulable on the formal plane. This is the technical problem of the preparation of the text which one encounters in the analyses of myths, narratives, or poems. But the procedures which one employs rests on the linguistic code common to the transmitter and receiver and essentially on the form of the expression. Can one give the same justifications when the modifications or alterations are based, or risk being based, on the substance of the content?

Therefore, it would be fitting, in order to clarify these points, for a rigorous epistemological analysis to be undertaken on the subject of the utilization of the notion of a model and on its metaphorical function, etc.

CRITICAL NOTE II: CONCERNING THE FUNERAL UNCTION

At the very least, this is the explicit meaning of the text: "...If she has poured this perfume on my body, it is in order to prepare me for my burial that she has done it." The unction is indeed an anointing for death which is practiced on a living and not on a dead body. Therefore there is an inversion of the order of the actions: it is not at all: 1st to die, 2nd to anoint the dead; but: 1st to anoint the living person, 2nd to die. However, one knows that the unction is also the ritual act of enthronement of the kings of Israel. Thus one reads in I Samuel 10 that at the time of the inaugural institution of kingship, Samuel took a small flask of oil and poured it on Saul's head, then he embraced him and said: "Has not Yahweh anointed you as the leader of His people Israel?" This enthronement is also performed by the falling of the spirit of Yahweh on the royal elect: "Then the spirit of Yahweh will fall on you, you will go into a delirium...and you will be changed into another man" (I Samuel 10:6). Thus one can wonder if the anointing at Bethany is not also an unperceived royal anointing (only its mortuary function has been decoded by Jesus). It is an anointing which, unlike the other anointing which precedes or anticipates the ritual moment of realization, here follows it because the royal messianic entrance had already taken place and the eschatological

prophesy had already been proclaimed. "Decoded" in this way
by the most discerning decoders, Mary's revelation conceals
an excess of meaning which the story does not reveal in its
literality. It appears on the surface in the present case
because the interpretation belongs to the story. But the
story contains the signs of a growth of meaning. They are
signs which call attention to the syntagmatic order, since
it is the ordinal position of the actions on the axis of
combinations which draw attention to this surplus of meaning.

But one must add a note which raises a new problem.
This is the knowledge of another text, that of I Samuel,
which shows (in Matthew's text which relates the anointing
at Bethany) a correlation with the messianic entrance. The
problem of the closure of the text, that of the relationship
of the text and the context, and the limits of this context
are also indirectly articulated in this text which we are
studying. This is because the knowledge of the ritual of
anointing belongs to the textual order, but it could also
arise from decorated monuments, bas-reliefs, or paintings
which would then enter, in some way or another, into the
perhaps endless interplay of textual references. [p. 50]

CRITICAL NOTE III: A DEFICIENCY IN THE REPRESENTATION

Moreover--and this is the main point here--the fact that
the resurrection escaped representation, if it was representation which the narrative deploys in its manifestation, the
fact of grasping the event in its negative results and not in
its sudden appearance, permits me to transfer the whole weight
of the narrative, its whole gravity--and thereby its signifi-

cance—on the angel as the vector of the word. And of what
word? That of the resurrection of Jesus. The narrative, by
not showing the event, separates itself from the representation in order to impart to the word what the representation
would have represented, the event in the world of the escape
of Jesus from the tomb and from death. The gospel texts
make the resurrection of Jesus something that cannot be
staged. They remove it from the fiction (or the fable) of
the narrative in order to entrust it to the discourse. It
is by refusing to relate it that this thing of the world,
this fact which must be proof and truth of all the later
preaching, which they make expressible in words, that is
to say composes it in a fundamental statement of discourse.
This is, in the text itself, the *reality* of the Good News.
We will return to the analysis of the angel's *discourse*.

CRITICAL NOTE IV: THE BODY-WORD

One should thoroughly investigate and situate this
permutation at diverse levels and points of discourse of
the constative and performative modalities in a larger
problematic. In any case, it is characteristic of this
element of meaning which seems to be important to us:
the double conversion of the referential quotation in a
proclamatory message and from a fact of speech to a speech
of fact. It is to this extent that the message in this
text constitutes a linguistic ensemble which has the value
of an injunction, an obligation, and a quasi-realization.
It is a *fact* which appears in and by the *word*.

Furthermore, the angel's discourse indirectly gives
a reading lesson in the interplay of the living word to

the women. It teaches them to *read* the facts and events,
like a text, where the spaces, absences, or blanks signify--
forever--some fillings or presences, but it signifies them
elsewhere: in Galilee, in the future--"You will *see* him;
he *precedes* you...." These are presences of which the entire "conclusion" of the Gospel is the quest and which will
only be found in the form of a descent and proliferation of
the word. Whatever teaching--the empty space--the impression
or the trace--left by a dead body uncovers is nothing else
than the inscription of the word, "I will rise from the
dead".

VI

JESUS BEFORE PILATE:
A STRUCTURAL ANALYSIS ESSAY

by

Louis Marin

As in our analysis of the arrival of the women at the
tomb, we have chosen for our guideline the text of Matthew
extracted from all the narratives of Jesus' passion and
resurrection, Mtt. 27:1-2, 11-31. The corresponding texts
of Mark and Luke ("corresponding", that is to say, telling
the same story) will be considered, as before, to be arbitrary variants. They will only be used to the extent to
which they present some significant differences from the
reference text. On the other hand, we have excluded Mtt.
27:3-10 (which tells about the death of Judas) from our
study. However, while this narrative is considered to be
of secondary importance to the surface continuity of the
text, it does indeed belong to the trial of Jesus by Pilate.
This decision to exclude this narrative, which is important
in certain respects and clearly deprives us of a possible
significant orientation, is in our view justifiably prag-
matic. In reality, to take into consideration the narrative of Judas' death would require that the parts which we
have extracted from the global narrative would have to be
reintegrated at the end of the analysis. This is because
a cursory examination of the ensemble of the narrative of
the passion and resurrection shows that there is a limited

97

correlation of this unit of the death of Judas (27:3-10) and
the denials of Peter (26:69-75) with three other prior parts:
Judas' betrayal (26:14-16), the announcement of Judas' betrayal (26:20-25), and the prediction of Peter's denial (26:
30-35). Thus the narrative of Judas' death would have led
us by degrees to consider the study of the global narrative.
But it does not necessarily follow that our decision to exclude it completely protects the unity and independence of
the text which we are considering. It is indeed certain
that, for example, the part which is called the "royal derision" here and closes our text (27:27-31) refers (according to the modalities which one ought to analyze) to the
messianic entrance into Jerusalem (e.g. Mtt. 21:1-11) and
the eschatological discourse (Mtt. 25:31-46). Moreover, in
the interest of a more precise and careful reading, we will
not hesitate to reintegrate the episode of Judas' death in
order to establish some significant correlations. In one
word, the part is not considered in our study in and of itself as a stage of the narrative studied but as being able
to supply useful and fruitful correlations when the opportunity occurs. Therefore [p. 52] it would be fitting
throughout this analysis to preserve in spirit the idea of
the arbitrariness and artificiality of the segmentation
which we have imposed on the surface continuity of the
text. But there is a "drastic" responsibility here which
we have decided to assume in order to insure the best results in the research.

Segmentation of the Parts

We have cut up the text into twelve parts. Here is a
table and the textual references of these parts:

(1)	(2)	(3)	(4)
Jesus passes from the Jews to the Romans. (27:1-2)	Accusation of the chief priests and the elders. Silence of Jesus. (27:11[1]-12-14)	Pilate's question: "Are you the King of the Jews?" Jesus' response: "You have said so." (27:11[2])	The division of the hero.

Jesus

Barabbas

Christ

(27:15-16)

(5)	(6)	(7)	(8)
Pilate's question to the crowd: "Jesus or Barabbas?" Silence of the crowd. (27:17-18)	The dream of Pilate's wife and its warning. (27:19)	The intervention of the chief priests and the elders on the crowd. (27:20)	Pilate's three questions to the crowd: "Jesus or Barabbas?" Condemnation confirmed by the crowd. (27:21-23)

(9)	(10)	(11)	(12)
The washing of Pilate's hands or his non-responsibility; the self-accusation of the crowd. (27:24-25)	The hero returns to his unity. Barabbas is released. Jesus is delivered. (27:26)	The royal derision: the parodic king, Jesus. (27:27-30)	Jesus passes from the Romans to the Jews. (27:31)

Although it might be awkward in the presentation of this enquiry to follow a synthetic rather than an analytic order, we prefer to show from now on (for interests of clarity) how these twelve parts are organized in large sequences which then directly enter into some significant correlations.

1 is opposed to 12:

Jesus is delivered by the Jews to the Romans (1). The Romans deliver Jesus to the Jews (12).

2 and 3 are opposed to 11:

The questioning of Jesus comes to a conclusion with the question of his kingship, which is affirmed (2-3). The condemnation of Jesus comes to an end with the recognition of his kingship, but in a parodic and derisory way (11).   [p. 53]

4 is opposed to 10:

The hero is divided into Barabbas and Christ (4). The hero regains his unity (10).

5 is opposed to 8:

Pilate questions the crowd and is unable to obtain a response. This is the first questioning of the crowd during which the crowd appears in its neutrality (5). Pilate questions the crowd three times and obtains a response which confirms the condemnation of Jesus (8).

We will set aside the case of sequence 9 which seems to us to be an inversion of 5 and 8 and at the same time is a consequence of the large central sequence.

6 and 7 form the central sequence around which the correlations are connected in some way, setting up a constellation of the oppositions. The following schema shows the general surface structure of the sequences:

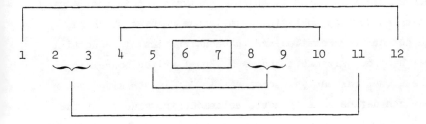

The segmentation of the text into sequences and their
relative regrouping into pairs of oppositions presupposes
that we have already made a careful reading which we have
left out of this presentation. There is a question here at
the same time of a result and a starting point. It is a result of a prior reading and the starting point for an investigation of the meaning in the signifiers which constitute these oppositions. The analysis from now on will ex-
tend from the level of the correlations 1/12, 2-3/11, 4/10,
etc. to the central kernel which sequences 6-7 form.

On the other hand, one will note the very unequal importance of certain sequences or regroupings of sequences,
and equally the necessity which we ourselves have found to
perform some scissions, cuts, and even some modifications
in the content of the text at certain points in the discourse. Thus, for reasons to which we will later return,
we have differentiated two sequences (2-3) in the large unit
which forms the questioning of Jesus. Moreover, what is
more important, we have been led to regroup the accusation
of the chief priests and the elders, and the silence of
Jesus (or the textual elements belonging to 27:12-13) into
one single sequence (2). In this way, one could suspect
this essential operation of a lack of precision in the
analysis which is the fragmentation of the syntagm. As M.

Benvéniste said about linguistic analysis, it is the *meaning*
which guides the analysis: "It is the meaning which has
guided our segmentation and the construction of sequential
pairs of oppositions", and as N. Ruwet writes concerning
the structural analysis of poetry: "It is striking that
one can define some semantic relationships exactly of the
same formal type as the two kinds of positional equivalences
(comparable and parallel) defined by Levin."

Coupling 1/12: this correlation is significant on the
spatial (dynamic) plane and on the ideological plane. In
effect, Jesus passes in sequence 1 from the Jewish world
(where he had already been condemned to death) to the Roman
world (where it is necessary for his condemnation to be
ratified). And sequence 12 reverses the [p. 54] meaning of
this movement *by showing the return of Jesus from the Roman
world to the Jewish world for his execution.*

One will note, as a matter of fact, a certain ambiguity
in Matthew with regard to the final sequence and its meaning. Therefore, the second part of verse 26, "He will be
delivered in order to be crucified", confirms our analysis,
but then it would be necessary to throw sequence 11 out of
our narrative, in which we have been and will be interested,
as the correlative term of sequence 3. According to the
point of view adopted, the last part of verse 31 is redundant with that of verse 26. But the difficulty itself is
significant—it will show, according to the methodology of
structural analysis, the quasi-formal necessity of the royal
derision sequence in relationship to those of the messianic
entrance, the eschatological discourse, or the crucifixion,
verse 37: "This is Jesus, the King of the Jews." (For
this latter correlation, see the text of John which is a

veritable commentary on the categories of being and appearing [Jn. 19:19-22] and our Critical Notes I and II).

These two farthest sequences which encase the ensemble of the text studied give us the two semes of one of the semantic axes of the narrative. This semantic axis is the death axis. The narrative begins with the plans for Jesus' death by the priests and elders. It closes with the departure to Golgotha. The two semes are those of "Jewishness" and of "Roman-ness" or rather by an explicative development of these terms which all the analyses devoted to the gospel texts and the *Acts of the Apostles* corroborate, those of "national particularity" and "supranational universality", or the "totality". The development of the syntagmatic line is made as a going--return articulated by three actors: Israel/Rome/Jesus, with a double condemnation to death at two positions on the line. There is a condemnation to death of Jesus, but there is also a condemnation of the Jewish people, to which we will return. Thus, at first glance, death forms the conjunction of two disjunct (opposing) semes of the semantic axis: particularity *vs.* universality.

The couplings which follow lead us into the trial properly speaking and first of all into the ensemble of examinations which one must treat at the same time "as a whole" because they constitute a whole which is well-determined and internally set forth. Because they are of a very different nature, these new internal oppositions within the ensemble are shown to be significant.

Coupling 2-3/11:

Sequence 2-3: This is the questioning of Jesus which is performed according to three poles: Jesus-Pilate-the chief priests and elders. However, the exchange only takes place between Pilate and Jesus, and it does not seem that the testimony and accusations of the priests are received by the Roman Pilate. Nevertheless, Pilate interrogates Jesus in the company of the chief priests and elders. This is ultimately what is found to be isolated as Jesus is from the beginning (cf. our preceding analyses, especially that of verse 17).

One variant from Luke is interesting to the extent to which it completes the schema which we see take form little by little. The accusations of the priests and elders are essentially of a political nature: "instigation to revolt" --"disobedience to Caesar"--"refusal to pay the taxes", and [p. 55] Barabbas is a political agitator. Jesus does not respond to the accusations of the chief priests but to Pilate's question: "Are you the King of the Jews?", Jesus responds: "You said so." Certainly this is an answer, but it is indirect. It is Pilate, not Jesus, who affirms that Jesus is the King of the Jews. Jesus' answer transforms Pilate's question into an affirmation by leaving everything in Pilate's hands. It is this complex interplay of silences and oblique affirmations about the question of Jesus' kingship and his "political" role that sequence 11, coupled with 2-3, repeats on another plane in a characteristic way. In effect, if Jesus' kingship had been clearly denied, one would hardly expect a clear recognition of this kingship in the correlated sequence or vice versa. Now there is nothing of the kind. Jesus' kingship has

been indirectly affirmed. The parodic royal affirmation is
also one of the ways of repeating and "bringing to a head"
the question of Jesus' kingship. In sequence 11, Jesus
appears as a king who plays the role of a king and appears
in the role of a king, but whose role does not at all conform to his being (cf. our Critical Note II).

(As a confirmation of the analysis of sequence 11, we
will note a trait which must be correlated with a corresponding trait which is found outside the limits of our text,
namely the derision of the prophet in Matthew 26:67-68 and
Luke 22:63-65. It corresponds to the eschatological prophesy of Matthew 25:31-46 which is a peculiar prophesy, since
it must be realized in a transcendant way at the end of
time. Moreover, one will note that the eschatological discourse conjoins the prophet and the king in the prophetic
word. This is a conjunction which the narrative of the
Passion and Resurrection of Jesus disjoins in the diachrony
and its episodes by reserving the prophet to the Jews and
the King to the Romans.)

In order to continue with the ensemble constituted by
the examinations, we will pass directly to the analysis of
the coupling 5/8-9. At this point, we should note the
special position of sequence 9, which we have described as
the most important, whose characteristic relationships with
sequences 7 and 8 it is necessary to perceive.

The questioning of the crowd by Pilate takes place
three times. The first questioning is represented by sequence 5 in which Pilate offers the *alternative--"Jesus or
Barabbas"--in one single question*. It is a question to
which the crowd does not respond.

(This silence of the crowd is not clear-cut in the
text, but one can assume it because of sequence 7, i.e. the
intervention of the chief priests and the elders on the

crowd for them to ask for the death of Jesus.) Sequence 5
corresponds and is opposed to sequence 8 in a very significant
way. Pilate poses *three questions* which reveal a gradation
from the alternative to the choice and from the choice to the
justification of the choice. In these three cases, the crowd
responds violently. It responds correctly to the first two
questions. It responds with its choice to the alternative.
It responds to the questioning of its choice by rejecting the
response which it had previously made. As in the preceding
coupling, it is indeed a question of an examination with three
poles: (1) Jesus-Barabbas, (2) Pilate, (3) the Jewish crowd.
But it has two differences: (1) the "hero" is divided, Jesus-
Barabbas, and (2) the exchange takes place between Pilate and
the crowd. The position of the crowd in relationship to
Pilate in sequence 5 occupies the position of Pilate in relationship to the chief priests and elders in [p. 56] sequence 3. One (Pilate) questions the other (the crowd) and
they are silent. But sequence 8 makes an interesting modification in this schema of exchange. It inverts the passive
and the active, i.e. the *"accusing"* crowd is opposed in 8 to
the *"accused"* Jesus in 2-3, while the crowd is characterized
by silence or *neutrality* in 5, which is Pilate's prominent
trait until the central sequence.

This is the reason for the importance of sequence 7 in
this ensemble. It is by the intervention of the chief priests
and elders on the crowd that the crowd (which was neutral or
silent in 5) becomes hostile with respect to Jesus in 8.

Consequently we can isolate a second semantic axis from
this ensemble, the *kingship axis*. The actant which comes to
pass through it·according to the syntagmatic line is indeed
the hero. But he is a hero who is divided at the same time
by his proper name, Jesus-Barabbas (that is to say, "Jesus

Son of the Father") and Jesus Christ, and by his value:
one is a political agitator and an aspiring king; the other
is the "King of the Jews" (cf. the messianic entrance).
This division of the subject-actant (or hero) as well as
his reunification by Barabbas' expulsion (he is freed) and
Jesus' condemnation in the crucifixion (*coupling 4/10*) permits one to distinguish the two disjointed semes that the
semantic king axis conjoins, namely *the profane and the
sacred*, or more precisely, political liberation and religious liberation, namely *the here-below and the beyond*.
On this point, the Gospel of John appears to be a veritable
"proto-semiotic" commentary on the Synoptic texts and provides us with some remarkable confirmations. On the one
hand, the semantic kingship axis is much more apparent in
the Fourth Gospel than in the Synoptics, just as if John
has brought the deep structures of the narratives of the
other three evangelists to the surface. On the other hand,
the semic opposition here-below/beyond is especially confirmed. Thus Jesus responds in Jn. 18:36-37: "'My kingdom
is not of this world. If my kingdom were of this world, my
servants would have fought that I might not be delivered to
the Jews. But my kingdom is not here.'--'Well are you a
king?,' Pilate asked him--'You said so, I am a king,' Jesus
replied....'" Moreover, as we have seen by analyzing the
coupling 2-3/11, two other semes segment the semantic king
axis. The first seme is the affirmation and the second is
the derision which are modalized on the syntagmatic line
according to the "implicit" and the "passive", if one can
say that. The royal affirmation is indirect in 27. It is
another who *calls* him a king. And the royal derision is
passive in 27:28-30. It is the soldiers who *treat* him as a
false king. (Cf. the detailed information provided on this
point in my Critical Note II.)

We can next return to the central sequences. They are
the only ones which do not have any correlations because
they are, in reality, correlated with all the other sequences which surround them. Their function is to transform the elements of meaning offered by the first "stages"
of the narrative. We have connected sequences 6 and 7 from
this point of view, although in another sense sequence 7
ought to be correlated with sequence 8, which follows it as
its cause, explanation, or justification. In effect, the
two sequences are paralleled by their function, respectively
on the semantic death and kingship axes. The dream of
Pilate's wife which is told to Pilate, not in its content,
but in its sign aspect (she said to him: "Do not become
involved in the case of this just man because I have been
very disturbed by a dream today because of him", 27:19). It
is this sign which gives the key to Pilate's conversion to
a "neutral" or quasi-positive term on the semantic death
axis [p. 57] and to the disjunction of the particularity
and universality semes. According to the diachronic order
of the sequential elements with regard to Pilate, there is
the sign given to Pilate following his amazement at Jesus'
silence towards the chief priests and elders (27:14).
There is also the feeling which he had that a conspiracy
had been hatched against Jesus (27:18) which immediately
precedes the affirmation of Pilate's absolute neutrality
in this case. His "disengagement" in 27:24 also indicates
the extreme distance between the actors Israel/Rome at this
point of the narrative and the disjunction of two semes
recognized on this axis at the spatial, topographical, and
dynamic levels.

Likewise, the intervention of the chief priests and
elders on the crowd is decisive since they persuade it to

pass to the "negative", whereas it had previously been neutral (cf. the silence of the crowd to the alternative question posed by Pilate). Therefore sequence 7 which is on the syntagmatic line corresponding in this way to the semantic kingship axis, as we have already seen, is the cause of sequence 8, just as sequence 6, on the other axis, refers to one of the two elements of sequence 9. Furthermore, it is at this point of the narrative that the two axes, death and kingship, are connected and intersect one another.

Starting from these first remarks concerning the main central sequence (6-7), we can suggest by deduction the existence of positions which are prior and subsequent to the narrative sequences which we have studied. These are the positions occupied by the actors of this narrative, but they have a different significant value from that which we have presented. They also enter into a positive or negative correlation with some sequence of the trial of Jesus by Pilate. Thus the crowd must have occupied a positive position with relationship to the subject Jesus on the semantic kingship axis. This positive position, which we have already discussed, is that of the crowd at the time of the messianic entrance into Jerusalem. And perhaps the crowd will later rediscover a positive position with respect to the hero, who is absent-present in the community, and this will be at Pentecost. But since it is no longer a question of the same Jesus, it is also no longer a question of the same crowd which then "becomes" the characteristics which the text gives it by the ending of the national particularity. The schema below shows the positions of the crowd on the king axis in the superficial structure:

King axis projected on the surface structure	t1	t0	t2	t3
	Messianic entrance	Neutrality: silence to Pilate's question	"Crucify him"	The first Pentecost (Acts 2:37-41)

In the same way, one can wonder if Pilate, or the "Roman-ness", has not occupied a negative position with respect to the hero on the *Death* axis and if it must not subsequently appear on the same axis in a positive position. An indication of this on the first point is given to us by John 11:48-51. This is the sequence where the chief priests and Phari-sees perceive the negativity of the Romans concerning Jesus. "If we do nothing, [p. 58] everyone will believe in him (Jesus) and the Romans will come destroy both our holy place and our nation....Do you not see that it would be better that one man die for the people rather than the whole nation perish." Thus there is indeed a negative position (perceived) of the "Roman-ness" on the death axis. One should, however, note the equivocal character of the actor Rome in all these texts. The positive Rome of the centurion from Capernaum (Acts 10-11) can be connected to the negative Rome of John 11:48-51. And we find the same ambiguity in the later positive position of the centurion at the cruci-fixion who, while being the complete negative agent of death, positively affirms the divine sonship of the hero (cf. Mark 15:39). We can, therefore, construct a schema of the death axis on the surface structure which is parallel to that of the king axis:

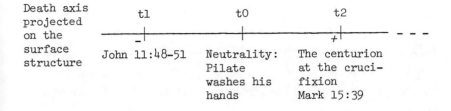

Death axis projected on the surface structure	t1	t0	t2
	John 11:48-51	Neutrality: Pilate washes his hands	The centurion at the cruci-fixion Mark 15:39

We have already noted the somewhat peculiar nature of
sequence 9 which is diachronically connected with sequence 8
which precedes it and of which it is a consequence. But it
can also be coupled, on the one hand, with the central sequence 6-7 and, on the other hand, with sequence 5, which is
the first "examination" of the crowd by Pilate. Sequence 9
is that of ratified accusation and condemnation. It is
characterized by the fact that Pilate does not accept the
accusations brought against Jesus, and he refuses to condemn or ratify the condemnation. It is also characterized
by the correlative fact that he transfers or throws aside
the Jewish accusation and condemnation. "I am not responsible for this blood, see to it yourselves."

On the other hand, the people accept the condemnation
of Jesus which Pilate transfers to them. Better still,
they confirm it, but they do so in the form of a self-
accusation or self-condemnation. "May his blood fall on
ourselves and our children." Even if the formula used is
stereotyped, this point is remarkable. The crowd which
was neutral in sequence 5 becomes negative in sequence 8,
and self-negative in 9. Pilate, however, who was surprised
by Jesus' silence in sequence 2-3, becomes neutral in 6
and passes to a kind of positive indifference in 9 since
he condemns Jesus by abandoning him and completely giving
up his responsibility for him.

This self-condemnation of the people in sequence 9 poses some important problems for the analysis. One can conceive this sequence as a kind of reduplication or redundance of the negative position t2 on the king axis, or even as a negative doublet contrary to the neutral-positive position of Pilate in the same sequence.

One possibility of the text would consist of rigorously articulating the semes of accusation, accuser/accused, non-accuser/non-accused on the semantic death axis which are considered as "vehicles" by the actors. The chief priests and elders are accuser/non-accused. Jesus is non-accuser/accused. Pilate would appear to be specified, especially after the [p. 59] narrative transformations, as neither accuser/nor accused. That is to say, Pilate appears to be a neutral term while the people which are also neither accuser/nor accused in the first stage of the narrative pass through a second stage where they are accuser/non-accused and end in sequence 9 (which we will consider here) in the position of accuser and accused. They are accused to the extent to which they accuse, i.e. they are a self-accuser. In short, they occupy the position of a compound term after transformation.

However, we will attempt to suggest an interesting correlation with the main sequence of the death of Judas which we have rather arbitrarily excluded from our text. In reality, this sequence is decomposed into three stages. First, Judas said, "I have sinned by betraying innocent blood." Second, the chief priests and elders replied, "What difference does it make to us; see to it yourself." Third, there is the death of Judas: he hanged himself in despair. We will leave to one side the other narrative elements which do not enter, at least temporarily,

into correlation with the text which we are studying. Now
we can schematize sequence 9 in a homologous way: Pilate
says to the people, "I am not responsible for this blood;
see to it yourselves." Therefore Pilate occupies in
relation to the people the position of the chief priests
and elders in relationship to Judas. The people, who accused and condemned themselves before Pilate, responded
(like Judas before the elders), "Let this blood fall upon
us and our children." Furthermore, Judas affirms the innocence of Jesus by accusing himself, while the people deny
this innocence. The narrative of Judas' death separates
the self-accusation and the self-condemnation. The narrative of the trial by Pilate conjoins the two with the
people.

Finally, Judas accuses himself of a *past* act, i.e. of
having accused Jesus, and he *henceforth* condemns himself.
By accusing Jesus and condemning him *henceforth*, the people
accuse and condemn themselves *hereafter*. Therefore the
table which summarizes this analysis of the situation of
questioning is given below:

Judas +	Chief Priests 0	Judas −
Self-accusation and affirmation of Jesus' inno-cence.	Indifference of the chief priests and elders: shift-ing the accusa-tion on to Judas.	Self-condemna-tion: Death of Judas.

Pilate O	People –	People ?
Positive indifference concerning Jesus: shifting of the accusation on to the people.	Self-accusation and negation of Jesus' innocence.	Self-condemnation hereafter.

In order to conclude this analytical work, we can quickly study the *coupling 4/10*. By releasing Barabbas in 10, Pilate opposes himself to the division of the hero which took place in 4. The hero regains his unity, but he does so by the elimination of his real heroic double, i.e. by exclusion and not by synthesis. The division which appears in sequence 4 shows the ambivalence of the hero, who is simultaneously a nationalistic agitator and a messianic king. The quotations used in John 11 clearly show [p. 60] this interlacing of the political and religious, and more deeply some semes of the here-below and the beyond, which are the poles of the semantic kingship axis. By eliminating the political agitator from the scene, sequence 10 leaves only the messianic king deprived of his political dimension present that the in depth seme "here-below" articulates in its opposition to the beyond. The hero *here-below* is a king of the *beyond*. Thus the king can then only be a parodic and disguised king at the same time, or again what conjoins in the parodic complexity (a parodic which is passive here) the semes of affirmation and negation on this same semantic kingship axis. In other words, just as we did a little while ago in connection with the three actors of the semantic death axis, we can attempt to articulate the semes of affirmation--affirmer/ affirmed, non-affirmer/non-affirmed--on the kingship axis insofar as they are "vehicles" of the unique and double hero actant. Jesus does not affirm that he is a king, but someone affirms it for him. Pilate says it about Jesus. This is sequence 3 in Matthew, for example. Jesus affirms that he is a king, but no one affirms it of him. It is the chief priests and the elders who reject his kingship (cf. the sequences of the messianic entrance and the eschatological discourse and more generally the basis of the reports of Jesus with the chief priests and Pharisees). The breaking of the conjunction is indeed the parodic scene where the kingship of Jesus is simultaneously affirmed and denied. In other words, it seems that there is no ambivalence in this scene in the "appearing" which enters into correlation with the ambivalence in the "being" which constitutes the royal affirmation of the messianic entrance where Jesus is a king and messiah and where he is what he does not seem to be.

We can therefore construct the semantic *king* axis in all its complexity as a conjunction of disjunct semes, here-below/beyond, affirmation/negation, being/appearing.

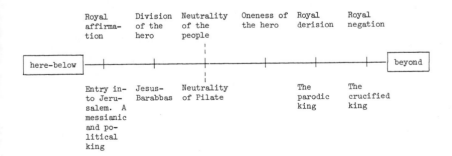

116

The semantic *death* axis will be constructed conjointly in the following way:

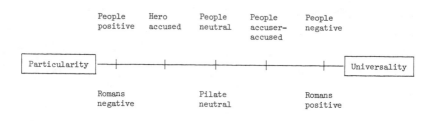

People   Hero   People   People   People
positive   accused   neutral   accuser-   negative
                                    accused

Particularity ——┤————————┤————————┤————————┤———————— Universality

Romans   Pilate   Romans
negative   neutral   positive

In conclusion, and as a working hypothesis for further research, one possible signification of the text studied could be the following. Everything takes place as if the sequences of Jesus' trial before Pilate had the function of solving two insolvable problems: [p. 61] First, how does one pass from a particular, closed, national community (1) to an open, supranational universality (2)? Second, how does one pass from a temporal messianic kingdom (*a*) to an eternal messianic kingdom (*b*)?

According to the semantic *death* axis in the text considered, the transformation from (1) to (2) is imperfectly realized in the surface structure by a compound term (*the Jewish people* = particularity: accuser--accused), and a neutral term (*Pilate* = universality: neither accuser nor accused).

According to the semantic *kingship* axis, the transformation from (*a*) to (*b*), in other words from the royal affirmation to the royal negation, is realized by the division of

the king into two "actors" and by the exclusion of the political king in favor of the other. In this sense, the royal
negation (b) is the place of a different royal affirmation,
its opposite being the eternal messianic kingdom. There is
a negation—affirmation process here where one can see a
characteristic mark of religious thought.

CRITICAL NOTES

I. The Dismemberment of the Text.

Having pointed out these correlations, however, it seems
necessary to us in this connection to note two possible directions (among others) in the significant organization of
our text. These details are not useless. They not only en-
rich the meaning of the text by enhancing its plurality, but
they clarify the problem of the construction of the sequences.
In reality, one can consider the narrative at the first level
—that of the actions which are described whatever their
nature may be—and reserve their content for a second analysis.
This is a distinction which is only possible at certain points
of the narrative.

We will give two examples drawn from the text studied.
The evangelist writes about Pilate in verse 18: "He knew
well that it was because of jealousy that he (Jesus) had been
delivered." The notation of Pilate's knowledge, that is to
say a reflection or an inner conviction within Pilate, must in
my opinion be distinguished from what this reflection or inner

conviction produced: the fact that "it was because of jealousy
that he had been delivered". At the first level, this knowledge of Pilate must first refer to the position of the narrator in relationship to his narrative and to his ability to
intervene in the narrative plot. It must second refer to
Pilate's position in relation to the dramatic situation as it
is told. The narrator gives us an indication of the "inner"
attitude of Pilate. By this reflection, Pilate is put at a
distance from the events of the narrative. It would have
still been the same thing if he had written: "Pilate knew
well that it was in order to please him...or that it was only
right...or that it was for the salvation of the people that
he had been delivered." Pilate's awareness in the narrative
of the motivation for the arrest of Jesus, whatever this
motivation may be, constitutes an element situated at a level
of analysis distinct from that where Pilate's reflection is
considered insofar as it requires a specific content.

In the same way, one can study the organization of the
questions and answers insofar as the actions of questioning
or answering, or the organization [p. 62] of the questions
and answers insofar as something is asked and something else
answered. Thus in the first case, we will examine the fact
that Pilate or the chief priests speak, posing some questions
and Jesus or the crowd respond or do not respond. For
example in the second case, Pilate asks, "Are you the king
of the Jews?" and Jesus answers, "You have said so", or
Pilate asks the crowd, "Whom must I release?" and the crowd
responded, "Barabbas". There is therefore a kind of action
in the narrative which has the characteristic of dividing
in two or the characteristic of requiring a double function:
the function of knowing, saying, questioning, and responding
and the function which plays the role in the narrative of what
is said, responded, or known.

A superficial reading of the text immediately reveals
the importance of the dialogues inserted in the narrative.
Each of them is introduced by "He said...he asked...he responded...he remained silent..." (once in a while they are
attributed to their actors: *Pilate* said...*Jesus* replied...
the *crowd* said...). These introductions are articulated in
an organization of meaning which is not homologous, at least
at first glance, to the one which appears after the correlations between the contents. Thus 2-3 (in content) are found
connected to 11 according to a relationship which one must
determine. Since Jesus confirms the affirmation of his kingship by Pilate in 2-3 and the soldiers turn this affirmation
into derision and parody in 11, 2-3 and 11 enter into correlation with 7-8 on the one hand and 5-9 on the other, according to the first level of analysis.

2-3	Pilate, the chief priests and elders *question* Jesus *three times.* Jesus *does not respond at all* or responds indirectly.
7-8	Pilate *questions* the crowd *three times.* They have been persuaded by the chief priests and elders. The crowd *responds three times.*
5	Pilate *questions* the crowd one time. The crowd *does not respond at all.* Pilate *questions* the crowd one time. (They have been persuaded by the chief priests and elders.)
9	The crowd *responds* one time.

One observes in the chronological succession of the narrative that 5 and 9 bracket 7-8, that is to say 2-3 5 7-8 9,
or else one observes that the two relationships displayed between these different parts of the narrative are in alternate

or intersecting positions. As far as the actors of 2-3 and 7-8 are concerned, one helps in the displacement of the chief priests and elders which passes from Pilate to the crowd, from questioner to the questioned, and conjointly one establishes the isolation of Pilate who is separated from the chief priests and rejoins Jesus in this position.

As far as the actions are concerned, they are organized according to two categories. One is that of the question and the answer (or the non-response = silence). The other which is that of oneness or tripleness: from 2-3 to 9, the narrative makes it pass from the *silence* of Jesus to the *response* of the crowd. But it is no less remarkable that, from 5 to 9, it also makes it pass [p. 63] from *one*/silence (non-response) of the crowd to *one*/response of the crowd, who is persuaded by its leaders, through the medium of *three*/responses. The isolation of the question--response, its oneness, marks it in opposition to its triple repetition as unusual compared with the ritual. It indicates thereby that Pilate's question and the response of the crowd in 9 constitute an essential stage of the narrative.

Let us add three remarks to this first direction of the analysis--to conclude very quickly. The first concerns the inclusion of segment 7 in this interplay of correlations. Let us take verse 20: "The chief priests and elders persuaded the crowds (to demand Barabbas and get rid of Jesus)." We have only tried to retain from this intervention--at this level of analysis--the conjunction, the agreement of one group of actors (the chief priests and elders) with another group of actors (the crowds). Henceforth, these are the ones, the whole ensemble, who are questioned and who respond. The "content" of the persuasion will be examined at another level.

The second concerns another intervention which we have
not clarified on this plane, that of Pilate's wife. We have
disjoined it because it belongs to another order of speech:
that which advises, warns, and which at the same time does
not require a response. Consequently, it would be improper
to consider the absence of an answer from Pilate to his wife
as significant. It does not follow that this segment is essential to the structure of the narrative, as the second organization of the meaning will make clear.

The third consists of noting that this level of organization justifies an overture and closure of the narrative
which are much more limited than those which the initial extraction had permitted us to see, namely from verse 11 to
verse 26. If the overture does not pose a difficult problem,
the first part of verse 11 can be considered to be a kind of
summary of verses 1 and 2. On the other hand, the new closure draws our attention to the remarkable independence of
segment 11 (verses 27-31) called "the coronation with thorns"
or "the royal derision". In its initial and terminal *actions*,
segment 11 constitutes a reiteration of verses 2 and 26 of
the "entire" narrative (verse 2): "After having bound him,
they led him away and delivered him to the governor Pilate
(in order to put him to death)." One will read in verse 27:
"Then the governor's soldiers took Jesus with them into the
Praetorium and incited the whole cohort against him." Verse
26 indicates the end of the narrative: "Pilate delivered
him to be crucified." This is repeated by the end of verse
31: "They (the soldiers) led him (Jesus) away in order to
crucify him." From then on, the parodic acts of the recognition of Jesus' kingship will repeat, but in a gestural and
ritual way, the dialogue or the questioning of Jesus by
Pilate, the chief priests, and the elders. What is the value
of this repetition? Only an analysis of the diverse parts of

the narrative according to the second orientation could provide us with the elements of an answer.

II. The Problem of the Sequence.

One must consider the implications of this type of reading on the methodological plane. They could be summarized by
three questions:

1) What is the validity of the segmentation into parts,
segments, etc.? [p. 64]

2) What is the value of the oppositions, inversions,
correspondences, homologies...revealed after the segmentation?

3) What is the meaning of the spatialization of this
reading?

For the moment, we will only deal with the first question
which is the most important one, because the dismemberment of
the text and its articulation must deliver its signification
in each operation. But how does one define the articulations
through which our analysis will successively pass? How does
one draw out the good points of the text from its continuity?
What are the criteria for an accurate segmentation? Is not
the operative yield of the analysis or pattern under the text
of a structure of intelligibility not only that of *this* text
but also of numerous other texts, each of which would constitute a particular representation and investment? But this
structure of intelligibility, far from being at the end of a
progressive and inductive analysis, is it not, in its beginning like the "dotted line" which would indicate where the
segmentation must be performed?

Thus the delimitation of the sequence poses a difficult
methodological problem. To be precise and to give an operative point of departure, one can consider that the minimal

sequential unit is apparently the process indicated by a verb or its equivalent.

Let us take Mtt. 27:2: "And after having bound him (Jesus), they (the chief priests and elders of the people) led him away and delivered him to the governor Pilate." This sentence includes at least three sequential units: the first, "after having bound Jesus"; the second, "they led him away"; the third, "they delivered him to the governor Pilate". Three actions are noteworthy: the act of binding Jesus, his reduction to a passive object (a movement directed by the chief priests and elders), and finally, the transfer of Jesus to Pilate at the end of this movement. These three actions are indexed in space and time. *In space:* by coming out of our text and by referring to verse 57 and 58 of chapter 26 in order to find the point of departure of the movement: the group leaves the palace of the High Priest for that of the Roman governor, Pilate, its point of arrival defined in our text. *In time:* verse 1 notes: "the morning had come...". These units are therefore at the provisional end of our analysis of the surface of the text. But they form a "gross sequence" in three of them. How does one determine the limits without being arbitrary or resorting to a vague intuition? It is necessary to appeal here to the notion of a conclusion or a closure of a process. Thus in the example which we have taken, one can consider that the sequence is composed of a movement which leads from a point of departure to a point of arrival, from the palace of Caiphas to that of Pilate. It is a movement in the course of which an individual is reduced to the state of an object which is transferred. At the same time, the action of binding Jesus prior to the movement belongs to the sequence only to the extent to which the person is delivered as an object. This action is an index and a function at the same time. But one can consider the sequence

ended when the object is transferred at the end of the movement since its end (in the teleological and temporal sense of
the term) is indeed this delivery. But here again, do we know
by verse 1 how the meeting of the chief priests and elders
envisages the death of Jesus? It does so by transferring
Jesus to Pilate so that the latter can judge him, that is to
say, confirm the condemnation to death already pronounced.
Likewise we are [p. 65] forced to include the action described
in verse 1 in this sequence, "The meeting against Jesus with a
view to his death".

	1	2	
Spatial-temporal index: *Palace of Caiphas* (outside the text), *the morning.*	Meeting against Jesus with a view to his death.	Movement of transference of the object	*Spatial index:* *Palace of Pilate,* the governor, the place at the end of the movement: arrival and death of Jesus confirmed.

	(a)	(b)	(c)
	to bind	*to lead away*	*to de-liver*

Reduction
of Jesus
to the
state of
an object.

One can consider that the sequence is concluded with the
end of the movement of transference created by the meeting.
But in another sense, it will only become reality at the moment
when Pilate will deliver Jesus to be crucified (in verse 26)
and when the soldiers lead him away to be crucified (in verse

31). It is at this moment that the end posed in verse 1
("the meeting *against* Jesus with the purpose of putting him
to death") is reached, and beyond these two verses the crucifixion. But it is remarkable that this end of sequence 1
consists of two actions identical to actions (b) and (c) of
verse 2: "Pilate delivers Jesus"; "the soldiers lead Jesus
away". The object transferred in verses 1 and 2 is re-transferred, in turn, in a movement of direction opposed to verses
26 and 31. The ultimate end of the sequence is thus a return,
a re-transfer, and a reversal of the movement of the sequence.
Thus if we decide to constitute verses 26 and 31, at least
partially, in a sequence correlated with sequence 1, it
realizes sequence 1 by reversing its direction. By this remark, we show the equivocal nature of the correlation between
sequences 1 and 12. (12) is in continuity with (1). It is
its chronological and logical end. But (12) is to a certain
extent opposed to (1), since Jesus is transferred as an object by the Jewish elders and chief priests to the Roman
governor Pilate in (1) and Jesus is re-transferred as an object by the governor's Roman soldiers to the Jews in (12).
Thus (1) and (12) are two sequences in the linear and logical
chronology of the text, but they form only one sequence in
its non-linear teleology since (12) is separated from (1).
On the surface of the text considered, (12) is separated
from (1) by every narrative which we are studying although
(12) and (1) constitute the anterior and posterior boundaries.
By correlating them, we fold the text back in some way on itself by its two ends. We have produced a density of the
textual surface by this folding.

Thus there are two significations linked to the end of
the sequence. In the first, the sequence is controlled by
the simple logic of empirical *consecutions*. If a question
is posed, one can expect that a response will be given or

that silence will be observed. If an object is demanded, one
can expect that it will be given or refused. In the second,
the sequence is determined by the organization of a network
of structural connections which one can summarize in the
example chosen by the expression "exchange of an object-
person between two groups". Consequently, the entire analysis
consists of setting forth these two significations, the first
and the second, starting with the double limit of the sequences, and making the directions of meaning in this interplay apparent. [p. 66]

III. A Study of One Opposition.

The coupling of the sequences 2-3/11 offers a good
example for studying the problem which we noted above, i.e.
what is the nature of the relationships between the diverse
elements of the narrative? How are (2-3) opposed to (11)?
The interrogation of Jesus is based on the question of his
kingship which is affirmed. His condemnation concludes with
the recognition of his kingship, but it is done in a parodic
way. They mock him by saying, "Hail, King of the Jews!" (v.
29). The two sequences put into correlation include a common
element: kingship. At no other place in the narrative is
this discussed. But the affirmation or the position of kingship assumes a different character in the two sequences.
Pilate's question on the subject of Jesus' kingship is found
by the response of Jesus to return to Pilate's indirect
position on his kingship: "Are you the King of the Jews?"--
"You have said so." The exchange of a longer dialogue seems
to be implicitly assumed. Jesus could have said: "I note
that you pose the question of my kingship over the Jews.

Therefore you speak of kingship and since I do not wish to
oppose you, therefore you affirm it." And for his part,
Pilate could have added: "You affirm what I said in questioning you that you are the King of the Jews."

In (11), Jesus' kingship is affirmed by the governor's
soldiers, but it is done on the gestural and ceremonial
(and not on the verbal) plane. For the soldiers as well
as for Pilate, there is a question of his kingship, but
the oblique affirmation of the governor has become a parodic coronation ceremony performed by his soldiers. There
are two differences between (2-3) and (11). First, there
is the difference between language and gesture or the single
question and the ritual ceremony. But there is also the
difference between the implicit and the parodic. Pilate
tells the truth: "Jesus is King", but he does so in passing without developing it, *explaining it*, or completely
realizing it. The soldiers crown Jesus king, but they do
so only *in appearance* because they are mocking him. The
affirmation is posed *implicitly* in the question (or language)
which nevertheless neutralizes it. The being is affirmed
parodistically in the appearing (or comportment) which nevertheless denies it (cf. Critical Note I). Therefore the opposition of the two sequences is based on the articulation
combined with the linguistic (affirmation vs. negation) and
ontological (being vs. appearing) categories. It is these
categories whose articulation we will find in the (ontological) opposition of (4) and (10) and in the (linguistic) opposition of (5) and (8). One could summarize this analysis
in the following tables which represent "the opposition" of
(2-3) and (11):

2-3 Affirmation -	11 Being +
Language	Comportment
Negation -	Appearing +

It is only necessary to add that in 2-3, where Jesus'
kingship is neither directly affirmed nor explicitly denied,
Jesus' answer, "You have said so", gives a *non-negative
dominant* to this *neutral* ensemble. In [p. 67] the same way,
one will note in 11 a *dominant of appearing* in the *compound*
ensemble where being a king and appearing to be a king are
simultaneously posed, which is another way of saying that
the opposing terms are not perfectly symmetrical and that
it would be advisable to define precisely *stricto sensu*
this orientation of the opposition relationship. If we be-
stow the general logical model of signification on these
particular contents, we obtain:

For Table I

S = Equivocation,
Ambiguity

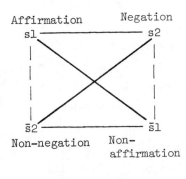

S̄ = Question

For Table II

S = Veracity

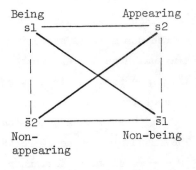

S̄ = Strangeness

Table I:

The asymmetry of the neutral axis S̄ with the dominant
s̄2 signifies that the relationship of implication s1 ... s̄2
is oriented s̄2 ⟶ s1. It is a non-negation which implies an affirmation: "Are you the King of the Jews?"
Jesus' kingship is neither affirmed nor denied. It is in
question (neutralizing value of the question): "You have
said so." There is a passage from a neutral to the non-
negative dominant, that is to say to the implicit affirmation.

The asymmetry of the compound axis S with the dominant s2 signifies that the relationship of implication s2 ... s̄1 is oriented s2 ——→ s̄1. There is an appearing to be king which implies a non-being king. The compound S axis is the veracious axis. Jesus appears to be what he is: a King. The appearing is coextensive with the being and the being is coextensive with the appearing. He is crowned king and he is king. But this crowning is derisory and parodic. It is the dominant of appearing s2 on the compound axis. The king which he appears to be is not the king which he truly is. In effect, he is crowned by non-Jews. He is not the King of the Jews. He is a universal king. The non-Jews affirm this in a parodic manner: "Hail, King of the Jews." They make him appear to be what he is not. In Table I, s̄2 ——→ s1 would designate the *implicity*. In Table II, s2 ——→ s̄1 would designate the passage of the truth from the parodic to the non-being which determines the *disguise* (= King of the Jews). Jesus appears to be what he is not, that is to say the King of the Jews. Consequently, one sees the opposition of (2-3) and (11): s̄2 ——→ s1 *vs.* s2 ——→ s̄1 very clearly.

One can point out throughout the gospel text the interplay of dominants of the compound S axis. *With* the dominant s1, it would designate the messianic entrance to Jerusalem (Matthew 21:1-11) and *without* a dominant s1, it would designate the last appearance (Matthew 28:18) and the eschatological return (Matthew 24:30-31 or 25:31-46). In effect, in Matthew, Luke, or Mark, Jesus is indeed designated as the King of the Jews at the time of his entrance into Jerusalem. But this is always done in the perspective of the messianic proclamation. This is the reason for these particular marks of appearing to be the (messianic) king, e.g. the ass's foal and she-ass or the refusal to correct the [p. 68] acclamations of his disciples. These are marks which will not be really perceived by the people. Therefore s1 ⟶ s̄2 (Jesus is what he does not appear to be) is an orientation of the implication which is that of a *secret*. In the eschatological discourse, Jesus, the Son of Man, *is* and *appears* to be a king with all the attributes and qualifications: "And one will see the Son of Man coming on the clouds of heaven with power and great glory. And with a trumpet blast he will send his angels to the four corners of the horizon to assemble his chosen ones from one end of the heavens to another." This eschatological king is a universal king: "All the races of the earth will lament." Verses 31-32 of chapter 25 are even clearer: "When the Son of Man will come in his glory escorted by all his angels, then he will take his place on his throne of glory. All the nations will be assembled before him, and he will separate them from one another...then the king will say...."

Moreover, could one recognize the articulations of the neutral axis s̄ in this particular investment which is "the kingship of Jesus"? Verses 37 and 42 of Matthew 27 could constitute a manifestation of it: "They placed the reason for his condemnation above his head, it read: 'This is Jesus, the King of the Jews'" and verse 42, the mockeries of the chief priests and elders: "He has saved others and he cannot save himself! If he is the King of Israel, let him come down from the cross now...." Jesus is not, nor does he appear to be a king in the crucifixion sequences. In fact, this analysis appears to us to be excluded for one important reason. It is only within the language that there is a question here of Jesus' kingship, and the two verses cited call much more attention to the notion of *implicity* indicated by the orientation of the relationship

of implication s̄2 ⟶ s1, than to that of a neutrality with
respect to the being and the appearing, the *strangeness* vis-a-
vis the kingship. It is a neutrality, if one wishes, but with
a non-negative dominant. It is a reiteration in another context and in another way of Pilate's implicit affirmation.
"This is Jesus, the King of the Jews." This description is
the reason for his condemnation. This affirmation is in
reality a negation: "Jesus affirms that 'He is the King of
the Jews' *whereas he is not*." So he is condemned and crucified. From the point of view of Jesus' judges, the affirmation includes an implication which displaces it in negation
(cf. the discussion of this subject in John 19:19-22). Nevertheless, at the level of the global text (in its reception)
as it is intended and wished by the redactor, the affirmation
is correct: "Jesus is King." But it has lost one of its
elements by its passage through the implication which imposes a negation on it, the designation of the people of
whom Jesus is the king, the Jews. One can make the same remarks about verse 42: He is the King of Israel (with the
implication: "He falsely pretends that he is the King of
Israel" and its mark in the text: the point of exclamation
or irony). It is by reference, on the one hand, to the eschatological discourse which (in the linearity of the text)
precedes the passages studied, and by reference, on the
other hand, to the affirmation of 28:18 at the time of the
final appearance ("All *power* in heaven and on earth has
been given to me. Go therefore and make disciples *of all
nations....*") that the signified excess can be read and consequently recognized as implicit in the affirmations of the
chief priests and elders at the time of the crucifixion. [p.
69] This text can only be understood in its meaning as *reread*. In order that it may tell the truth, *from the beginning, one must reread it*. One must be free from the linear

discovery of the succession of events and episodes. In one word, it is necessary that this narrative be a *rereading* which is always already known and nevertheless new in the upheaval of events which every narrative displays. Perhaps at this point the profound articulation of prophetic and narrative discourse can be perceived in what one could call the *recitative-narrative.*[1]

III. A. The Retroactive Reading.

The last problem suggested by the preceding appendix was connected with the question which we have already noted: that of the "spatialization" of the text. What is the meaning of this type of reading which no longer respects the temporal principles of the narrative linearity and irreversibility and which transposes or transforms these principles into spatial forms--which may strictly speaking compose a text-- of envelopment, integration, and hierarchical (intra-textual) subordination? In effect, sequences 6-7 constitute a well- defined focal point of the networks of oppositions which sur- round and envelop it. And nevertheless these spatial or representative forms permit an order of reading. One will begin by reading 1/12 then 2,3/11, etc. At this point, there- fore, *another kind of temporality than the common temporality of the "line" appears traversing time.* We refer on this point Starobinsky's remarks in *Le Mercure de France* 350 (Feb., 1964), p. 254, concerning F. de Saussure's *Anagrammes*: "This read- ing does not develop according to another *time* (and in an- other time): specifically one leaves the time of the consecu- tivity characteristic of habitual language." To which Jacques Derrida, who quotes Starobinsky, adds: "One could probably say [it is] characteristic of the habitual concept of time

and language" (*De la grammatologie*, p. 104). This is the same
problem we have attempted to grasp in the "tempo" of the reading of the table by [p. 70] distinguishing several levels of
temporality which enclose one another and form a topological
structure of the temporality of reading.

IV. Pilate's Three Questions

We have pointed out in our analysis that Pilate's three
questions to the crowd concerning Jesus simply do not have
the iterative value of the superlative. They observe a gradation (i.e. an alternative--choice--justification of the
choice) which implicitly marks Pilate's·passage from a semi-
hostility to a positive indifference. They indicate the
difficulty of apparently posing a term which may be absolute-
ly neutral. We will still attempt to draw attention to the
triplication of the question which evokes Peter's *three*
denials in the courtyard of the High Priest's palace. An
important text from L. Gernet in the *Anthropologie de la
Grèce Antique*[2] could help us to begin with one of the codes
from which Pilate's three questions could be constructed.
This is especially true because the problem which L. Gernet
studies is that of the temporal models in juridical thought
in general and in the trial in particular.

The idea in question is that of a positive or negative
effective power of time. Time "multiplies" (thus the model
of the interest provided by the increase in livestock) or
"erases" (thus Aeschylus' Orestes declares: "My impurity is
washed away").[3] How can a rational juridical mind integrate
this effective power of time while preserving and going beyond its mythical-religious aspect?

One will note again a series of very particular facts, but rather characteristic of
what we call the turning point and some more
or less intentional and twisted proceedings,
to which it can give rise. We borrow them
from very ancient Roman law. The Romans are
the experts. It is a matter of triple acts
or acts which muct be performed three times
in order to be effective.[4]

L. Gernet gives several examples of this juridical tripleness:
the ritual tort at the door of the defaulting witness must be
repeated three days: "The woman comes into the hands of her
husband...at the end of a year, unless she has stayed out
three nights in succession, etc."[5] Gernet continues:

Despite the diversity of intention which one
perceives, they (these provisions of the law
of XII Tables) have something in common. One
knows that the number, but especially the
number three, confers an effective power on
human action: when this religious mind
emerges in the law, it requires tripleness.
But there is something else: the 'three
times' must be consecutive. Now the idea
appears here of a concentration of the time
at the conclusion of a juridical *operation*.
The duration which is more or less vaguely
conceived but is felt to be necessary for a
conclusion is at the same time symbolized
and actualized in a short space of time and
by virtue of the triple repetition....The
operative virtue of a temporal symbolism
is certainly not something unheard of....
What the ancient Roman law offered in particular is what, with a view to a proper
juridical efficiency, it used while trans-
posing an ancient view to it whose significations it almost patently accentuated.[6]

[p. 71]

It is perhaps likely that Pilate's three questions are
ascribable to a juridical disposition analogous to those which

Gernet analyzed. But it is more important for us to transpose the referential sociological indications which we have noted into the articulation of the text. Pilate's questions textually indicate, better than the interventions of the chief priests and elders, the change of the Jewish crowd, or of the people who (between Jesus and Barabbas) chose Barabbas, who chose the crucifixion, and finally refused to justify his condemnation, condemning him for that very reason especially more effectively. The textual temporality is symbolic of a logical transformation which is at the focal point of our text: the passage from the neutral to the negative.

We can make some similar remarks about Peter's three denials (Matthew 26:69-75). The chronology of the text is again a time symbolic of the logical change from a positive Peter (the defender of Jesus) to a negative Peter ("I do not know this man") with an increasing gradation: first, public negation (v. 70); second, negation with an oath (v. 72); third, negation with an oath and curses (v. 74).

What L. Gernet analyzes (as a juridical act which aims to utilize by a rational rule the archaic effectiveness of time in order to be fulfilled) is in our analysis a "textual act" which uses the narrative and its surface peripeties in order to carry out the logical operations necessary for its actualization.

V. A New Correlation.

From this point of view, the episode of the two robbers who were crucified with Jesus (Matthew 27:38 and 27:44; Luke 23:39-43; Mark 15:27 and 15:32) will be an interesting correlation. In Matthew as in Mark, the robbers crucified, one on

the right and the other on the left, appear to be the representatives on the cross of the chief priests, the scribes,
the elders, and the people. Like the two extreme positions
of the nation (cf. Matthew v. 41), the leaders and the rabble
joined forces to insult him. On the other hand, the dichotomy
is more complex in Luke. The good robber recognizes Jesus as
the king of a kingdom of the beyond, while the evil robber
repeats the insults of the people and the soldiers: "If you
are the King of the Jews, save yourself." We find here at
the same time the division of the hero and the recovery of
his oneness by the exclusion or expulsion of one of the contraries, but it is reaffirmed in another way.

VI. One Variant of the Central Sequence in Luke 23:7-12.

Our analysis of Matthew's text has isolated a central
sequence of the narrative where a double action of the same
kind (but it is reversed) exerts itself on the two privileged
actors, the people and Pilate. In the case of Pilate (sequence 6), it is the mediating intervention of his wife,
"Do not have anything to do with the case of this just man",
which is caused by a dream. In the case of the people (sequence 7), it is the intervention of the chief priests and
elders who "persuaded the crowds to demand Barabbas and get
rid of Jesus". This is therefore the second stage of the
[p. 72] narrative after sequence 8, which is characterized by
the general and opposite transformation of the prior sequences.

Now the intervention by Pilate's wife disappears in Luke.
The same thing is true of the chief priests and elders' intervention on the crowd because the crowd does not constitute an
entity separated from the chief priests and elders (cf. 23:4:

"Pilate then said to the chief priests, and to the crowd....";
or v. 13: "Having therefore summoned the chief priests, the
leaders, and the people...."). On the other hand, an important sequence does appear referring to the meeting of Jesus
and Herod. It functions as a doublet of the meeting of Jesus
and Pilate, but it is substituted for that sequence where
Pilate's wife intercedes with her husband on behalf of Jesus
(sequence 6 in Matthew), and it is integrated with the sequence where Jesus undergoes the test of the royal derision
(sequence 11 in Matthew).

There is a double modification here:

First of the Schema of the Characters:

Matthew

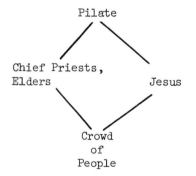

Luke

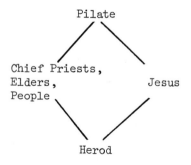

One will note that Luke's schema is subtended by a series of topographical oppositions:

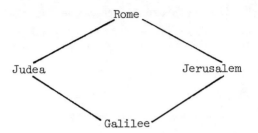

Jesus revolts against Rome and Caesar, Judea *and* Galilee (Luke 23:5). The Roman Pilate is located in Jerusalem where Herod, the Galilean King,is also found at that time (v. 7). Jesus is a Galilean, but he is tried in Jerusalem (v. 7).

It is the old North and South opposition which reappears here with its double mediation: Jerusalem is the focal point and in this focal point and beyond it there is Rome.

Second of the Sequential Schema:

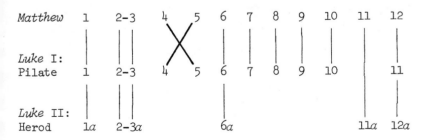

[p. 73]

The sequential schema is doubled for Luke's narrative,
i.e. one of the lines of the narrative refers to Pilate--Luke
(I), the other to Herod--Luke (II). One will note a point by
point correspondence of sequences 1, 2, 3 between Matthew,
Luke I and Luke II, a correspondence of sequences 7, 8, 9, 10
between Matthew and Luke (I), and a correspondence of 11, 12,
and 12a between Matthew and Luke (II). In Luke, the royal derision is not performed by Pilate but by Herod (Luke 23:11).
On the other hand, one should note the intersecting correspondence of sequences 4 and 5 in Matthew and Luke (I). Pilate's
first question to the crowd in Matthew, "Jesus or Barabbas?"
(to which the crowd does not respond), becomes Pilate's question to the crowd, the elders, and the chief priests in Luke's
"Is he a Galilean?" Matthew's sequence 5 corresponds to Luke's
sequence 4. The reason for the correlative crossing of sequences 4 and 5 is that Jesus is also divided in Luke but he
is not divided between Christ and Barabbas, but between being
a Jew and a Galilean. The ambiguity of the hero is not personal. It does not take place in his proper name but in his
"tribal" or "national" membership. This is the reason for the
reference to Herod and the reiteration on line II of sequences
1, 2, 3 in Luke's narrative. Jesus passes from the Romans to
the Galileans (1a). Herod questions him; Jesus is silent (2a);
the chief priests and the scribes accuse him (3a). Sequence 6
introduces an important element of signification. It appears
in Luke II and in the succession of the narrative between 1a
and 2a, but it agrees well with Matthew's sequence 6:

1. Herod wishes to meet Jesus--he hopes
   that Jesus will perform a miracle--
   this miracle is not performed.

2. Pilate's wife has no relationship with
   Jesus. She receives a dream--a warning
   sign which she does not want. She transmits this sign to Pilate.

Sequence 6 in Matthew and sequence 6 in Luke (II) are
indeed homologues. But one will note by their consequences
that they are inverted: with respect to Jesus, the hostility
is hidden by Herod's parodic admiration--this is sequence 11a
--positive indifference on Pilate's part--these are sequences
7, 8, 9 in Luke (I).

The rest of sequence 6a in Luke (II), the conséquence of
6, displays a positive relationship between Pilate and Herod
which follows a disjunction (cf. Luke 23:12). Herod and
Pilate become friends from the enemies which they were, while,
on the other hand, Pilate and the Jewish people of Jerusalem
(including the chief priests and elders) become opponents from
the (at least implicit) "friends" which they were.

It is time to draw some consequences from this tedious
analysis. If, as we think, the whole insoluble problem of
these narratives is to achieve the passage from a closed
national and religious community to an open "supranational"
universality and from a temporal kingdom to an eternal messianic kingdom, then the Herod episode constitutes an additional
mediation. It is first an addition: the episode functions
well as a mirror trial of the "trial" before Pilate with
which one could do without (cf. Matthew or Mark). But its
elimination would be made at the price of a surface contradiction. How would one *apparently* explain the episode of the
royal derision, and then the meeting with Herod, the *true* King
of Galilee?

The Herod episode is second a mediation: Herod, and
Galilee with him, represent an ambiguous Jewish community.

It is certainly Jewish, but its center is not Jerusalem. In the passage from the particular to the universal, from the temporal to [p. 74] the eternal, and from the national to the "supranational", Galilee constitutes between Jerusalem and Rome a stage--a recourse which shows itself to be negative in the parody and the disguise. The accent remains on Rome which polarizes the concepts of universality and "supranationality". It is Pilate's wife who receives a sign without asking for it. Herod who desires and asks for a sign receives nothing. It is a beginning, but it is outside of time and politics whose completion will be accomplished at the time of Peter's approach to the centurion of the Italian cohort (Acts 10-11). While on the political and anecdotal plane, the conjunction between Herod, the Tetrarch of Galilee, and Pilate produced by the mediation is immediately performed over the heads of the chief priests, the elders, and the people of Judea.

NOTES

1. By posing the question, "Are you the King of the Jews?", to Jesus, Pilate reveals that Jesus' kingship is in question for him. Neither affirmed nor denied, Jesus' kingship is neutralized by the act of questioning. A negative or positive answer is possible to this question. As for Jesus' answer, it attributes an affirmation to Pilate which is neither Pilate's nor Jesus'. Jesus does not affirm that he is a king, but he thinks that Pilate has called him a king by posing the question of his kingship to him. This affirmation of Jesus' kingship over the Jews is thus an affirmation which no one attempts to make but also one which no one attempts to dismiss. It is an affirmation without a subject. In other words, what Pilate says (by posing his question) exceeds his speech, not in its content but in its form. The (neutral) interrogative is assertive by this excess of the signified over the signifier, which Jesus' answer brings to light: "You asked about my kingship over the Jews? I did not make you say it." The neutrality of the one who is questioned consequently implies an affirmation. But it was necessary that Jesus and Pilate cooperate in its transformation. It is an affirmation without a subject, but it is also an affirmation with two subjects which float between "you" and "I".
       One will find the same excess of signified over the signifier in other forms in the parodic coronation. By crowning Jesus King of the Jews ("Hail, King of the Jews!"), the Roman soldiers (or non-Jews) deny him this qualification by "pretending" to affirm it. But their comportment has (like a little while ago with Pilate's question) exceeded in its meaning the way in which it signified it. The non-Jews crown Jesus as the king of the Jews exceeding in its derision the "Jewishness" of his kingship and they present him in this way as a universal king (or at the very least as the king of the non-Jews). The parodic interplay permits the oblique position to exist.

2. Louis Gernet, "Le Temps dans les formes archaïques du droit," *Journal de Psychologie* 53 (July–September, 1956), 379–406. Reprinted in *Anthropologie de la Grèce antique*, Paris: Maspero, 1965, 261–287.

3. *Ibid.*, 282.

4. *Ibid.*, 283-284.

5. *Ibid.*, 284.

6. *Ibid.*, 284-285.

VII

AN ANALYSIS OF
THE "TEXT" OF THE PASSION

by

Claude Chabrol

We will give the perspectives and limitations of this
study at the very beginning.

(1) It is not concerned with establishing some definitive results of an analysis but with the formation of an operational model which must be compared later with the three
gospel texts.[1] This comparison allows us to correct the model
and to make apparent what it cannot account for.

(2) At first sight a paradoxical consequence is inferred
from this conception. We have assumed that the three gospel
texts (Matthew, Mark, and Luke) were three substitutable
variants of a single "meta-text" which is given to us as a
veritable object for analysis, although properly speaking
this text does not exist as a single *text*.

(3) One could rightly wonder about the extreme impover-
ishment of the text which results from our contempt of the
differences peculiar to each gospel text, in short, about the
incomplete character of our analysis.

--But one must understand that an analysis which attempts
to construct an operational model cannot procede otherwise.
It would be useless to attempt at the very beginning to take
account of all the levels (including the stylistic level)
and all the details of the manifestation.

--It is only once a structural hypothesis of a coherent ensemble has been put into use in a deductive method, which will attempt each time to integrate new specific elements into their places, that one could pose these questions.

I. *From the Narrative Structure to the Semantic Structure.* (The Models of Lévi-Strauss and Greimas.)

We will not give a new definition of these models in this article. The application which we will make of them is so incompletely worked out that one can easily reduce it to the functioning of one [p. 76] homologous structure. As T. Todorov has said about Lévi-Strauss, it is a matter of grouping the narrative statements which have the same inversed or posited semantic content. In other words, a paradigmatic structure of the semantic content being assumed, it is necessary to find the semantic opposition (which is often homologous) in the syntagmatic succession of narrative statements which has produced them.

The results which we have obtained thus far can be represented[2] in this way: a second higher stage of amelioration follows the first stage. One must precisely determine what creates the superiority of this second stage. With regard to this, one will place into opposition the symmetrical and/or inverse statements of the first and second stage:

	I	II
A	Ignorance of that which they say of themselves (by the Chief Priest and Sanhedrin) (a)I Jesus is explicitly silent (a')I	Knowledge of what they receive from others (the apostles, the women, and the Emmaus pilgrims) a(II) Jesus (and his spokesmen) explicitly speak a'(II)
B	Request of a "prodigious" sign by the Jews (b)I Request not explicitly met (b')I	Non-request of a (prodigious) sign (by the apostles and disciples) b(II) "Non prodigious" sign explicitly given b'(II)
C	Inability of the false witnesses to produce the condemnation of Jesus + repetition of an enigmatic message (c)I	Inability of the women and the Emmaus pilgrims to produce recognition of the risen Jesus (+ inadequate presence of Jesus with them. He does not eat $\frac{before}{with}$ them) c(II)
D	The condemnation ("he has blasphemed") originates from the heart of the old Community (High Priest, Sanhedrin)-- (with the help of Jesus who acquiesces) (c')I The action by the Elders of the Sanhedrin (d)I Negative sanction by all the old Community (d')I	The definitive recognition (with the help of Jesus who eats $\frac{before}{with}$ them) originates from the heart of the new Community c'(II) The evangelization (to come) of the apostles d(II) Positive sanction by all the new Community (to be obtained)? d'(II)
E	Jesus is implicitly consecrated king by the Jews (e)I Implicit glorification ? (e')I	Jesus states his power himself e(II) Explicit glorification e'(II)

General Commentary

(1) Each of the five basic statements (A, B, C, D, E) shows itself to be a complex homology (which is based on several units of meaning) in which the sub-statement which is first designated (a, b, c, d, e) implies those which follow (a', b', c', d', e').

(2) Therefore one statement A presents itself in this way:

$$\left\{ \frac{a(I)}{a'(I)} \quad :: \quad \frac{a(II)}{a'(II)} \right\}$$

or I and II refer to successive stages. There is a term for term opposition of a(I) *vs.* a(II) and a'(I) *vs.* a'(II).

One will immediately note several difficulties. In the first place, numerous elements of the text studied do not appear. This lack of exhaustiveness threatens the analysis or at least threatens its results.

To the extent to which we are more interested here in an investigation of the power of the structuration of diverse methods, it has still seemed possible to us, despite everything, to give these partial indications.

--A second difficulty, which is perhaps more important, lies in the use of the term *statement*. It is not a question at any stage of a more or less large unit of the text exposed, but of a metalinguistic definition of a certain number of passages from the text (or outside it) which already accentuate some bundles of pertinent units of meaning, in other words, where the commutations are shown.

--Finally, the relationships of opposition or implication of the sub-statements a(I) *vs.* a(II) or a(I) $\longrightarrow$ a'(I)..., etc. are not always of the same kind and the same extent.

Thus (A) opposes: "Knowledge to Ignorance",

"Speaking about oneself to Receiving
knowledge from another",

"Being explicitly silent to Transmitting
a knowledge explicitly".

On the other hand, if (C) indeed opposes: "condemnation to
recognition", it seems that one is insisting on a symmetry
which is not inversed but identical: the "insufficiency" of
that which comes. from the periphery of the community (false
witnesses, women, pilgrims) and the "sufficiency" of that
which comes from its heart (the Sanhedrin and apostles). This
trait is repeated in (D) where d'(I) is only opposed to d'(II)
by the negative or positive character of the sanction.

--The negation therefore operates differently from one
basic statement to another, which creates a problem with regard to the legitimacy of the formation of our columns. We
will leave the resolution of this difficulty unsolved for the
moment. (The negation can be based on the ensemble of the
proposition which is taken as a whole, or it can be based on
only one of its parts.)

Commentary on the Statements

Statement (A): a(I) is placed in a prominent position
which is shown in more detail in the Jewish and Gentile trials.
There is an inversion of roles between the one who poses the
question and the one who must respond. Those who interrogate
Jesus do not make inquiries about the hero in order to obtain
a knowledge which they could not possess. [p. 78]
They simply want to confirm their knowledge in order to
verify it ("Are you the Christ, the Son of God? Are you the

King of the Jews?").[3] Therefore they appear to be in possession of a knowledge which no one could have transmitted to
them since they refuse to receive the one who had to give it
and its messages to them. We will compare this knowledge
which is not transmitted to that of the Gerasene demoniac
(cf. Mtt. 8:29) who cried to Jesus, "What do you want with
us, *Son of God*?" Without developing this important axis
here, to speak (or act) by oneself in the New Testament is
assumed to be a negative sign. One must speak "for, instead
of, in the name of".

--The form itself: the question is pertinent. We will
not repeat what has already been said above. We will be content to point out that to question knowledge which already
exists can only be a sign of doubt or a *qualificative misunderstanding* (cf. all the quotations from Isaiah in the New
Testament such as in Mtt. 13:14-16: "You shall indeed hear
but never understand, and you shall indeed see but never perceive....They have blocked their ears, they have closed their
eyes.").

--One can summarize a(I) in the following formula: Knowledge (not-known) where the modalization is revealed by the
questioning position and the "non-transmitted" character of
the Knowledge.[4]

--a(II) is directly opposed to a(I). It must therefore
be defined as Knowledge (known). This works well since the
women after the resurrection (like the Emmaus pilgrims) *receive* the object of Knowledge without ever having asked for
it.

Jesus or his representatives (the angels, etc.) transmit
the knowledge (i.e. the role of Christ, the necessity for his
death and resurrection, the conformity of these events with
Scripture).

The opposition of a(I) *vs.* a(II) establishes that of a'(I) *vs.* a'(II) which will clearly follow from it. a(II) implies a sender of the knowledge; therefore Jesus must explicitly speak. Unlike a(I) which denies the sender, Jesus must be "suppressed" and therefore be explicitly silent. It is not very important that Jesus affirmatively respond to the question which is given to him for what he says cannot be understood and *known*.[5] The misunderstanding produces a veritable silence.

--Statement (B) is closely connected to (A). If doubt were expressed in the question of Jesus' identity, the request of the Jews must take the form of a quest for a guarantee. This is revealed in the demand for a sign b(I).

This demand for a sign is explicit when Luke tells us that Herod "wanted to see him perform some miracles". It is implicit when it is inscribed [p. 79] in a derisory way (i.e. the mockeries, the jokes) after the appearance in court before the High Priest, the soldiers, and male servants who demand that he "prophesy" [ed. note, see Mtt. 26:68]. Those who pass by and shout to him on the cross: "If you are the Son of God, save yourself and come down from the cross." (or when the chief priests say, "He has saved others, and he cannot save himself, let him come down from the cross now and *we will believe in him*.").

One should compare this demand for a sign with all those which precede it in the New Testament and especially those of the scribes and Pharisees: "Master, we would like for you to give us a sign" (Mtt. 12:38; Lk. 11:29-32; Mk. 8:11-12) which is elsewhere qualified as a "sign which comes from heaven" (Mtt. 16:1; Lk. 11:16-29).[6]

Besides being an obvious resemblance, this comparison permits us to point out a new determination of the sign demanded; it must be supernatural or "prodigious" (e.g. to perform some miracles on command or descend from his cross).[7]

Although it is impossible to develop this point further, one should note an inversion in his relationship to the deity. Jesus must prove himself by his ability to perform some supernatural acts. (Is it perhaps only conceivable to have a struggle between magicians or gods in a pantheistic [and not in a monotheistic] religious world?)

--A is opposed to (b)I; b(II) must be defined as a non-demand for a sign, which obviously excludes every additional quest for a "prodigious" characteristic. The apostles and the disciples never ask Jesus to give a sign as a guarantee or as proof of his nature or mission.

--But on the other hand, the apostles and disciples receive a sign: "the resurrection"--b'(II). The bond of implication b(II) $\longrightarrow$ b'(II) appears to be very strong. The non-demand for a sign requires the reception of a sign, just as the non-questioning of Jesus' identity requires the reception of knowledge.

--One should no longer be amazed to discover that the demand for a sign, b(I), henceforth corresponds to the refusal to give the sign expected, b'(I).

Note (1). One must note, however, that if there is an explicit refusal to give the sign expected, this refusal does not take the simple form of silence or inaction. It would be easy to show that Christ is in the process of supplying the signs which are asked of him. He *has prophesied* by correctly prophesying the misunderstanding of the Jews, his condemnation, his death, and his resurrection. He is *indeed the saviour* since he brings salvation by dying on the cross. He *"will save himself"*, not by coming down from the cross, but by coming out of his tomb.

In summary, some signs are given by Jesus (in this text as well as in the entire New Testament), but they are not received. The non-response is in fact a non-reception. But [p. 80] there is an inversion on the plane of appearing, and a pre-supposed non-reception requires the perception of a non-response.

Note (2). If a prodigious sign were demanded in b(I), the sign given in b'(II) must be "non-prodigious". But the resurrection from the dead could appear to be a kind of prodigy. This hypothesis is confirmed by the absence of this deed in the text.

No one has helped him, no one has witnessed this most important event [ed. note: i.e. Jesus' actual departure from the tomb], and even the narrator is silent about it. What is produced is only "the absence of a body". It is this "absence", this empty sign which will function contiguously as an "equivalent" for the resurrection.

--In summary, it is the transmission of an object of value (it is not important for us to know precisely what this value is here) which is in play here. This object of value can only be received, or *given* in the strict sense of the word, to the one who does not ("explicitly") request it. Every explicit quest for this object disqualifies the subject, who cannot receive the gift; and it makes him appear to deny the axis itself of the transmission and therefore of every sender.

One could summarize statement (B) in the following formula: sign of value (not known) *vs*. sign of value (known).

--Statements (C) and (D) develop the consequence of statements (A) and (B). On the one hand, one has a Knowledge (not known) and a sign of value (not known): $a(I) + a'(I)$ and $b(I) + b'(I)$ which assumes a *negation* of the sender and his representative. This negation comes to be revealed henceforth in the "condemnation" (c[I], c'[I], d[I], d'[II]).

On the other hand, we will see that the *affirmation* of the sender and his representative must correspond to a Knowledge (known) and a sign of value (known), therefore it is a "recognition" (c[II], c'[II], d[II], d'[II]).

But this negation or affirmation cannot immediately be produced by the text. A helper is needed. Statements (C) and (D) therefore show the constitution of the helpers (C) and their necessary action (D). The need for these helpers is not to be found at the narrative level (where they are only possible and disposable). In fact, this need is inferred, as we will show, from the semantic universe which subtends the text.

--Statement (C) poses the inadequacy of certain "possible" helpers, e.g. false witnesses, or the women and Emmaus pilgrims, in order to succeed in determining the *real helpers*: the chief priests and the Sanhedrin, on the one hand, and the apostles, on the other.

One can make the hypothesis that this division reveals a social distinction in which one recognizes a hierarchical conception of a community where the center (or upper class) is opposed to the periphery (or lower class) of the community.

This hierarchical conception imposes *at the very least* a duplication of all the operations between the sender and receiver according to the following process: [p. 81]

```
Divine a  --              gift
                 sender ————————→ privileged receiver


Human b   --              circulation
                privileged ————————→ final receiver
                receiver      gift
```

Note. It is impossible to develop all the consequences of this duplication here. We will, however, show the main points. Axis (a) constitutes a hero (or a class of hero)[8] who is a mediator par excellence. This axis is that of the *divine* or that of a *direct* relationship with the "present" deity. Axis (b), on the other hand, establishes only an indirect relationship to the "absent" deity, it appears to be *human*.

The qualification of the privileged receiver appears therefore to be twofold. It is "divine and human" (because it shares in the Divine and the Human).

According to the dominance established in this compound contradictory term, one would have for example (for the Old and New Testaments):

1) "Human > divine": chief [*importants*] priests

2) Human = divine: Patriarchs, Prophets, Kings

3) Divine > Human: Jesus

This duplication is apparent if one compares (C) and (D). The condemnation by the privileged receivers (the Sanhedrin and chief priests): (C)I must be followed by a condemnation by all the Jewish people (D)I. Likewise, the recognition by the privileged receivers (the apostles) (C)II must be followed by the recognition of all the "new" community D(II) thanks to the action of the apostles.

It is not very important that D(II) is only sketched out or reported in the gospels. Its necessity is posed. D'(II) (recognition by all the new community with the help of the apostles) will be realized in the "Acts of the Apostles". This leads to an important consequence. The "text of the Passion" cannot be closed with the end of the Gospel, the Acts of the Apostles also belongs to it (or at least some passages to be defined belong to it).

--One must still show how the inadequacy is represented.

The false witnesses almost repeat a "parabolic" or enigmatic message of Jesus: "I can destroy the temple and rebuild it in three days" (Mtt. 26:61), while the High Priest asks him "in plain language" if he is indeed the "Son of God" and he clearly responds with the affirmative (Mtt. 26:63-64).

The pertinent opposition to the level of the messages themselves is therefore "enigmatic *vs.* clear" which produces the inadequacy or the adequacy of the testimony.

--The women and the Emmaus pilgrims (at least in Luke, who seems to be the most explicit)[9] receive a less complete message than the [p. 82] apostles, and this message is moreover transmitted by a Christ who is less present.

--Only the apostles are entitled, at the same time, to a complete message. They are entitled to receive an explanation of the resurrection in comparison with the Scriptures and to the explicit and non-instantaneous presence of Christ who presents himself to them in this way and who is no longer hidden (in an angelic representative or in a person who is not identifiable).

--Moreover, Christ definitely establishes a contract with them. He eats with them (which reminds them of the

eucharistic contract) and the evangelization to come develops
from that as a consequence.

Note. One can certainly note that the women and the
pilgrims receive an explicit or implicit secondary mission
to transmit the message to the apostles, which is a sign of
a secondary contract.

--This trait leads us to state a new point. We have
attempted to take account of the inadequacy of the testimony
and the help of the false witnesses, the women, and the
Emmaus pilgrims by the hypothesis of a "privileged sender"
which is inferred from a hierarchical conception of the
society. But conversely, one must now understand the necessity of repeating, for example, the sequence: (appearance +
message + mission[10]). In other words, what are the reasons
which make the repetition of the relationship of donation between Jesus and some multiple actors other than the privileged
receiver (the apostles) indispensable, when we know that these
relationships cannot be enough?

--They seem to be connected with a fundamental characteristic of this discourse. The transmission performed by the
apostles (for example) would be based less on the knowledge
or the sign of value than on its mode. They will not have
to circulate a knowledge which is received by themselves
alone, but they will have to *make known* a knowledge which is
received by many but not known.

--Moreover, that only reflects the way in which they
have themselves received this knowledge. It is not our purpose here, but it would be easy to point out all the gospel
passages which show the non-comprehension or "the doubt" of
the apostles *before* the end, with respect to what they receive and even of what they say.

--From the negative (condemnation) or positive recognition to the glorification, there is a necessary step which statement (E) expresses.

The oppositions which form it are the following: (implicit glorification *vs.* explicit glorification) (act by men *vs.* act by Christ himself and the deity).

The implicit glorification (in a derisory way) is obvious. Jesus is invested with the insignia of kingship: a "purple cloak", a "scarlet chlamys", and a "crown of thorns". He is crucified with the inscription: "This is the King of the Jews" above him. The derisory mode only hides the evident character of the glorification here.[11] It implies it and permits the non-knowledge of the knowledge. [p. 83]

It is still necessary to note that the Jews who glorify Jesus do so by giving him the signs of a terrestrial kingdom.

--On the other hand, Jesus himself says at the end of the gospel: "All power in heaven and on earth have been given to me" (Mtt. 28:18). He also says that by repenting in "his name" that healing could be obtained or even: "For my sake, behold I will send the promise of my Father upon you..." (Lk. 24:49). Thus Jesus himself qualifies his power as being on the *celestial and terrestrial* but especially on the religious (and not temporal) plane.

--But the "ascension" which immediately follows this self-glorification ought perhaps lead us to re-examine this analysis. Jesus does not rise to heaven by himself, instead the text says that he was "removed" or "carried away". The final glorification is first performed by the deity, and Jesus submits himself to it.

--For the importance of this point, we will simply note that a divine glorification is opposed to a human glorification.

Note. This point of view, however, must be precisely defined. One finds a self-glorification (or at least its announcement) in the Jewish trial of Jesus: "But from now on the Son of Man will be seated at the right hand of the power of God" (Lk. 22:69). This "explicit glorification", which is perfectly clear, is completely misunderstood and taken to mean its opposite. In reality, it is understood to be an important prevarication: "the blasphemy". Therefore we have two kinds of glorification before his death:

    a) an announcement of explicit glorification made by Jesus himself and not known (by the Jews),

    b) an implicit glorification made by the Jews (and therefore it is also not known).

The first *announces* in advance what cannot yet be (since it lacks the decisive test of the death and resurrection), a "celestial kingship"; and the second *very soon* realizes a "terrestrial kingship".

One could infer a new hypothesis from that to be verified: the non-knowledge of the knowledge, for example, will be connected to the *anticipatory* character of its transmission. That would allow us to understand that "almost" everything is communicated (knowledge and value) before the main test and yet is unacceptable before it.

One will even note that the glorification, which was understood before as a "terrestrial kingship", can be considered to be a metaphor of the definitive glorification. The non-knowledge consists here in not taking the metaphorical expression for what it is (cf. the mistake of the apostles who take the expression, "Beware of the leaven of the Pharisees" in the literal sense, Mk. 8:15).

Tentative Conclusion

The text of the Passion is still far from being analyzed.
Numerous elements have still not yet been put into place.
Among them, everything which inscribes the Alterity over
against the Jewishness has still been neglected. However,
one is aware of the importance for the definition (the delimitation) of the "community's" final receiver, and which takes
place under the names of "Pilate" and the "centurion".

--It appears to be necessary to us, in order to take
account of the Alterity, to make a "detour" via a text from
the Acts of the Apostles: the arrival of Peter at the home
of the centurion Cornelius (Acts 10:1-48). [p. 84]

Analysis of Peter with Cornelius (Acts 10:1-48)

From the first reading, it appears obvious that the dimension of the geographical distance is noteworthy. Peter
is in Judea (in the village of Joppa) and the centurion
Cornelius is in Samaria (at Caesarea). The reduction of
this distance is the obvious object which will first attract
our attention.

1. At the beginning, we have a representative of "Jewishness" who resides in a "Jewish" province par excellence
and a representative of Alterity, a Roman gentile, who resides in a "foreign" province. One can assume that there is
a geographic opposition between the provinces:

Judea *vs*. Samaria which represents the opposition:

Jewishness *vs*. Alterity

Therefore the object of this text will be, beyond the
reduction of the geographical distance, the abolition of the
"distance" from Jewishness to Alterity.

--In order to verify this hypothesis, we will compare
this text with the episode "of the healing of the daughter
of a Canaanite woman" (Mtt. 15:21-28). It is said: a) that
Jesus went from the area of Magdala in Galilee (into) the
area of Tyre and Sidon, and b) that a pagan mother came to
him *by leaving her territory* in order to ask him to heal
her demoniac daughter.

There is an apparent contradiction in this passage.
Jesus enters a gentile province, but the gentile mother
must depart from her "pagan territory" in order to meet
Jesus. This apparent contradiction can only be explained
as the actualization of a neutral term ("neither inside nor
outside"). This trait allows us to reconstruct the true
surface statement:

> --Jesus goes to the foreign province//but he
> does not enter it.
> The gentile mother leaves her foreign terri-
> tory//and enters into Galilee.
> --Therefore the reduction of the geographical
> distance takes place by the movement of the
> representative of Alterity to the representa-
> tive of Identity, although the latter has
> started an opposite movement of neutraliza-
> tion by himself.

--These first indications can be confirmed if one compares this new text with "the healing of the Centurion of
Capernaum's servant" (Lk. 7:1-10 and Mtt. 8). In Luke as
well as in Matthew, we find no indication of a provincial
geographical opposition. The scene takes place at Capernaum

in Galilee. But the geographical opposition is replaced here by an opposition of habitat and localization.

> --Jesus who goes to the house of a stranger//
> does not enter it and the healing takes place
> "at a distance", by intermediary persons.

If Matthew establishes a contact between Jesus and the centurion, it is done by the coming of the latter to meet Jesus outside of his house.

> --Therefore let us summarize these determinations:

1. Jesus goes to a foreign province//but he does not enter it.
2. Jesus goes to a foreign home//but he does not enter it.
3. The gentile mother leaves her territory//and enters into Galilee.
4. The centurion leaves his home//and goes to Jesus (or his representatives).

> --These are opposed to those which are produced from our text in Acts. [p. 85]

> In reality here:

5. Peter goes to a foreign province//and he enters it.
6. Peter goes to a foreign home//and he enters it.
7. The centurion does not leave his province//he remains in the foreign country.
8. His representatives go alone to Judea in order to bring Peter back.

Note. If the opposition between the representation of Peter and Jesus is clear (5, 6), the same thing is not true for the centurion and his representatives (7, 8). The sending of representatives outside his territory and his home must already indicate a "certain" negation of the "Alterity".

This is verified by the positive qualifications with respect to Jewishness which are attributed to the two centurions in general (cf. the intervention of the Jewish elders of Capernaum), "He deserves that, for he loves our nation, he has built our synagogue" (Lk. 7:4-5), or in our text: "Cornelius was pious and God-fearing; he gave large alms to the Jewish people and prayed incessantly" (Acts 10:2). We will return to this important point later.

--Therefore one will note for the moment that the reduction of the geographical distance in our text takes place by the movement of the representative of the Identity to the representative of the Alterity, although the latter has started an opposite movement of neutralization by himself.

--In order to clarify this first approach, we will now consider a second element which is especially important: "the abolition of the food restrictions" and the connection which it shows to the Identity *vs*. Alterity opposition.

In the narrative the statement of the vision of all the animals and the injunction ("sacrifice and eat") is immediately followed by the statement of the arrival of the representatives from Cornelius and the injunction "go therefore... depart with them without hesitation".

Therefore the question is to know whether this connection of consecution is a logical connection, in other words, if the abolition of the food restrictions from Leviticus (Lev. 11) is a necessary condition for the reduction of the geographical distance which the opposition Identity *vs*. Alterity represents?

--If one compares the vision and the injunction which Peter receives with some words of Jesus on what can *defile* a man (Mtt. 15:10-11 and Mk. 7:14-16), the pertinent elements will appear.

Peter refuses to eat all the animals because some of them are unclean (Lev. 11), and he would then be defiled by them and make himself unclean. He is answered: "What God has purified, you must not call defiled" (Acts 10:15).

This statement can only be clarified by a comparison with the teaching of Jesus:

"What goes into the mouth of a man cannot defile him, but it is what comes out of his mouth which defiles a man."

In other words and "in plain language", no food can defile a man, which is an apparent negation of Leviticus 11. The *impurity* will not be connected (as the Old Testament puts it) to a failure to observe the prescriptions.

One will note in this connection that if the New Testament does not allude to any "serious" infraction of the alimentary prescriptions by Jesus and his disciples, it does pay particular attention to set forth all the minor "infractions": [p. 86] "eating without washing his hands, not washing before lunch", "eating with some publicans and sinners", "having table contacts with a sinful woman", and "never fasting".

To these infractions for which he is criticized, Jesus responds, "You cleanse the outside of the cup and dish, but *your insides* are filled with graft and malevolence." This is also an indirect negation of the purification ritual decreed in Leviticus 11:33: "Every earthen vessel inside of which something unclean (blood, the skins of unclean animals) falls, its inside will be unclean...(and must be purified, etc.)."

--Thus the semantic category "Purity *vs*. Impurity" is represented in the distinction:

1) (animal) foods suitable for consumption *vs*. foods not suitable,

2) and in the "proximity or distance" especially in the taking of food: the meal in the presence of community members is made "unclean" by their mistakes and especially by their

occupation (e.g. a publican, harlot, or *blacksmith*) or their contacts with the foreigner.

Note. This category, which is at the center of the Old Testament religious system, immediately leads to some important consequences in the "hierarchical" structuration of the community and its relationships with the "outside" of the community.[12]

--All the rites of purification statements appear to be operations which allow one to reduce the "impurity" which members of the community acquire from being in contact with unclean groups and especially with the foreigner (besides also inviting him, to the extent to which he attempts to live in the territory of the community, to "purify" himself by respecting the minimum food regulations which are incumbent upon the "Host").

--We will summarize these first results in this way:

<u>Identity</u> · · <u>Alterity</u>
Purity · · Impurity

This fundamental homology is what the text of Acts and the New Testament attempt to deny and transform. It establishes a fundamental polarization whose religious and representative center of the Jewish community is or must be completely pure and necessarily opposed to a center which is "external" to the community and totally unclean. Two consequences must be emphasized:

In so far as the "outside" of the community cannot only coincide with a group living in the community but "excluded", the uncircumcised for example, but also in a wider sense with all the foreign nations, a division of the religious work is

inferred where the Jewish people appear to be the religious
people par excellence, a community of priests for all nations.
That reveals a new sense of the community which is conceived
as universal and hierarchical. Each group in this universal
community (according to [p. 87] its position in the hierarchy)
is a little less clean than the one which precedes it and a
little more cleaner than the one which follows it. This is
the reason for an excessive work of purification in order to
indicate the difference and a progressive conception of purity
and impurity.

Conclusion

Our text, like those which we have quoted from the New
Testament, must therefore "shape" a geographical or local distance which increases a religious distance and which is inferred from the opposition "Purity *vs.* Impurity" which represents and establishes at the same time the distance from the
Identity to the Alterity.

--Just as the term of "distance" can only be realized by
excluding its contrary "proximity", every negation of the distance must tend to affirm the proximity. The texts of the
New Testament and Acts show us a preference for the "proximity"
by the taking of food in common, the meal. In this way, one
should better understand the importance attributed to the episode of the meal with Cornelius.[13]

--The next question is to recognize what appears in the
form demonstrated by this meal with the foreigner and at his
home. This cannot be done without referring to the elementary
structures of signification which subtend this text. One can
now set up the structures which are given *"at the point of departure"*.

A) Semantic axis of the "geographical or local distanciation":

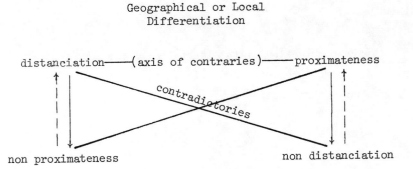

Geographical or Local
Differentiation

distanciation——(axis of contraries)——proximateness

contradictories

non proximateness   non distanciation

Non differentiation
(neither proximity, nor distance)

B) Semantic axis of the ritual "purity" or ritual differentiation:

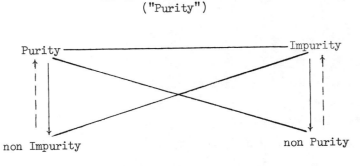

Ritual Differentiation
("Purity")

Purity ——————————————— Impurity

non Impurity   non Purity

Non "purity"
(or beyond the "Purity")

[p. 88]

Note. Since French lacks a general term which could take account of what is common to purity and impurity at the same time, we will use *"Pureté"* [= Purity] in quotation marks in this sense.

--The combination of (at least) these two axes permits us to reproduce the third semantic axis, that of the "national or community differentiation":

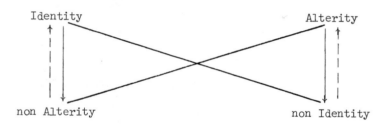

Community
Differentiation

Identity   Alterity

non Alterity   non Identity

Community
Non differentiation

--The question can now be repeated. It is a question of describing the working of the text on these structures. We will take it up by examining the precise content of the "negation" in our statements. In other words, what is the term (or terms) affirmed in these structures?

--In the healings of the daughter of the Canaanite woman or the servant of the centurion, Jesus went to a foreign province (or home) but does not enter it, while the mother

or the centurion (or his representatives) "left" and went to
him.

--Jesus could not therefore affirm the "proximateness":
"being together with the Foreigner and at his home", since
by coming to him the representatives of the alterity force
him to a "non proximity" although he had (by his first movement) repudiated the distance therefore posing the "non distanciation". The combined result from the point of view of
the "distanciation" can be formulated as an affirmation of
the neutral term: "non distanciation", that is to say neither
proximity nor distance. Let us say local or geographical non
differentiation.

--Apparently the opposition with Peter's conduct was
strong since he went with the foreigner into his territory
and home. In other words, at first glance, the text poses
the "proximity" or proximateness here.

But, as we have already pointed out, the proximity
realized in this way is not made with a true representative
of the Alterity.

--On the one hand, some representatives of the centurion
Cornelius have come to Peter. This movement already represents a major negation of their "Alterity". Moreover, Cornelius is qualified by the narrator as a pious (man) and a
"God-fearer" who gives large alms to the Jewish people and
prays incessantly.

--This qualification, which implies his respect of the
food regulations imposed on a "foreign" host (cf. Acts 15:20-
21), makes Cornelius a character who has at least repudiated
the "Alterity" in himself without having affirmed the "Identity" (of which circumcision is the mark). In other words,
the content of the qualification which he obtains by denying
the [p. 89] obvious impurity (which is connected to disrespect

for alimentary presecriptions, etc.) can be formulated in this way: (non Impurity ⇄ non Alterity) where a bond of double implication is revealed between the first and second terms.

--If one now examines Peter's qualifications, some analogous traits will appear. Peter lives with a "blacksmith", in other words, a man whose profession is to work with the skins of animals. Therefore a blacksmith is perpetually subject to contact with unclean substances. This information does not seem to be accidental to us. Peter can no longer affirm a perfect "purity" in this "unclean" place. He implicitly realizes the term "non purity".

This is confirmed by the test of the vision which directs Peter not to respect the traditional regulations concerning food by assuring him that this disrespect will not lead to "defilement", that is to say to "impurity".

In other words, the content of the test of the vision is an injunction to deny his "purity" (without going so far as to pose the impurity or affirm the "non-Purity").

--One will now better understand the importance of the "minor" infractions committed by Jesus and his disciples. They do not reveal the "Impurity" but the "non-Purity". One ought to place the "non-Identity" or the negation of Jewishness on the axis of differentiation. In this way one obtains a formula for Peter which is opposite but complementary to that of Cornelius:

$$(\text{non Purity} \longleftarrow \longrightarrow \text{non Identity})$$

If one compares these two formulas:

$$\left\{ \begin{array}{ccc} \text{non Impurity} & + & \text{non Alterity} \\ \text{non Purity} & + & \text{non Identity} \end{array} \right\}$$

one notes that they systematically reveal the negative terms
of the contradictories and that they designate the neutral
terms of two semantic axes: "non Impurity and non Purity"
and "non Alterity and non Identity".

This must be understood as the negation of the semantic
category of "ritual differentiation" articulated under the
contrary terms of Purity and Impurity which may be like the
affirmation of a "beyond the Purity" and in other respects
like the negation of the category of "community differentiation", that is to say like the affirmation of the "community
nondifferentiation".

Assuming this to be true, the "proximity" established
by Peter finds its meaning. It is a negation of the category
of distanciation itself. It is a "non distanciation"[14] or a
geographical or local nondifferentiation.

--One can wonder about the reasons of a work which tends
to neutralize the opposition which it is based on in each
structure. This neutralization first appears to be a waste
of meaning. It makes [p. 90] the categories which organize
a system of signification irrelevant.

--It only finds its *raison d'être* attributed to the
possibilities which it opens in the new "higher" elementary
structures. In reality, each semantic category and its contradictory can belong (because of their basic logical status
in relationship to the terms which articulate them) to a
higher elementary structure according to the following schema:

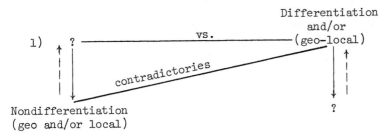

1)

? ———————— vs. ———————— Differentiation
and/or
(geo-local)

contradictories

Nondifferentiation
(geo and/or local)   ?

172

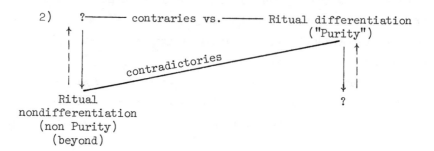

2) ?——— contraries vs.——— Ritual differentiation
                                      ("Purity")

contradictories

Ritual
nondifferentiation
(non Purity)
(beyond)

?

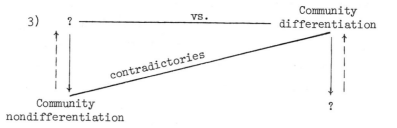

3) ? ——————— vs. ——————— Community
                                   differentiation

contradictories

Community
nondifferentiation

?

--The advantage of placing the neutral term of the structures *at the beginning* now appears in its positive aspect. In
fact, it is a question of an operation of negation of the semantic categories at the beginning which must make possible
the affirmation of their "contraries" which are still inde-
scribable in the first system. [p. 91]

--We would then have an important starting point here
for the analysis of the transformations of systems and the
elementary structures which constitute them.

--To attempt to define the content of these new opposing
categories would go beyond our purposes. Nevertheless, we

will point out the elements of later research in a hypothetical way.

By emphasizing the *"external"* Purity and the actual *"internal"* impurity of the Pharisees, Jesus produces under some
"old" names the new terms to which elsewhere he gives a functional definition (as in Mtt. 5:21-7:12): "Do not be angry
with your brother, do not desire the wife of another, do not
swear, do not render evil for evil, but do good for evil,
love your enemy, give alms in secret, pray in secret, fast
in secret, do not judge, etc."

From functional definitions like these, a new religious
system could be inferred (which is still not "named") where a
"kindness" (?) or a "charity" (?), which is individual and no
longer social, could be substituted for the ritual social
"Purity" which first put man into a direct relationship with
the deity.

Likewise, one could extract the significant elements of
a new hypothetical term which is opposed to the "community and
national differentiation" from the "definitional" declaration
of Peter to Cornelius (Acts 10:34): "Truly I perceive that
God *shows no partiality* but *that in every nation* any one who
fears him and practices justice is acceptable to him" or else
from that of the Jerusalem "brothers" who were persuaded by
Peter (Acts 11:18): "Thus *to the gentiles also*, God has given
the repentance which leads to life!" This new hypothetical
term would perhaps be something like a "universalism" of the
community of individual believers, which would be clearly
different from "the hierarchical universalism of the community of nations" which is evoked in the Old Testament for the
end of time.

Note. One must clearly note an essential point beyond these unverified hypotheses of the content of the new terms. If the elements of a definition are given, the absence of new *names* is not without significance.

--It facilitates the transformation of the structures. In effect, by evoking, for example, "the *internal* purity" or "the new *justice*", the text attempts to preserve the old signifier and to give it a totally new and different signified. This will first appear "in addition" and "super- imposed" in relationship to the old signified. This explains the presence of paradoxical statements which claim to recon- cile some opposing signifieds (cf. the notion of the *accomp- lishment* of the Law) or which present the new as superior to the old--but of the same order.[15]

--This permanence of the signifiers, which is character- istic of the Old Testament in the New Testament, not only has great importance for every stylistic study of these texts; but it also reveals *a law of the diachronic transformations of the systems which could be expressed in this way:* [p. 92]

1. The new system must first apparently be written down in the old system which is only supposed to be accepted by the reader.

2. The new system attempts progressively to neutralize the ancient articulation of the meaning. It empties the old signifieds by making them "irrelevant".

3. It gives some definitions (which are often more negative, oblique, and functional than qualificative) of its new articulations without producing the names which would correspond to them. In other words, it designates or consti- tutes the new signifieds by keeping the old signifiers.

4. The unwieldiness of the signifier shows well that a text cannot have a single or even a closed signification

(that will only be possible for texts in artificial languages where a precise and only one signified corresponds to a specific signifier). Despite a new semantic and narrative structure which puts a new isotopy into a dominant position, the keeping of the old signifiers produces a polyvalent signification because it "preserves" the traces of the old signifieds. Therefore it is at least possible for them to signify anew in the text and to "haunt" it.

Conclusion

We will temporarily end our analysis of this text from Acts at this point. Our goal was not in fact to completely and totally describe it, but to call attention to the fundamental and elementary structures of the content in it.

After having dealt with these structures, our analysis of the text of the Passion can be picked up again. We will now attempt to consider the episode of the trial before Pilate in detail and to show how these structures clarify the neutralization which takes place.

III. *The Trial of Jesus before Pilate (Matthew)*

Matthew's text first suggests a strict correspondence of the trial before the Sanhedrin and the trial before the Roman governor on the same level of the surface statements.

Jewish Trial (Sanhedrin)	Gentile Trial (Pilate)
1. Testimony of the false witnesses.	1. Accusations of the chief priests and elders.
2. The High Priest is surprised at the silence of Jesus.	2. Pilate is surprised at the silence of Jesus.
3. The High Priest asks him if he is "the Son of God".	3. Pilate asks him if he is "the King of the Jews".
4. Jesus acquiesces and is glorified.	4. Jesus acquiesces + (?)
V. The High Priest calls his answer blasphemy.	V. The governor is "surprised".
VI. The Sanhedrin declares that he deserves death.	VI. Pilate asks, "What evil has he done?"

[p. 93]

Statements 1, 2, 3, 4 could make one believe that the "gentile" trial is only a simple duplication of the Jewish trial which supplements the first (e.g. by adding, among other things, the royal to the religious messianism).

--Therefore one would again be confronted with a negative test where the opponents show themselves to be unable to receive what they have received and of understanding what has been said to them (implicitly or not). This inability is described in the same way by an explicit request for knowledge and signs.

--But what defines a test is given above all in its (or their) consequences. But there is a profound difference between the two trials (statements V and VI here). If the consequence of the Jewish trial is the affirmation of the break and lack, the consequence of the gentile trial is quite a different matter.

--Therefore in order to define the precise content, it is necessary for us to repeat the analysis of the whole text and to reflect upon the apparent parallelism of the beginning.

Repetition

--Pilate, like the High Priest, can only "ignore what he *himself* says"[16] when he asks Christ if he is the "King of the Jews".

--Like the High Priest, Pilate encounters the non response of Jesus or his silence. In order to modify this beginning position, it is necessary that an operation of negation take place. The latter can be reconstructed beginning with two textual elements which evoke a *transmitted knowledge which is not asked* and is well-known by Pilate.

1. "He *well knew* that it was because of jealousy that he had been delivered."

2. And the message from his wife: "Do not become involved in the case of this *just*..., I have been very disturbed by a *dream* because of him."

--These two elements indicate that Pilate has received a knowledge which is just a little more explicit ("jealousy", "the case of this *just*"), but it is enough since it has been understood and will have an effect.

--One can affirm that the negation of the beginning statement "ignorance of what he says of himself" necessarily implies the affirmation which is explicit or not (cf. Luke who does not mention any reception of a knowledge) of a "knowledge received from others" and therefore from the sender.

This positive statement must be assumed if one wishes to take account of the "positive" consequences which follow:

--Pilate passes in effect from "astonishment" to the conviction of Jesus' innocence through the triplication of his question to the Jews:

1. Whom do you choose, Barabbas or Jesus?

2. What do you want to do with Jesus?

3. What evil has he done?

--The Jewish community under the influence or with the help of the elders (statement dI and d'I, see p. 147) confirms the negative sanction three times. It is useless to stress the "juridical" character of this repetition here which Louis Marin has emphasized in other respects [cf. pp. 134-136 above]. [p. 94]

--We will only note that this question which indicates a juridical judgment is the means of an exchange. Pilate by it refuses to "judge" and appoints the Jewish community as the only judge.

--Therefore he exchanges the position of a judge for the complementary position of a witness. The content of this testimony is what we will attempt to clarify.

--The triplication of the question is the chance for the Jews to confirm their sanction three times and for Pilate to reproduce his testimony three times.

--It is necessary, however, to pay particular attention to the basic form of the "question"--"testimony".

"Whom do you choose, Barabbas or Jesus?"

This choice (which is proposed by Pilate) forces the Jews (who want to condemn Jesus) to prefer the robber. Thus an important inversion materializes which is often proclaimed by the New Testament:[17] the Jews treat the innocent man like a robber and the robber like an innocent man (which is confirmed by the presence of robbers crucified at the same time as Jesus).

This inversion leads to another which we have noted above. Those who judge the innocent man as a robber, judge themselves. They *qualify* themselves implicitly.

--Thus Pilate by his question (like Jesus by his answer to the High Priest) forces the Jews to demonstrate their blindness and their incapacity to receive the knowledge and the object of value.

--But even more profoundly, what is important is what results from the "pseudo-choice" proposed by Pilate. We are aware of the indecisiveness of the critical tradition concerning the name of the prisoner: "Barabbas" or "Jesus Barabbas", depending on the manuscript. Be that as it may, the similarity of the names appears very clearly if one recalls that *Bar abba* in Aramaic means "son of the father" which is a name that is well suited to Jesus.

--In other words, if the proposed choice is a false choice, it is at first:

1. that the Jews who want to condemn Jesus can only choose the second alternative, (and especially:)

2. that in any case they can only choose him directly or in person by an "intermediary" *name* (at least if one accepts this hypothesis).

--This result would confirm what we noted above about the glorification. After all, the Jews cannot fail to recognize Jesus, but they cannot know their "recognition". They must imply it and conceal it under the derisory or the enigmatic. Their inability with regard to the text does not rest on a knowledge but on the knowledge of the Knowledge.

--One will not be surprised that knowledge of their speech act (which they commit by proclaiming "Let his blood be upon us and our children.") escapes them. This "act" seals the "retribution" which sanctions their condemnation of Jesus. [p. 95]

--On the other hand, Pilate explicitly wants to erase any possibility of a negative "retribution" with respect to himself by washing his hands.

Second Repetition

This first arrangement still remains very inadequate. We must understand the reason for the change in the testimony of Pilate. It can only become visible if one inscribes this text

1) among those which oppose and reconcile the representatives of Alterity and Identity in the New Testament and Acts,

2) in the syntagmatic continuity where it operates.

One would note that an elementary structure of signification is given in this way at the beginning:

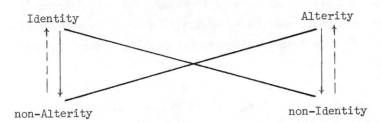

Community
differentiation

Identity   Alterity

non-Alterity   non-Identity

Community
(nondifferentiation)

The working of the text would produce a neutralization of
the semantic category (e.g. Differentiation) by successively
posing the sub-contraries (or contradictories).

Having the affirmative of the neutral term as a result
(e.g. Nondifferentiation), this working would open the possibility of a new category and therefore of a transformation of
meaning.

--It will be up to us to show that a superficial commentary, which can be designated under the expression of the
"indifference" of Pilate, is an intuitive grasp of the Nondifferentiation which he represents.

--In the syntagmatic chain of the text, the sequence of
Jesus' death is bounded by the testimonies of two foreigners,
that of Pilate and that of the Centurion (and of his men) just
after Jesus' death. They are opposed, on the one hand, to the
negative testimonies of the Jews and, on the other hand, to
the "absent" or "mute" testimonies of the Apostles and the

182

women. That is to say, they represent the positive transformation in advance and make it possible.

--It is "in advance" because the central test is formed
by the Death + the absence of the body, and this "absence"
gives meaning to the Death for the Apostles. In other words,
the representatives of Alterity can testify without having
received the major sign. In this way, the implicit qualification of *sacrifice* is established for his death, at the
same moment at which his death is stated. Since this qualification is the anchorage point of the transformation, one
must note the privileged position of those who produce it,
i.e. the representatives of Alterity.

--In order to understand the content, we will compare
the results of this problem [p. 96] with those we have obtained in our analysis of "Peter with Cornelius".

--At the beginning the actor Pilate is a representative
of Alterity in the trial, but (and this is more notable) he
is also a representative of Identity. He syncretizes two
different and opposing actants.

--Of course it is obvious that he is a "Representative"
of Alterity since he is the Roman governor and the Jews suggest that he judge Jesus as an incitor of a revolt against
Rome (cf. Luke 23:2) which is implicitly contained in the
title "King of the Jews" (which explains Matthew's silence
on the details of the accusations).

--But Pilate is also a "representative" of Identity, in
any case, since he assumes the role of the High Priest and
becomes an essential helper of the "Jewish" negation of the
divine sender and his representative. Moreover, it befalls
him to proclaim the royal messianism: "You are the King of
the Jews", which is a typically Jewish conception of the
messiah.

--But Pilate, thanks to the Knowledge which he has received, produces a negation of the two terms: Alterity and Identity.

a) He does not take any appropriate action concerning the accusations of revolt. He is not a true representative of Rome.

b) He is anxious to affirm that he is not a helper of a condemnation which he does not understand. This is indicated in the consequence: Pilate could not be held responsible for the Jewish negation.

Thus Pilate repudiates the Alterity position in (a) and the Identity position in (b). He produces in this way a non-differentiation (non Alterity and non Identity). One can say again that Pilate denies the representative of Identity and Alterity in himself and is affirmed as the representative of Nondifferentiation.

--This is a determinative position, as we have seen, which makes possible the passage to "universalism". By denying the semantic category which establishes the difference and opposition of communities, the trial before Pilate clearly reveals the connection in the transformation between Jesus' sacrifice and the necessary affirmation of the possibility of a non-differentiated, universal community as the new final sender.

NOTES

1. We are referring to Mk. 14:1 to 16-20; Mtt. 26:1 to 28-30; Lk. 22:1 to 24-53, in the Cerf edition translation established under the direction of L'École Biblique de Jérusalem.

2. We refer here to the first analysis of the text of the Passion which will appear later.

3. One will note that the question is neither *Who are you?* (a question of identity) nor *Who do you claim to be?* (a modalization of the question of his identity). A study which could distinguish the assumed statement from the posed statement (following O. Ducrot) would be very useful for our purposes.

4. The non-transmission of the Knowledge acquired is an overthrow of the Sender-Receiver relationship where the receiver repudiates the sender and therefore destroys the axis of communication.

5. As elsewhere, the use of the parabolic discourse which affects the transmitted message reveals itself as a modalisator and produces it as Knowledge (not known) and therefore enigmatic (cf. the response: "Only the sign of Jonah will be given to you." Mtt. 12:39; 16:4; Lk. 11:29).

6. This sign which comes from heaven and which explicitly guarantees the divine mediation of Jesus is given in the Transfiguration where God explicitly says: "This is my beloved son, listen to him" (Mtt. 17:5). One ought to note that it is apparently given to the apostles, and particularly to the reader.

7. This is confirmed by the "Temptation in the Desert" (Lk. 4:1-13) where the devil demands a "prodigious" sign from Jesus in order to believe that he is indeed "the Son of God".

8. In the religious order, this duplication permits one to understand the constitution of one part of the (more

or less vast) community as a mediator between the Divine and the Human or: the religious institution (the clergy).

9. By the word "explicit" we mean that the text revealed by Luke is the one which best enumerates and actualizes this statement of the meta-text.

10. One should compare this recursive process with the self-enchainment of the syntax described by Chomsky.

11. The latter is so obvious that John 19:21 notes the *failure* of the demand from the chief priests to Pilate concerning the wording of the billboard whose contents, according to them, should be replaced with the words: *"This man has said: I am the king of the Jews."*

12. Louis Dumont in *Homo Hierarchicus*, London: Weidenfeld and Nocolson, 1970, 71-85 points out a very similar utterance by the Indians.

13. The criticisms of the "circumcized ones" from Jerusalem are expressed in this way: "Why (they asked him) *did you go* to uncircumcized men and *eat with them*?" (Acts 11:3).

14. This result must lead us to reconsider the semantic content of "Samaria". It must no longer be defined as external, but as "neither internal nor external". This is the reason for its "strategic" importance in the system of an overture to the external.

15. All these paradoxical statements could make one believe that the term referred to is a compound conjunctive term: "the one and the other" (at the same time) where a dominance can be introduced, when it is fundamentally a question of posing its contradictory--the neutral term: "neither the one, nor the other".

16. It does not matter if this accusation is prompted by the elders. For him as well as for them, it is a "knowledge" which cannot have been transmitted to them considering their position.

17. Cf. the words of Jesus at the time of his arrest: "Have you come out, as against a *robber*, with swords and clubs to capture me?" (Mtt. 26:55).

VIII

THE LEGIBILITY OF THE "SCRIPTURES"

by

Edgar Haulotte

The application of the methods of structural analysis
to those texts called *Scripture(s)* (with a capital "S") poses
some new aporias to the critical form of present exegesis,
whose hermeneutic is based on the methods of historical
criticism.[1] Conversely, does the application to these texts
of formal categories and models (which have been conceived
somewhere else) permit one to account for their peculiar semantic substance and isolate the structure in them?[2] The
legibility of this body of writings brings into play a
series of questions which are situated at the intersection
of two problematics. These texts, which were originally
disjoined and often restricted by their historical (or diachronic), geographic and ideological situations,[3] have been
compressed during their transmission in terms of a common
algorithm by a kind [p. 98] of selective practice which
excluded a multitude of parallel (or actually "apocryphal"
or lost) texts to form, when all is said and done, a configuration in which all the parts simultaneously exist, the
Bible.[4] This process of selection and conjunction between
texts, which the official authority of the Jewish or Christian traditions has only verified,[5] creates another question:
that of its *closure*. This corpus was transmitted without
change from the 2nd century A.D. and possessed meaning in
diverse types of tradition. While being spread into differ-

ent cultures, it did not lose its original character. The
successive rereadings, versions, commentaries, glosses, and
usages of all kinds did not take its place and are not substituted for it (as Islam has done with the Koran[6]).

The studies collected here are situated in the field of
these rereadings by the simple fact that they adopt the limits
of this corpus. Does this field of reading have a structure
different from that of the Scripture? Is there a diachronic
relationship between *two "structural states"*[7] which takes
place between the Scripture and rereadings? Or is there instead only one structure which exists (that of the Scripture)
and produces some multiple *usages* (or some plural traditions)?
The texts transmitted by the Christian tradition introduce one
final problem (which is a kind of repetition of the preceding
one) within the corpus. The "New" Testament is juxtaposed to
the "Old" Testament simultaneously as a closure and opening
of its meaning (or its "fulfillment"). The rereading of the
first "text" is fulfilled as a new scripture where the "old"
appears to be a *quotation* of the "new" (types, antitypes
[Heb. 9:24], figure, prophecy). The question can be posed
in two ways, without necessarily considering their diachronic
situation within the same closed configuration. Either one
makes "use" of the other (but who can truly say which one
uses the other?), or the relationship of one to the other is
that of two different "structural states" (but the two states
are kept in tension in the same [achronic] field).[8] Whatever
the semantic levels may be, the problem of the legibility of
this corpus always amounts to recognizing how the *transforma-*
tions are performed between one "structural state" and another (or between one structure and its "usages"). [p. 99]
In other words, it is a question of seeing how the *integra-*
tion of the different levels function in diachrony and ach-
rony (i.e. what is the *agent* in it?).

Can one account for this by some categories and models
which are homologous with experimental categories and models
which have been useful in other areas? Is it possible to
apply a general linguistic model to this particular corpus?
One can only respond to these questions with a strategic
approach which always includes a theoretical aspect symmetrical to a practical aspect. The method will be as
follows: (I.) The fact of the *closure* of this corpus and
its persistance as a *producer of meaning* introduces a
specific problematic. There is a gap between a form (defined by its closure) and its *epistemic field*. (II.) This
problem produces another: what is the position of the
"reader" towards the *"narrator"* and the *"author"* and what
becomes of the reality effect and the temporal dimension
which is so prized by the exegete? (III.) Basically, how
is the *production of meaning* realized in a reading where
nothing is at stake? It is here that the analysis of the
categories and models will have the most important position.

I.

CLOSURE AND OPENING

For the New Testament as well as for the Old Testament,
the "canonical" list was progressively formed by the spon-
taneous selection of texts which were received and read in
public as the "Word of God" or the "rule of truth" (the
latter was the only meaning of the word *canon* until 360 A.D.,
with the exception of Origen). Each text is explained in the
same way by a *practice* which it always reveals in its texture.

(For example, the transmitter knows the reaction which his choice of "genre" or register will produce in others, e.g. a psalm, oracle, or a historical narrative which is closely based on a liturgical form [e.g. there is a division of the people into two groups in order to imitate the action of division, fundamental to some narratives about the Covenant, the procession to the Ark, to the Temple, or to the sepulchre of Christ], "gospel" or letter). The *protocol* of reading is often indicated at the beginning (a psalm to be chanted with the accompaniment of some musical instrument, the proclamation and address and act of thanks at the beginning of the Epistles, at the end of the Gospels of Matthew and John, the prologue of Luke and the Acts of the Apostles). The Scriptures are addressed to a type of reader who is united with a society to "listen", celebrate, and understand, and which forms a "discourse" with a collective aspect (which is sometimes stated by one member of the congregation in a homiletic or charismatic form, cf. 1 Cor. 11:17ff. and 13-14). Readings are distributed in an annual cycle (from Passover to Passover, in the Christian as well as the Jewish tradition) which repeats that about which the whole corpus speaks. The diegesis [= narrative structure] is accompanied by a *mimesis*. The reading of the narrative of the Christian Eucharist gives the complete model of this type of reading, where *the gesture is interpreted in the word*, according to the specified protocol: "Do this in memory of me." "This *is* my body and this *is* my blood." By this practice, the present reading is therefore capable of producing the *inaugural* structure anew, without altering the surface of the signifiers, on the contrary, by *producing* them.

This structure could indefinitely create an infinite number of [p. 100] linguistic manifestations. How does one explain the fact that the manifestations may be limited in number and that some contemporary or almost contemporary texts (like the *Didache* and the *Epistles of Clement* of Rome, which conform to the "rule of truth") are not, however, included in the scriptural corpus but on the contrary, are disqualified from it, by taking the corpus as a field of reference? Let's take it step by step. Every series of signifiers is a plural manifestation. Thus the relationship of man to the "beginning" is expressed in Gen. 1 by a scale of seven days, and it is expressed in Prov. 8:22-31 by a juxtaposition (Wisdom, which was created before anything, finds its delight to be with men). The "beginning" appears in Ps. 136 with the repetition of a hymnic formula including *"he is good"* (cf. Gen. 1) which is followed by a refrain repeated in seven successive narrative elements: *"Because your love is eternal"*, etc. One finds about a dozen variants.[9] The "titles" of Christ are the result of combinations between two extremes. Christ is a man *glorified* by God and taken up to heaven (cf. Elijah) / *and* a being who *preexisted* before man (cf. Wisdom). The four gospels are four manifestations of one genetic stock. Some correlations and permutations are produced in this way between the elementary units of the plane of the signifier. The narrative on the bread of life in John 6:51-58 is a transcription of the narrative of the Eucharist which is missing from its "normal" place (Jn. 14-17 only presents a discourse). The manifestations are therefore multiple but limited. This is neither caused by chance nor by an arbitrary authority. The works of A. J. Greimas on "Structure et historie" [An Eng. trans.

of this article which originally appeared in *Les Temps Modernes* 22 (1966), 815-827 will appear in *Structuralism and Biblical Hermeneutics*, see my next work in this series.] and "The Interaction of Semiotic Constraints" (*Yale French Studies* 41 [1969], 86-105) explain this phenomenon of restriction very well (reprinted in Greimas, *Du sens*, 109ff. and 150ff.). What is manifested corresponds to the only meaning-effects which are possible in the contextual settings. The closure is due to the interaction of different systems which produce the semiotic manifestation. By comparing the other three linguistic manifestations of the same genetic tradition (i.e. Mtt., Lk., and Jn.) with Mark and some comparative documents which one has at his disposal (Jewish and Jewish-Christian literature, etc.), "redaction history" shows how the invention of syntagms by each one is realized by a selection following the possibilities of a "milieu". In prologues at the beginning of his two books (Lk. 1:1ff. and Acts 1:1ff.), Luke reveals his objective and his constraints: *akribie* [= ακριβῶς], logical order, confirmation of a *katabasis* (the *Gospel of Luke*) by its *anabasis* (*Acts*). The "history" of the primitive "churches" is the semantic field where the function of the "Lord", "prince of life", "architect", etc. is exerted in an inaugural way. John is aware of the selection: "Jesus has performed many other signs in the presence of the disciples which are not related in this book..." (Jn. 20:30); "Jesus has done many other things. If one told them in detail, I suppose that the world itself would not be enough to contain the books which could be written" (Jn. 21:25). As for the *Epistles*, their role is to elaborate new signifying elements with respect to problems posed by real life, by correcting the signifiers made here and there when they are not homologous with the structure of

earlier teaching and the tradition which he has transmitted, e.g. "everything is lawful for me", but "everything
is not helpful" (1 Cor. 6:12). The most elaborate list of
"appearances of the Lord" is not found where the terrain
would be the most [p. 101] favorable (i.e. the narrative
fabric of the Gospels), but where a challenge of the (genetic) "apostolic" status of Paul required the manifestation of
a precise, technical series. Paul is the last of those who
have "seen" the Resurrected One (1 Cor. 15:1-11). "Only
those segments are taken into consideration and retained
which can function as signifying segments which contain
some contents, that is to say, which can help in the constitution of the signs of this language." This process is
clear with regard to sexual relationships (see the table,
p. 223 below). Among all the throws of the dice which the
combinative would permit, only some are effective.

Some important consequences follow from these analyses.
First there is the *historicization* of these texts. The restriction of the meaning-effects (the fact that what is
manifested from the "life of Christ" and the life of the
"churches" [e.g. in *Acts* and the *Epistles*] is only a partial realization) implies an "historical" perspective in
the reading of these texts. The closure takes place to the
extent that we are separated from those who have participated
in the writing of the event, which receives an *inaugural*
character.[10] Moreover, the elaboration of these texts corresponds each time to a precise "usage", and they are the
object of a discourse which one kind of reader spreads and
which *owes its signification to this communication.*[11] The
analysis of the legibility of this corpus must therefore
take its function into account from the point of view of its
reception.[12]

But this closure of the plane of signifiers in a book
(which is quantitatively one and where the infinite virtualities are only partially manifested) exercises an essential
function in the opening of the semantic field which is peculiar to it and permits it to overlap some completely different
social and historical texts, unless its structure is modified
by its transference. This fixed linguistic space (where all
the parts simultaneously exist and where each can serve as a
place to begin, e.g. the Old Testament or New Testament, the
Gospels or Epistles, etc., but which immediately set into
motion a system of very precise correlations and permutations)
functions as a work of art in relationship to the superimposed
discourse which makes it *legible*.[13] A multiplicity of systems
are represented (patriarchial, royal, or prophetic figures;
successive forms of the Exodus or the Covenant; infancy or
resurrection narratives; historical creeds, the titles of
Christ...) composing among them "an epistemic configuration
which can be formulated". Diverse "theologies" of the Old
Testament and New Testament exist which are coherent from
different viewpoints: the Covenant, confessions of faith,
etc. *The figure has the function of giving one access to the
epistemic configuration which is not entirely manifested any-
where and which, however, supplies its legibility to each
figure.* The coherence of partial manifestations results
from the coherence of a knowledge which is historically
situated and transmitted (tradition) and which uses the combinative virtualities by limiting them to those which are
adapted to the [p. 102] production of the figure (according
to the well-known *Sitz im Leben* of historical "form" criticism). The intersections between Gen. 1 and Ps. 136, for
example, are based on a tradition which is interested in
making the manducation [Ed. note: a rare ecclesiastical

Eng. term meaning: "the act of eating"] borrowed from the taking of daily bread in a celebration connected with the cosmos and/or the history of the chosen people. What the scripture produces and reveals only becomes a real "text" by the explanation of the knowledge which is implied by its readers. But the inscription of the figure in a fixed and limited form prevents the successive readers from hypostatizing themselves in independent systems of signification. This is a temptation which "theologies" do not escape when they stop returning to the reading. By presenting itself as a fabricated object and by acting like a *figure*, the form keeps the epistemic field at a distance and the reader from its truth. Reading does not consist of discovering some signifieds but of composing the signifiers, that is to say the real "text". The interaction of the eucharistic narrative with a "sacramental" context is a good example since its rereading according to its protocol articulates the referential field which comes from its historical roots and produces a real discourse, unless the narrative is separated from the referential exteriority.[14]

The *visible* goes through the *legible* within the semantic space of the Scriptures (so that the "faith" of the reader may be "strengthened", as Luke's prologue says, Lk. 1:4). Is it necessary for this appearance to be spoken in order to be visible? Henceforth the problem presented is that of the "*figurability*" (*of the word*) *of the* "*god*", who reveals himself--although it can be said of him that he is neither here nor there, neither this one nor that one (Lk. 17:23; 21:8). The figurative configurations, which produce an epistemic system that cannot be manifested in itself, are therefore "fictive" (or an object of fabrication); but this production assumes that the system is figurable. In other

words, if this "god" "reveals himself" by his "word", it is
in the relational network woven between the diverse levels of
the Scripture by a certain kind of integration. Does this
analysis permit us to see how this network functions? We
will restrict ourselves to the New Testament.

II.

"AUTHOR" AND "READER"

The "text" oscillates between the "author" and "reader"
like an "obscure" plane or a "mirror".[15] The utopian or
opposite image ("which gives things a space which is beyond
them and transplanted"[16]) is the only (figure) which the
"author" and the "reader" utilize in the process where the
structure appears. "Remember the maxim: 'Keep to what is
written'" (1 Cor. 4:6). [p. 103] "If anyone dares to add...
or remove the words from this prophetic book, he will be
plagued with the afflictions described in the book, or deprived of his *access* to the tree of life and to the holy
city...described in this book" (Rev. 22:18), cf. Deut. 4:2.
What is the "light" which shines in the darkness? What is
the image in the mirror?

Jesus has not written anything, nor has he left any
trace of a legal reform (like Moses) or a great undertaking
(like David). His history is an "auditory history", i.e.
"the writing of the event".[17] He has left the hasty and precise inscription of his acts and words on the sensitive back-
ground of Jewish socio-religious codes. What he is, he does
and says. "Who do men say that I am, and who do you say that

I am?" marks the turning point of his public ministry in the
Synoptics. His speaking is more decisive than his silences:
"It has been said to you...but I say to you...." But when
he does not repeat the words (which someone says) that he
has said, his silence produces the strict antonym which condemns him: "He blasphemes"; and that constitutes the turning
point of the trial. Pilate asks, "Are you a king?" The Jewish authorities want Pilate to write as his epitaph: *"He
has said:* I am the king...." But Pilate, whom Louis Marin
describes as neutral (see above, pp. 112ff.), writes: "(This
is) the King...." He decrees death (by mistake) for an infraction of the order: "What is written is written."

Everything takes place as if the proper meaning of this
being was to be stated by others. It is from listening--
which is a fusion of the event and its signs--that the first
scripture is born, and one has a strict example here of the
law that scripture can only be born by the death of what it
is relating. Its designation as a "testament" is not accidental. The figure of this being is hidden in the multiple
discourses which support this scripture, instead of being
aloof like the gods of other religions and mysteries. The
"verbal condition" of God has been discussed.[18] The enunciation of this being includes Alterity as a constitutive content.[19] But for that very reason, its enunciation can never
be reduced to a statement. It consists of producing the
signifiers and therefore *continues as an act of enunciation*. In other words, the being who explains himself in the
configuration of this original scripture presents himself as
prior to every exposition, and his "death" does not indicate
the end of his "discourse" but its *transcription*. The choice
of paradigms in this Scripture takes account of this change
which is doubly supplied by the meaning in such a way that

the "visibility" of the being in question is never abolished.
On the contrary it is *maintained*, although it is transformed,
by the legibility of its Scripture. The gap between the
epistemic field and the figures of the inscription, far from
prohibiting, open the way to this "presence" which a certain
type of reader recognizes and which is nothing else than the
pre-sense--the meaning prior to its being put into circula-
tion and which is only delivered in the message whose proto-
cols the Scripture reveals. [p. 104]

The Transmitter of the Message and the "Author"

The transmitter of the message has some influence on
the history itself of the event. He often loses his identification with respect to the semantic field opened by the act
of writing, e.g. the prologues of *Luke* and *Acts*, the address
of the *Epistles*, and John's conclusion. In *Revelation,* the
transmitter ("John"--Rev. 1:4; or "I"--Rev. 22:16) is distinguished from "the Spirit who speaks to the churches".
Paul makes a distinction between "what the Lord says" and
"what I, myself, say". The "points of view of the narrator"
analyzed by T. Todorov[20] display certain meaning-effects:
the *omniscient point of view* [*vision par derrière*] (the
"disciples" in Matthew understand everything); the *limited
point of view* [*vision avec*] (the disciples do not understand
anything in Mark and the "messianic secret" is explained by
the choice of this perspective); the *outside point of view*
[*vision du dehors*] (this is the case where the narrator does
not want to know anything about what happens). The fourfold
Gospel is a remarkable example of a *stereoscopic* viewpoint.

Several formulas follow one another in Jn. 16:16-19:

> 'A little while and you will see me no
> more; and then again a little while, and you
> will see me.'
> Then some of the disciples said to one
> another, 'What is this that he tells us, "A
> little while and you will see me no more, and
> then again a little while, and you will see
> me." and "I go to the Father"?'
> They said: 'What is a little while? We
> do not know what he means.'
> Jesus knew that they were longing to ask
> him, so he said to them: 'You are asking
> yourselves what I meant by these words: "A
> little while and you will see me no more, and
> then again a little while and you will see
> me."'

The narrator is neither John, the Apostles, nor Jesus. It is
also not an impersonal agent. The identification of the
"author" poses the most critical question in the constitutive
phenomenon of the structure of the Scripture taken as a whole
and which one could call the *semantic precipitate*. It appears
in several forms in the Old Testament as well as in the New
Testament, but let us continue with the New Testament.

1. Some small constitutive units, which were originally
isolated and atemporal are at the basis of the composition of
the gospel narratives. These units may be a *logion* or a very
limited series of *logia* which are connected by their sound or
tonality (or their sheer difference) or by a short narrative
syntagm. These elementary segments change their positions
and functions according to the Gospels. About a dozen narratives in Matthew are constructed redundantly around a quotation such as: "Thus the saying of the prophet was fulfilled."
Each of these elementary units are like convex mirrors where
the entire configuration is (pre-sensed) presented: word +

act. It has been "remembered" or reproduced for this reason. The Emmaus narrative (Lk. 24) refers to the last gesture of Jesus (the breaking of the bread and disappearance) and leaves a place in the communication whose climatic (inaugural) point is the logion which ends the narrative (Lk. 24:34): "The Lord has risen and *he has appeared to Simon*" (this last sememe appears elsewhere only in 1 Cor. 15:5).

2. Another kind of short enunciation exists at the beginning [p. 105] of the work of Paul who, not having "known Christ in the flesh", still proclaims his "gospel" on a basis which conforms to the earlier tradition. The semantic virtualities of the event (of which the entire surface of the New Testament is a plural manifestation) can be summed up in one basic formulation: the *profession of faith*. Paul gives one of the oldest statements about it in 1 Cor. 15:3ff.:

> I have transmitted to you in the first place
> what I have also received: *That Christ died--*
> for our sins--in accordance with the Scriptures,
> that he was put in the tomb,
> that *he was raised*--the third day--in accordance
> with the Scriptures,
> that he appeared to Cephas....

A consequence develops at great length from this matrix.[21] This phenomenon of *precipitation*, which is the reciprocal of that phenomenon which was first described, is however also innate (or inaugural) with regard to the discourse.

3. Between the two, the enunciation of the *Kerygma*, as we see it in the "discourses" from *Acts*, presents the semantic equivalent of the formula of the Pauline creed in a diachronic form, with some variants according to whether the audiences are Jewish or non-Jewish (Acts 2:22ff. or 17:24ff.).

These three cases confirm Claude Lévi-Strauss' formula:
"The chronological order of succession is absorbed in a non-
temporal material structure."[22] Its function here is to in-
augurate a *repeatable* enunciation. By the infinite number
of metonymic transformations of which this act of enunciation is capable, it opens the field to the development of
meaning wherever it is repeated according to its protocol.
Who is the "author" of this enunciation? He cannot be any
one of the characters, the witnesses who are introduced,
nor an impersonal being. Historical criticism, in agreement with its presuppositions, prefers to view him as the
"community" (i.e. the anonymous but personal being who has
elaborated the statement). But we think instead that the
true "author" is to be identified with *the agent who maintains the correlation* between the configurative systems and
the epistemic field. His image is situated on the side of
the theologoumenon which intervenes in the text just when
that which one can call (following J. Derrida) "the *differentiation*"[23] [= *différance*] appears: the *Spirit* (with a
capital "S"). The semiotic analysis of the following three
texts confirms this presumption:

> *1 Cor. 12:3:* 'No one can be speaking
> under the influence of the Spirit of God and
> say: "Jesus be cursed" (= "Let him be
> hanged!") and no one can say "Jesus *is* Lord",
> except under the influence of the Holy Spirit.'

> *2 Pet. 1:19ff.:* 'You would do well to
> *consider the* prophetic *word* as a lamp which
> shines in a dark place until the day dawns and
> the morning star rises in your hearts...No
> prophecy of the Scripture is a matter [p. 106]
> of personal interpretation, because no prophecy
> was ever uttered by man's initiative, but the
> impulse of the Holy Spirit makes men speak on
> behalf of God.'

> *Rev. 2 and 3* have as a refrain: 'Who-
> ever has ears, let him listen to what the
> Spirit is saying to the churches....' But
> this Spirit and each 'church' are related,
> with the result that the sender and receiver
> together produce the same word: 'The Spirit
> and the Bride say, "Come", and whoever
> listens (i.e. the reader) also says, "Come!"
> ...' (Rev. 22:17).

In the depth as well as on the surface of these texts,
this theologoumenon sets in motion and organizes the image
without any figuration which materializes in the narratives
and the basic formulations. Thus the constitutive kernels
[Ed. note: kernel = a transformational linguistic term]:
the "Resurrection" and "Eucharist" can be dealt with from a
redundancy: "Why do you persecute *me*?", Jesus said to Saul
(Acts 9:4). According to the text repeated three times in
Acts (Acts 22:8-9 and 26:14-15), the "me" is identified as
the "churches" and the churches are identified as the "body"
of Christ. We can begin with an *invariant*. Jesus says,
"This *is* my Body" in the narrative of the Eucharist. The
relationship of *this "body"* to the readers who read *this
text* in accordance with its protocol (they are "a body")
corresponds with the relationship of Jesus to his own "body".
The scripture describes the event and forbids one to touch
it; it permits one to see and read it in a communication
which the Old Testament has already described (Deut. 4:9ff.):

> While the mountain burned with fire to
> the heart of the heavens..., you then *saw*
> no figure. There was only a *word*.

In both cases, the integration (which is effective) implies the intervention of an operant whose function is to
make the apparent exist and to open the way to the "prior

meaning" of which nothing can be said except what the text gives beforehand[24] by its "verbal framework".[25] This operant is represented *in* the Scripture as Spirit (or Wisdom: 1 Cor. 1:18-3:22). Do these linguistic manifestations permit us to make any other use of what this theologoumenon *represents*?

The analyst is urged here to make a *decision* about his methods which is symmetrical to the decision of recognizing the petinence of this "operant" or not. Is not this Scripture hidden in sands and urns, like the Qumran and Massada scrolls? But is this possible? This is a decision which gives life to the *langue*--and which permits the iteration of a limited number of *permanences* in the redundancy of a single structure (cf. "Jesus is Lord") producing meaning through the small historically situated spectacle that it presents (cf. A. J. Greimas, *Du sens*, 104f.). *This decision is agreed upon by the "author" and the "reader"* ("The Spirit and the Bride say: 'Come!'"). The distance between appearing and being is maintained by the physical restriction of the reader to the form of the text.

The Image of the Reader

An image of the reader is formed (during the reading, which we always assume is faithful to its protocol) which agrees with the establishment of the [p. 107] correlations between the diverse semantic levels. We will only note the focal point. If death is not the end of the discourse by which the "narrator" speaks but is a transcription into a visible form of which the Scripture is the legible manifestation, the same thing is true (inversely and in a mirror)

for the reader. He is associated with this transcribing
operation which endlessly expands the semantic universe
(for him and everything which forms one body with him: man
and cosmos, Rom. 8). In other words, the Scripture opens
an organic series of readings where the *possibility* (a possibility well executed at the level of the structure) is implied for the *"langue" to be transmitted completely* by a
certain economy of the performances *in the parole*. The
enunciation--"arrival of the Logos in the flesh" or "resurrection of the body"--performed in the decoding of Jesus as
"Lord" denotes in an inaugural form that the system of the
langues has (received) the gift of being realized in an ("infinitely plural") *parole*. The "discourse" held in this way
(whatever the form may be) is the beginning of this gift.
The Pentecost narrative (Acts 2) or the enigmatic chapter 4
of *Ephesians*, as well as the end of each Gospel, represent
this gift. The image of the reader in his home has an "eschatological" character: a glass of water presented or
justice done today is equivalent to the Kingdom of God and
to meeting Christ (Mtt. 25:31ff.). The reading of Scripture
at high noon--the banquet and the day when everything is rec-
onciled--leads one to *think it is fiction*.[26]

The effective power of such an act in the image of the
reader appears in all its radiance in the Eucharistic narrative in 1 Cor. 11:23ff. The "body of Christ" (while becoming meaningful by the reiteration of the narrative according
to its protocol) becomes a semantic space.[27] But does "a
pure narrative agent" necessarily remain? This "body" does
not introduce itself as "a being which is present somewhere
and which escapes from the interaction of the *differentiation*
[= *différance*]."[28] Its narrative position refers to the
difference of the being in question in relationship to the

physical anchoring of the reader in a particular cosmic context. But the combinative of the narrative (its iteration) is such that it also refers to a meaning "prior to the meaning" and to this infinite possibility which was previously described and which is not recoverable by a representation. The enunciation requires an *anamnesis* (which does not consist of going back in time but of yielding to the pre-sense, which is nontemporal despite its historical roots) and the intervention of the agent of the integration, the Spirit (*epiklesis*). Henceforth the *parole*: "This is my body..." becomes the word and the word becomes the "thing".[29] Its iteration is, if one wishes, (a sign in which) the thing (is) completed,[30] or a presence which is no longer delayed. Thanks to the text [p. 108] (or to its practice in the present historical context), the image of the reader is not engulfed in the "dazzling whiteness" which could produce without him the relationship to the (resurrected) being. The present discourse (the *logos*) transforms itself into something different than itself (into its accomplishment: *mythos*), but not in order to eliminate appearance and to recover it as an epiphany of the Absolute. The act of "thinking it is fiction" at high noon (e.g. the celestial Banquet) makes a new decision (i.e. a "conversion") possible in such a way that the path to the truth will no longer be the same as the earlier path (cf. Matthew's note: "for the remission of sins" = communication with the *being* through the *alterity* is open to all the manifestations which the context permits). We see that *desire* is the mediator of the communication and plays a large role in the discourse that separates the reader from the surface of the Scripture.[31]

One can analyze the image of the reader in this semantic universe from another angle.[32] The subject of the statement which reads: I am (with you...), etc., appears to be the same as the transmitter of the gospel message. But he is combined with the subject of the linguistic discourse, and at every moment "I" is at the same time the subject in the statement (I am the good shepherd, I will go up to Jerusalem) and the subject of the enunciation (He said). There is no "he" but there is a *you* for the reader, although *I* remains as the transmitter *hic and nunc* of the message. But these two subjects are situated within one single code of the expression—which has the effect of preventing their simultaneous presence. Jesus is/is not present. He is presense/present in the Spirit: "As I have departed, I shall return" (Acts 1:11 and Jn. 14-16). Thus in the episode where Mary Magdalene is seeking the body of Jesus: "*They* have taken him away", Jesus who is seen (but not recognized) is addressed as "you". "Tell me where *you* have put him." Recognized, Jesus says, "Do not touch *me*....Go, tell your brothers...." The narrative is produced by the logical confusion between the missing body as *he* and *I*. This "he" and "I" are the "you" for the reader which permits the communication to exist from the beginning. Therefore one is dealing as a rule with a text where the sender of the message, who is also the subject of the enunciation, also continues to be in the position of the subject of the statement (the theologoumenon of the *Spirit*/Jesus raised from. the dead in *body* and Spirit/living *word*).

III.

PRODUCTION OF MEANING

Theory.

The preservation of the Scriptural corpus, through its multiple usages (the eastern and western traditions, patristic, medieval, and modern exegeses, Catholicism and Protestantism, etc.) as an (inaugural) referential field of meaning attests that there is a profound difference between the stage of its genesis and the stage of all its usages which one can describe, according to A. J. Greimas' expression,[33] as two successive structural states. [p. 109] This difference between the structures explains why the project of returning to "what happened"[34] is an illusion. There is a gap between the structural state of reading and the structural state of the Scripture. Reading of necessity produces a displacement (or a series of transformations) which belong to it, and the text is not clarified if one is content to restrict oneself to the static surface structures.

The problem posed by this "gap" can be expressed in many ways. We will be content to formulate some terms and conclusions before passing on to a series of manipulations.

According to the problematics of A. J. Greimas: What is "the *translinguistic subject* whose intervention accounts for the diachronic transformations which disjoin the structural states?"[35] Or, if one follows J. Kristeva, we are dealing with "a trans-linguistic apparatus which redistributes the order of the langue by connecting a communicative *parole* referring to direct information with different types of earlier or synchronic statements". Or in short: What is the fundamental structure which also supports the whole

corpus and each elementary unit (e.g. a logion, creed, or
basic enunciation such as: Jesus is Lord) in its closure
in such a way that the complex syntax which articulates the
whole can be extended to some different usages—by a transformation which makes the visible endlessly legible anew?

The fact that this Scripture may be supported by a
tradition which finds its meaning in its reading and which
precisely uses this gap in order to produce it brings one
element of total response to these questions. This trans-
linguistic subject manifests itself by a linguistic discourse. It has no other reality than *that by which the
readers* (potentially: a man) *reach their reality*. In
other words, since it is a question of the trial [*procès*] of
the "word of God", the reality of God *is objectified* by the
reality of man. This is what *Lord-Jesus* represents, insofar as the relationship between the two names expresses the
fundamental structure of this corpus. The earlier questions
are therefore transformed as follows: What is semiotically
necessary in order that the semantic reality may be *this
aspect* of the reality of "God" which exposes and risks itself in this communication? Or rather: What difference
does the Scripture need with regard to the rules of the
general structure of the *langues*? The terms of this question show that it is difficult to find the original paradigm which projects itself at the same time on the whole
series and on the smallest syntagm by producing the specific
relationship between the "author" and "reader" which we have
outlined. This text, which claims to reveal by its appearance the existence of God, also shows how man is made up of
more than the totality of his contradictions. From the fact
of this double inscription (this double meaning), it frequently overthrows, even in the narrative sequences, the

usual interaction of the oppositions: *the oppositional terms are often unusual, and the contradictories can transcend their reciprocal exclusion.* Finally it should be noted that the New Testament especially does not present an enigma to be read, in the sense desired by western discourse since Oedipus.[36] One knows *in advance*--since the [p. 110] reading has this death/resurrection as a starting-point which is the starting-point of the Scripture. The question of truth is therefore not posed as elsewhere in the evolution of meaning, but another relays it. How does the *poetic* sense of the network appear (for the world and "me"). The semantics of the text always assumes a moment when it is actual, that is to say when the subject of the statement coincides with the subject of the enunciation, with the result that the syntagmatic statement is rarely predicative. In "This *is*...", the verb is about the nature of being not of doing. The text, if one wishes, remains "the inscription of its production" and is considered "as an irreducible production in the representation".[37]

Applications.

As L. Marin has noted here (p. 92 above), by what means does one apply some formal models to this text without producing the "loss of [its characteristic] semantic substance"? If the semiotic practice simply brings the formal models into play as "the selective and combinative appearance of a general abstract model", whatever binds this text into continuous performative parole is misinterpreted, we do not see why this vast configuration is not emptied of its meaning in order to be covered with the sands of the desert. On the other hand, if one arbitrarily applies the interaction of categories, oppositions, and combinatives (whose validity has been tested

in another linguistic area) to it, the result of the production risks being irrelevant. Moreover, historical-
critical exegesis has had much difficulty in avoiding this
twofold danger. However, putting it into a structural form
has always been advantageous for the production of a logical
verification.

Paradigmatic Oppositions.

The great number of paradoxical statements, even in the
New Testament, leads us to suspect that we are dealing in
some way with a derangement of an almost systematic "meaning":
"Harvesting where one has not sown"; "The smallest will be
the greatest"; "Render unto Caesar..."; "I have come not to
bring peace but the sword"; "To him who has it will be given,
and to him who has not it will be taken away..." Certainly
this derangement is based on a rule immanent to the *langue*.
However, more than other corpora and in a different way, this
corpus presents a surface where only the *boundaries* or fron-
tiers of the small or large spectacles which it presents are
to be read. The figuration does not end.

If there is something legible on the surface, it is a
permanent network of paradigmatic relationships whose plan
immediately seems to be a series of syntagms. The difficulty
is that these paradigms are only boundaries. The study of
each could fill an endless number of monographs. For example,
Formerly (= *archē*, or Law, or elements of the tradition, or
the stage before baptism, etc.) */Henceforth* (new creation,
etc.: the *archē* is also on this side); *Already* (filiation,
heritage, descent of the Spirit, etc.) */Not yet* (consummation, etc.: cf. the text cited from 2 Peter 1:19ff.); *Type*
(Adam, Abraham, events in the desert, etc.) */Antitype* (new
Adam, faith, "spiritual" rock from which the water gushes

out, etc.); [p. 111] catalogues of *virtues/vices* which
function as openings/closings according to the invariant
of the general structure but which have no coherence in
themselves. A systematic inventory of these oppositions
does not exist. Although they are situated on the surface,
their development should be clarified by the creation of
less visible paradigms. They are generally deployed in
constellations or concentric series of transformations:

> *Promise/fulfillment* form a disjunc-
> tive/conjunctive schema which appears in
> the Old Testament, generally remains true
> for the Old Testament passage in the New
> Testament, and which determines in large
> part the invention of the syntagms in the
> New Testament. For example: Small pic-
> tures in Matthew are built on some twelve
> 'quotations' which are introduced by the
> words: 'Thus it was fulfilled...'
> One finds in some texts, for example
> (in a constellation around this schema),
> two equivalent schemas which date from
> the catastrophic period of the Exile
> (Jeremiah 31:31; Ezekiel 36:26ff.):

> *Old/New*

> Law written on a *stone*/in the *heart*

> *flesh/spirit*

> Now is this paradigmatic succession
> reversible or irreversible? It is both.
> The fact that the Jewish tradition keeps
> the meaning (*in abeyance*) at the same
> time that the Old Testament corpus shows
> by the same practice that the Torah and
> the Prophets cannot be transformed into
> the "new" without losing its meaning.
> It is quite a different matter for the
> one who knows the reading of the "new".
> The discourse which the reader (who is
> acquainted with the "new") holds with

himself is structurally different. There
is therefore the possibility of a *structural change in the same signifiers.*
'Abraham (= promise) has seen the day of
Christ (= fulfillment).' What is the
nature of this correlation? An achronic
theologoumenon, 'I am', appears in the context of Jn. 8:56 which is the means of
passage from one structure to another.
The meaning is irreversible at this level
and the type of correlation described by
A. J. Greimas (*Du sens*, 114) can be
applied here: S_1--R--S_2 where S_2 can be
the transformation of S_1 but not vice-
versa. Now if one considers the last
schema, one sees that (*from the viewpoint of the New Testament*) this transformation consists of fulfilling the
'promise' of a radical and definitive
passage from the 'flesh' (or external
rule) to the 'spirit' (the communication
becomes its own Law to itself in terms
of a decision combined on the one hand
and the other, which is the event con-
figured in the 'new' Scripture). This
analysis corroborates the assertion of
Claude Chabrol about the 'permanence of
the signifiers characteristic of the Old
Testament in the New Testament'.

This change of the meaning of the Old Testament in its

signifiers shows that the Scripture is not the place of

a programmed exchange between a sender and receiver situated

in a closed system of communication. Some sememes like the

"purpose" or "will" of God can be misleading if one attributes

the meaning to them which they have in western culture. This

"plan" is endlessly modified or rather is combined with the

improvisations of man, since its semantic reality is revealed

in the series of operations by which man comes to his own

reality (the word). It is true that the syntagms (where they

are deployed) follow a [p. 112] paramentrium which Matthew

expresses in a disconnected way: "That you may be *perfect* as your heavenly Father is perfect"/or: "The will of the Father is that *not one* of the smallest ones *be lost*." This "purpose" is opposed within the discourse so that the man who keeps it loses the sense of it. This kind of surface sememe represents an algorithm which functions at every depth of the Scripture. Man has the ability at any time to make a change in his life (e.g. the form of his communication, his openess to the meaning) in such a way that this communication is not reducible to the totality of its contradictions. This means that there is an irreductibility of the "discourse" to the systems where it is shaped or the opposite of a programming. Or to take another paradigm drawn from Mtt. 5:37 and James 5:12, the word of man is *yes/no* at the same time. The "word of God" makes him able to say yes *or* no. That is to say, man is able to clarify the ambiguity of the message, not by leaving it, since the production of meaning is made by it; but *this* production *is not simply equivalent* to the communication itself. We could obtain the same result by analyzing the categorical interaction of *being* and *appearing*[38] in the sapiential (i.e. wisdom) genre of the parable, in the resurrection narratives (the Emmaus narrative [Lk. 24] is constructed completely on this interaction), or in the production of the Last Judgment scene in Mtt. 25. The *consummation* of time (of the discourse) consists of making the being appear (as present prior to its exposition)--as a rigorously precise word, that is to say as *equivalent to its inscription* ("word of God"). Such a "word" leaves nothing behind.

A study of the opposition between *blessing/curse*, which is often repeated, leads us further. We find it in various forms in the New Testament: for example, in the

inaugural discourse of the beatitudes in Lk. 6 (Blessed are
the poor..., but woe unto the rich...). We find it in Luke:
Blessed is the womb that bore you! / Blessed *rather* are they
who hear the word of God and keep it! (Lk. 11:27-28), where
the disjunction is only between two different approaches;
and we even find it in the appearance to Thomas in the form
of an opposition where *seeing/believing* and *believing/with-
out having seen* (= by the legible discourse) indicates two
stages opposed to the blessings. The logic of the discourse
precludes the first (Paul calls it *sarkinos* in opposition to
another which is called *pneumatikos*). The functioning of
the blessing/curse paradigm has been subjected to some important diachronic transformations before it was connected
to the New Testament. The two terms are symmetrical with
respect to the liturgy which celebrates the Covenant in one
basic context where the people divide themselves into two
groups in imitation of the paradigm. The earlier trans-
gressions of the Covenant code (= curses) are "forgiven"
because they (the people and the code) continue ("standing
upright before Yahweh") (= blessings). But who knows what
their faithfulness will be in the future? This indecisiveness of the meaning is consummated in the reiteration of a
permanence. The "word of Yahweh" *remains* while pointing
out of what Israel consists (this "discourse" receives its
strength from the atemporal situation which characterized
the liturgical discourse, which is inaugural there, cf.
Gen. 1 and Ps. 136). In an era when the imminence of a
global catastrophe appeared to be inevitable to the "prophets" [p. 113] because of Israel's internal sociological
disorder, the order of the terms is reversed: *curse precedes blessing* (Deut. 4:25-31). There is a change of meaning then: it *changes* from the certainty of a catastrophe

(curse) to another *certainty* (the blessing will surely
follow). Henceforth the earlier paradigm is reversed:

"Desertion of Yahweh" by Israel:	"Yahweh does not desert":
curse (exile)	blessing (return from exile)
= exile from the word	= return of the word

An irreversible invention is produced in the text between the
two stages. Israel loses its particularity during the exile
and discovers the world of other people (Mesopotamia). Henceforth the earlier state appears to be weakened (while it was
absolute in the celebration of the Covenant), and the universal stands out as a category of the "future". Henceforth the
discourse is preoccupied with the future. In the course of
the writing of this paradigm, we can make out the following
sequence for the prophets at the end of the Exile:

closing, weakness, past / opening, eternal, strength, future

"Let us not think any more
  of the past"   / "See the future"

-- desert...   -- water, roads...

                                         (Isa. 43:18-19)

And the "genres" are adapted to the semantic change. The
Pentateuch is closed, while the sapientiel or apocalyptic

discourse is developed. To the extent to which the earlier signifiers receive a new signified, the rereading begins to produce a scripture with some new signifiers. Prophecy, at its highest point, modifies the configuration of the "people" to such an extent that it produces the famous figure of the "suffering servant" who revealed on a broader scale what the contractual system of the Covenant included in a limited way in its effectively demonstrated combinative (Isa. 53).

Communication Categories.

The danger of using ready-made categories (which have been taken from somewhere else) for the analysis of this original field of communication is that they may impose an artificial development on the meaning. It seems to us that the principles formulated by J. Kristeva in two studies in the book, *Théorie d'ensemble*, are valid for this Scripture. This Scripture introduces the *difference* into the interplay of categories which it always uses, which makes them well-suited to induce the epistemic field which *figures* it *without* representing it. Therefore it ceaselessly produces a kind of revolutionary practice, examples of which it is easy to compile for the time-space, sociological, and legal settings; the syntactic functions; and even the morphology. Topology and chronology have the *flash of dice thrown upon a mirror*. A biography of Jesus' ministry is as impossible as that of the patriarchs or Moses. Eden or the "Sea of Reeds", the places of the major "events", cannot be easily *located* from our references. The same thing is true for the boundaries of the Promised Land (Deut. 1:1-9) or the place of the resurrection *despite* the accuracy of the figure. Louis Marin[39] has described the *reducer of desire* role which "utopian" space plays in the configuration. The use of legal categories constantly requires an explosive result which frees the communication [p. 114] from their natural constraint. This process reaches its climax in the criticism of the *nomos* [= Law] in Paul's work (the exegetical surface descriptions are constantly renewed, but they do not succeed in accounting for it).[40] As for the constitution of the grammatical "persons", the permutation from the "I" to "he" remains a problem for the exegete in a large number of Old Testament narratives. The effects produced by changes of the paradigms at the syntactic and morphological level can only be alluded to here. However, a structural type of analysis in all these cases permits us to say that it is not only the variants or non-functional stylistic figures which produce meaning--the function itself can account for it. But the data from (critical) exegesis is also necessary for an accurate determination of the categories and oppositional terms so that the transformational models can function at the very beginning in an economical manner.

Oppositional Terms.

The studies collected in this volume show the distortions performed by the biblical text on the oppositional systems which elsewhere guarantee the procedures within settings which can be formalized such as: contract, judicial trial, exchange, politics, religion, death. There is rarely an equivalency between the operant and the result. For example, the *contract*: the narrative isotopy of the healing of the blind men which was studied by Guy Vuillod (pp. 48ff. above) is twofold. Is there really a "contract"? In such a setting, freedom is only "an interaction within an inexorable structure". But what does the equivalence between

being poor/being healed and/*arrival* of the messiah signify
here? The contractual aspect of the relationship is a way
of considering the access to this arrival (the movement);
it is not the result (it is not equivalent to his arrival
but to his appearance). The narrative assumes the "sign of
Jonah" which is proclaimed later. It is an anteposed [ed.
note: this is the adj. form of the grammatical term, "anteposition"] message. The writing of this text implies an
intertextuality. The being which enters into a relationship
with the blind man *accepts beforehand* the breaking of the
"contract". In other words, this setting is broken as soon
as it is posed, and *the blind man is not at any moment in
the position of an object of exchange.* The setting which
appears is rather that of a Covenant. "If you believe" is
not a conditional stipulation but the means of access to the
sight (*ut sit!*) of Jesus, such as it is. The trial of Jesus
is quite another matter, but the contract which takes place
there (between Judas, the chief priests, the people, and
Pilate, which is implicit or explicit) only has men for
partners. Jesus is placed by them (or between them) in the
position of an object, just as the soldiers play with dice,
etc.[41] This is why this trial is inverted, as early as the
beginning, into an anti-trial. Claude Chabrol describes it
quite correctly here as an "anti-trial" by showing how the
neutralization of one [p. 115] semantic category allows the
transformation of the meaning to take place (pp. 148-49 above).
But does the category of "retribution" appear to be different
in this development of the meaning than on the surface? Repeating his own narrative, Luke declares in Acts that "the
Jews" ("you") have acted *in ignorance* (Acts 3:17--Lk. 23:
34). This *they* (i.e. the Jews) is an *I* for the evangelical
image of the reader of the trial. "They" can only admit

their "guilt" (in the self-trial) to the extent to which "I"
acknowledge being subject to a forgiveness (= beginning of
the reading, which corresponds to that of the writing of the
narrative). The appearance of retribution is not a false
conception; it is in the narrative to the extent to which
its polysemy requires a code of an apologetic reading or an
anti-Judaic controversy. To this extent, the text simulates
the sudden appearance of fictive records on the opposite
side of the reader. This "retribution" assumes a form of
the blessing/curse paradigm which has never been shown than
where it is disputed by the discourse/ which refers to it.
Perhaps this is a false fold whose western trace is Oedipus.
Can this code be considered to be one of the operators of
the meaning?[42]

This process in every case brings an opposition into
play between a negative movement which is symmetrical to a
positive term--and by saying that we have already made a
choice in favor of the "hero"--which *transgresses* with "us"
the end of every discourse by condemning it to an irreversible degradation. How does the transposition function? We
will suggest here, by a kind of suitable (an)achronism, that
one imagine that what is concerned *is* (already) the object
of a reflection in the *text*, whose (present) semiotic analysis must *appear* as the *citation*. How can one determine the
terms? By an analysis of a specific configuration like the
following: "Once I am lifted up (= cruciform), I will draw
all men" (Jn. 12:32), or even its homologue in Philippians 2
(*debasement/elevation*). The opposite is also possible: *ana-
basis/katabasis* (Eph. 4).

Basically it is the *hierarchical* structure of the whole
apparatus which the Scripture redistributes in a disconcerted
order, not on the surface, but at the level of the signifier

and signified, knowing and not knowing, temporal and eternal, profane and sacred, visible and invisible, life and death, etc., or where our hallowed linguistic institutions[43] are overwhelmed. *These oppositional terms are not exclusive.* Are they to be maintained? Yes, to the extent to which the application of a transformational model assumes, as an operative, a system of communication, which is (if not) closed, (at least) stable. [p. 116]

Models.

Desire, participation, and communication seem to account for the threefold "aspect" of the "life in communion" described three times in *Acts* (chaps. 2, 4, and 5). And one can apply the transformation rules which result from them to the Gospels. We will give only one approach:[44]

The Axis of Desire:

R1: *Jesus and the Disciples.* Jesus loves the disciples. The narrative makes the passive transformation appear at the end: the disciples love Jesus.

R2: *The Disciples and Jesus.* The disciples love Jesus at the level of being but not at the level of appearing (= suffering messiah). When the disciples become conscious of the level of being (the Passion), they take action against this love (Judas: Peter's denial, the flight of all of them).

The Axis of Participation:

R3: A relationship is established between Jewishness/Jesus/Non Jewishness. When the Jews become conscious that the relationship Jesus--non-Jews is identical to the relationship Jesus--Jews, they take action against Jesus.

The Axis of Communication:

R4: This is the relationship God/Apostles
where the Apostles are the confidants of
Jesus. If Jesus becomes the agent of a
proposition created by R1 (God is loved by
non-Jewish peoples), Jesus changes his confidants: after the meeting with the Roman Cornelius in Acts 10, Peter and the twelve
apostles disappear from the "apostolic" field.
That does not explain the "election" of Paul
who takes their place, but it does explain
Paul's position in the narrative and the mys-
terious disappearance of Peter (Acts 12:17).

On the other hand, the *homological model* proposed by
T. Todorov (*Communications* 8, 1966, 131) only seems to be
profitably applicable to the Gospels if one inverts the
terms:

Instead of $\dfrac{\text{Jesus}}{\text{Israel}} \: {\large\frown} \: \dfrac{\text{acts of Jesus}}{\text{rejection of his acts}}$,

the sense requires:

$$\dfrac{\text{gift(s) of Jesus}}{\text{people}} \: {\large\frown} \: \dfrac{\text{rejection (death of Jesus)}}{\text{act(s) of Jesus}} : \dfrac{\text{Resurrection}}{\text{message}}$$

The transformation of the Passion into the
Resurrection is what permits this last relationship to exist. Jesus' death is the
starting point of the message. Without the
resurrection your "faith" is in vain and the
message is also in vain. But the resurrection is only real if it has the effect of
being communicated/a correlate of the *gift*
which Jesus is/gives. The tradition of
this gift is written down (communicated)
as Scripture. It appears semantically by
transgressing the (customary) logic of the
actions.

A systematic practice could say if the models proposed by A. J. Greimas (*Du sens*, 160ff.), which are invaluable for the micro-universe of the Old Testament, are also useful for the New Testament, where the insurrectional movement of the "Spirit" travels through all the circuits without resting on a particular "people". Faith/non faith is not opposed to life/death. Faith (or life) presupposes non faith, instead of excluding it, since the life of Christ is only *manifested* by his death. Faith [p. 117] also passes through death to become itself....The same thing is true for faith/non faith in relationship to law/lawlessness. The Law is precisely the place of unbelief. But lawlessness (in the same Pauline text) is also the position of unbelief (Rom. 3-5). What is contradictory at one level becomes a necessary transition to another level. The same thing is lawful and forbidden, according to the combinative of 1 Cor. and Mtt. 5. How does one formulate the transformational model which can account for the sexual relationships in 1 Cor. 5:1-13? The following table presents the problem:

Within (Christian culture)

Prescribed relationships

(goals starting with an
indicative): v. 7*b*
"Our Paschal lamb *has
been* sacrificed" *between*
"brothers" (believers).

= "chaste"

   "cleansed"

     "we"
5:7*b*-8

Outside (?)

Prohibited relationships

(excluded):

on the part of the
"brothers"

= judgment by "you"

   5:1, 11

Quotation from the Old
Testament: v. 13*b*

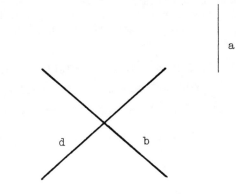

   c   d   b   a

*Relationships not pro-
hibited:*

= non judgment (by "me")

   judgment by "God"

   5:12-13*a*

= standards in "this
    world"

   5:9-10

*Relationships not pre-
scribed between "brothers":*

= not-cleansed: *"you"*
   being under an *imperative* as believers in
   the Paschal Lamb,

but forming a community of
sinners who have to be
cleansed,

5:2-7*a*

The deed performed by the Paschal Lamb, or
its reiteration in the community appears to
be indicative in the first position and imperative in the fourth position--the grammatical mood of the verbs belongs to the
oratorical process of the whole passage.
First Corinthians 5:7-8 seems to go back
to a paschal liturgical hymn. The succession of syntagms is indicated by *a, b*
("we": our Paschal Lamb/let us celebrate
--"you": situation spiritually external
to the "new lump" which is the community),
c, d. The last verse neutralizes the contradictories: v. 13*a* ("Those outside, God
will judge them"), but the quotation which
follows (v. 13*b*: "Remove the perverted
ones [= non-sense] from your midst")
vigorously maintains a contradiction by
subverting, however, the positions of *"inside"* and *"outside"*. As for "this world",
its [p. 118] situation is remarkable. It
establishes a position inside and at a de-
ferred distance (judgment/non-judgment).

To conclude, the following formulation from the prologue
of the Gospel of John and Romans 5:1-11 could be suggested as
an experiment in order to account for the development of meaning in the Scripture:

$$\frac{\text{human condition}}{\text{gift (received/transmitted)}} \ \overset{\frown}{} \ \frac{\text{divine condition}}{\text{human condition}}$$

The first term is equivalent to the relationship which unites
competence and performance in a linguistic structure. Consequently, the relationship of actuality shows how the theologoumenon agent of the correlations between successive or
achronic structural states in relation to the situation of
the type of readers referred to (the human condition) is

equivalent to the relationship of the "langue" to the "parole". Its being is to be spoken. The paradigms which we have analyzed can be expressed as a "gift" in a twofold sense--originating from a "decision", which is itself twofold.

June 1970

NOTES

1. N. Lohfink, *Sciences bibliques en marche*, Paris: Castermann, 1969, 56f.: "Historical research and interpretation naturally coincide when it is a question of texts which bring us closer to historical events...." "Man is placed in the world...of a text, that is to say, in the last resort in the world of another man. *The perspective of the writer in the past and the perspective of the reader now are confused.* If that occurs or if the interpreter manages to obtain this result with his hearer, *biblical scholarship has found its meaning.*" (Italics ours.)

2. Here is a list of works which are cited many times in this article: R. Barthes, "Introduction à l'analyse structurale des récits", *Communications* 8 (1966), 1-28 [English trans.: "An Introduction to the Structural Analysis of Narrative", *New Literary History* 6 (1975), 237-272]; *idem*, "L'effect de réel", *Communications* 11 (1968), 84-90; *idem*, "L'écriture de l'événement", *Communications* 12 (1968), 108-113; *idem*, "Drame, poème, roman", in *Théorie d'ensemble*, Paris: Seuil, 1968, 25-41; *idem*, "Comment parler à Dieu", *Tel Quel* 38 (1969), 32-55; *idem*, *S/Z Essai*, Paris: Seuil, 1970 [Eng. trans.: *S/Z*, trans. R. Miller, New York: Hill & Wang, 1974]; *idem*, "L'analyse structurale du récit. A propos d'Actes X-XI", *Recherches de Sciences religieuses* 58 (1970), 17-38 [an Eng. trans. will appear in *Structuralism and Biblical Hermeneutics*, see the bibliography, p.325 below]; *idem*, "Par où commencer?", *Poétique* 1 (1970), 3-9; J. Derrida, "La différence", in *Théorie d'ensemble*, Paris: Seuil, 1968, 41-66; A. J. Greimas, *Du sens. Essais sémiotiques*, Paris: Seuil, 1970; J. Kristeva, "La sémiologie: Science critique et/ou critique de la science", in *Théorie d'ensemble*, Paris: Seuil, 1968, 80-93; *idem*, "Problèmes de la structuration de texte", *ibid*, 298-317; *idem*, "L'engendrement de la formule", *Tel Quel* 37-38 (1969); L. Marin "Réflexions sur la notion de modèle chez Pascal", *Revue de Metaphysique et de Morale* 3 (1967), 89-108; *idem*, "Notes sur une médaille et une gravure", *Revue d'Esthétique*, N.S. 22 (1969), 121-138; *idem*, "Le discours de la figure", *Critique* 270 (1969), 953-971; *idem*, "Essai d'analyse structurale d'Actes 10, 1-11, 18", *Recherches de Sciences religieuses*

58 (1970), 39-62 [An Eng. trans. of this article will also appear in *Structuralism and Biblical Hermeneutics*]; T. Todorov, "Les catégories du récit littéraire", *Communications* 8 (1966), 125-151; *idem, Introduction à la littérature fantastique*, Paris: Seuil, 1970 [Eng. Trans.: *The Fantastic*, trans. R. Howard, Cleveland: Press of Case Western Reserve Univ., 1973]; *idem*, "Les études de style", *Poétique* 2 (1970), 224-232.

3. Thus the kernel [= a transformational linguistics term] of the sapiential [= wisdom] writings revealed in *Qohelet* (or *Ecclesiastes*) has no (or almost no) relationship with the institution of the Covenant, which is a focal point for the Torah, Psalms, and Prophets. Or again,·*Matthew* knows nothing about *Luke*.

4. This organic collection of texts presents itself as "frozen" in this way, according to the formula of N. Frye, *Fables of Identity*, New York: Harcourt, Brace & World, 1961, 21. The Jewish tradition established its official list of books in Hebrew a little after the Christian tradition had fixed its canon. The Christian canon included certain Greek books from the Jewish-Hellenistic diaspora in the Old Testament (for example, *Sirach* or *Ecclesiasticus*, whose lost Hebrew original has been reconstructed in its quasi-totality thanks especially to the discoveries at Qumran and Massada. It was therefore in use in the first centuries B.C. and A.D.). This Christian tradition juxtaposed a New Testament to the Old Testament. The catalogue of books *read in public* in the Roman "church" about 180 A.D. (i.e. The Muratorian Canon) agrees with the present "canonical" list of the Roman Catholic tradition.

5. The selection was made empirically. The authoritative books were those which were spontaneously recognized as the "Word of God" and generally read in the largest number of the "churches". The Qumran community, for its part, already distinguished those texts on which one meditates "day and night" from closely related but not homologous texts (e.g. the *Genesis Apocryphon* [1 QApGen] and the *Testament of Moses*, etc.).

6. The Protestant Reformation was based on a "return to the Scripture" and its diverse practice led it to consider certain books as "deutero-canonical".

7. In the sense of A. J. Greimas, *Du sens*, 112f.

8. The usages of the Jewish tradition are diverse (cf. the Jerusalem and Babylonian Talmuds), but the corpus remains intangible.

9. Paul Beauchamp, *Création et séparation. Étude de Genèse*, Paris: B.S.R., 1969.

10. In the sense of R. Barthes in *Communications* 12 (1968), 111.

11. Cf. J. Kristeva, *Théorie d'ensemble*, 299ff.

12. H. R. Jauss, "Littérature médiévale et théorie des genres", *Poétique* 1 (1970), 97. This point of view is also necessary for the fantastic folktale, whose essence (i.e. hesitancy about the meaning) is not always represented in the narrative. The analyses of the Scripture by R. Barthes (*R.S.R.* 58, 1970, 36f.) and L. Marin ("Women at the Tomb", p. 92 above) show how the discursive figure is often focused on its own transmission in such a way that "the words become things".

13. Our analysis is based entirely on L. Marin's "Le discours de la figure", *Critique* 270 (1969), 953-971.

14. Cf. L. Marin, *ibid*, 970. The accuracy of the metonymic transformations also depends on this rule of reading. Its transgression explains why W. Marxsen's formula, "*Die Sache Jesu geht weiter*", appears to be unable to transcribe the scripture of the resurrection. To say: "The cause of Jesus continues" does not account for the figure inscribed in the text.

15. 2 Peter 1:19 (see the text, p. 201). 1 Cor. 13:12: "Now we look obscurely into a *mirror*, but then it will be face to face." 2 Cor. 3:18: "We all with unveiled *faces* reflect the glory of the Lord as in a *mirror*; we are *transformed* into this image...."

16. M. Foucault, *Théorie d'ensemble*, 13.

17. Cf. R. Barthes, *Communications* 12 (1968), 108-114.

18. G. Vahanian, *La Condition de Dieu*, Paris: Seuil, 1970, 80-83.

19. In the trinitarian formula worked out in a Hellenistic context during the Third and Fourth centuries, this

alterity is revealed by a remarkable paradigm in the formulation of the triune God. The Father is not the Logos, although these two are "consubstantial". The Holy Spirit, the third term, is neither the one nor the other, and yet it is "consubstantial" with them. The latter exists as a paradigmatic projection on the syntagmatic succession of the formulation.

20. T. Todorov, *Communications* 8 (1966), 141f.

21. The "hymns" (2 Tim. 2:11) have the same function. The whole Law is found in the interaction of two "commandments" (to love God/neighbor); and the rabbis combine all the Scriptures, like certain texts of the New Testament, in the enunciation: "God is one."

22. These three phenomena are also common in the Old Testament. The "historical" structure of the Covenant can be converted into the odysseys of Wisdom (or the Spirit) connecting man to the "beginning"--which have a logical character, even when a segment of the "history" of Israel appears in the story.

23. J. Derrida, "La différance".

24. J. Kristeva, *Théorie d'ensemble*, 90.

25. M. Foucault, *Théorie d'ensemble*, 19.

26. Ph. Lacoue-Labarthe, "La fable (littérature et philosophie)", *Poétique* 1 (1970), 56ff.

27. The formula is from R. Barthes, *S/Z*, [Eng. trans.], 61.

28. Cf. J. Derrida, *Théorie d'ensemble*, 45-51.

29. According to Khlebnikov, the puppet "sunshine" would not make sense if the true sun disappeared (*Poétique* 1, 1970, 110). If the operation was not successful in the reading of the Eucharistic narrative, the image of the reader would be "fantastic" (cf. J. P. Sartre's little story quoted by T. Todorov, *The Fantastic* [Eng. trans.], 174); but it is not.

30. It is therefore not necessary to resort, as scholasticism has done in a Hellenistic problematic, to the

operants which are the "sign" and the "symbol" (*signum/res/res tantum*, etc.). The "thing" always escapes. Semiotic analysis permits us, on the other hand, to break loose from these hierarchical structures and to arrive at a meaningful truth outside of them, i.e. its production (not a simple indefinite exchange).

31. Cf. Louis Marin, "Women at the Tomb", pp. 83-86 above and *idem*, "Le discours de la figure", 964-966.

32. According to the analysis of A. J. Greimas, *Du sens*, 66f.

33. *Ibid*, 112.

34. In the sense referred to by the quotation in note 1 above.

35. A. J. Greimas, *Du sens*, 112.

36. R. Barthes, *S/Z*, [Eng. trans.], 62-63.

37. Cf. J. Kristeva, *Théorie d'ensemble*, 94, 299, 303f., 309ff., 315.

38. One need only refer here to the studies by Claude Chabrol, chaps. III and VII, L. Marin, "Jesus before Pilate", chap. VI, and G. Vuillod, "Exercises on Some Short Stories", chap. IV above.

39. L. Marin, "Le discours de la figure", 964-968.

40. The *Law* is articulated in "history" (i.e. in an historical preamble--which refers to the creed--presented as a preliminary blessing from God). The "legal" apparatus (on the plane of the appearing) refers to the decision to conjugate which is the Covenant (the plane of being). The (Covenant) Code "comes" from God by the mediation of an assumed "history"--for the purpose of assuming the (present/future) contingency of an historically situated context. The Law has no other purpose. It is an open system which has, like every true form, a closed appearance.

41. L. Marin, "Jesus before Pilate", p. 123 above.

42. This retributive schema can apparently have other meanings, for example (if one is permitted to consider the absurd)--one can compare the two opposing statements from

Mtt. 6:14f. ("If you do not forgive, you will not be forgiven") and 5:38 ("It has been said to you: An eye for an
eye...; but I say to you..."--the logic of the "same" must
be broken). The key is found in Mtt. 5:48 ("Be perfect as
your Father..."). Nevertheless, the schema of the "same"
often indicates the presence of a marginal code. In this
way one can explain the redundancy of v. 31 to v. 26 in
the narrative of "Jesus before Pilate" which was noted by
Louis Marin, p. 102 above (the derision sequence would not
belong to the kernel of the narrative).

43. One can almost call them "literary genres", cf.
Guy Vuillod, p. 47 above. The transmitter uses the "genre"
which has the meaning-effect he desires, but there is always a difference. The disjunction between *political* (temporal)/*eternal* noted by L. Marin ("Jesus before Pilate"),
seems to us to belong to "religion", not to the performance
accomplished which is (for the "author" and the "reader")
the "word" in question ("All power *comes* from 'above'").
Or else, the categories of religion, the sacred, etc. only
enter into the Scripture in a relevant way to the extent
that a competence is accomplished/excluded by the performance of the "word".

44. T. Todorov, *Communications* 8 (1966), 136-138.

IX

A CONCLUSION

by

Louis Marin

In conclusion, we would like to pose three questions
which are related and intertwined with one another to such
an extent that they may appear to be repetitious. They form
the intersecting point of one problematic which is itself in
the process of being questioned. These questions which we
are formulating, without concealing their hypothetical character, deal with three apparently unconnected problems: 1) the
position of the reader with respect to his text or the status
of the discourse on the biblical text; 2) the position of the
biblical text with respect to mythical discourse, as far as
their respective analyses are concerned; 3) and finally, the
position of semiological and psychoanalytic discourse with
respect to the biblical text. We think that these three
questions are mutually related to one another to the extent
that the reading position which the biblical text requires
defines it as different from the mythical narrative and at
the same time requires a kind of analysis which would be
appropriate to the mythical narrative. Finally, semiological
discourse, by reverting to the text itself, shows its similarity to certain forms of psychoanalytic discourse.

However, we must emphasize above all that this problematic only begins to receive its meaning and importance with
the first analyses of the texts, their difficulties, their
unintelligibilities, or their strengths. By segmenting them,

233

we run the risk of appearing to possess a philosophical super-
structure which exegetes as well as semioticians are justified
in rejecting. Therefore one must consider this as a preliminary and tentative reflection on some enterprises which are
themselves tentatively executed in the texts which appear to
us (in a still intuitive and confused way) as constituting a
"proto-semiotic". It is a "pre-semiology" which is certainly
aware of itself but which aims at another purpose and expresses
itself in a non scientific practice. That does *not* mean that
semiology has the pretention of being a scientific practice.
Perhaps it is in fact the last form of this semiology (which
is no doubt unrecognizable) which the biblical text produces
as it develops. It appears to us that to define this problematic concerning some fundamental questions as broadly as possible is a useful contribution to this investigation.

There is one last remark to be made. The "we" used in
these pages neither designates [p. 120] a party, club, nor
sect as the diversity of the enclosed articles clearly shows.
It does not designate the spokesman for a collective subject.
It is a "we" which signifies an "I" who is participating in
his turn in a research group whose only common interest is
the biblical text.

I

What is the discursive position of the careful reader of
the biblical text? This is perhaps the preliminary question
of every structural analysis which is attempted. By the discursive position, I mean the status of the discourse that the
reader conducts with the text which he is reading. Speaking
of a language object, it is not enough to say that this discourse is metalinguistic and thus occupies the status of

exteriority or transcendance with respect to the object
studied. This is because this object is still a language,
and it is a language of the same nature as that discourse
which one uses to discuss it. Even if these discourses are
deployed at different levels, this homogeneity creates some
bonds and a complicity which it is impossible not to express
in a thematic form in the metalinguistic discourse itself--
and in no other text more than the biblical text. This is
all the more true since one will find some metalinguistic
positions in the text which will show that the text has already begun to produce its own reading and has already begun
to comment on itself at the very time when it was formulated.
The discursive position of the reader signifies therefore the
nature, form, and structure of the relationships which exist
between the primary discourse (or the narrative which is read
in this text) and the reading itself of the narrative to the
extent to which it is uttered in the discourse. A second
definition is therefore necessary. By "careful reader", I
mean the one who refuses the naïve action of a simple reading
with the grain [or woof] of the text. A "careful reader" is
one who questions the text, that is to say *re*reads it. And
by this rereading he studies and works on it. Consequently
he agrees to listen to the reminders and multiple echoes
which lead him to some depths where it seems what he has read
the first time is broken up and regrouped without ever being
resolved. This reader must accept a twofold constraint. To
be sure there is that which originates from the object of
reading which he constructs by his reading, but which determines it in turn and limits it by some impassable and insur-
mountable injunctions which belong to this text and which, in
essence, would not refer to another text but to a hybrid
existence between the concrete and abstract and the singular

and general, or to a model or a class of texts where this text would disappear. The reading is, however, a construction of an object, and as such, it is regressively and progressively *constitutive* at the same time.

And we can see a double epistemological problem beginning to appear here which is anthropological and transcendental at the same time. 1. *The Anthropological Problem:* One of the aspects of the problem of interpretation is that it is called exegesis or literary criticism. A screen (which is also the code that the culture to which he belongs offers to him and imposes on him) is interposed between the text and the reader without his knowledge by a mystification of which he is the first victim. Deciphering the text then amounts to unwittingly coding the reading. The very movement by which the text is "understood" is hidden by its understanding, unless taken from a new [p. 121] cultural or historical perspective. This reading is read (that is to say deciphered) in its turn thanks to a secret code which it would be necessary to know once again. And the *ad infinitum* movement of interpretation would begin which is nothing else than that by which cultures (the cultural stages or the groups within a culture) offer their products of thought, and exchange them in an endless permutation. Every decoding of one by another is a coding for a third, etc. Is it possible to set the constitution of the relationships of meaning over against this infinity of interpretation, assuming: (1) that the meaning of a textual element is defined by its function, that is by its possibility of entering into correlation with other elements of the text and with the text as a whole; and (2) that these correlations are finite in number? There is indeed a fundamental problem posed here, which is created by this double methodological decision, because in the name of what principles shall I arrange the constellation of correlations?

Aren't these articulations of the text culturally determined? Aren't they already interpretations? And, on the other hand, what fundamental arithmetic in this particular text will determine the finite number of significant correlations?

2. *The Transcendental Problem:* In fact, the only possibility left in the validity of the opposition of meaning and interpretation consists of applying it to the transcendental sphere of the constitutive reading and to the *a priori* possible circumstances of the textual object in its significance. This is the second aspect of the epistemological problem and the second visage of the constraint which affects the reading. This second aspect is that of a transcendental subject and a source of objectivation by categories, laws, and schemes of operation by which, in the name of an objectivity transcendentally justified, this singular empirical object (which is the text) is dissolved. It is dissolved because it is not at this fundamental level that *this* text is read and articulated in its meaning. The forms and transcendental logical relationships only assure its conditions of possibility, that is its foundations in the exercise of reading or constitution of the text. The constitution of the text is continuing at another hierarchically subordinate plane which is empirically and culturally invested with particular significations. These significations are divided according to diverse levels of a constitution organically determined by some particular science and some appropriate field of knowledge. Now, this is indeed the key problem which the second type of constraint poses here. What are the relationships existing between the transcendental and empirical or between the possibilities of the constitution of the text and this constitution itself? How can the interpretation in its "culturality" and its psychological and ideological forms be estab-

lished in a transcendental form of meaning. This is the
problem which Cassirer posed in his *Philosophy of Symbolic
Forms* and which is encountered for example in the iconology
of Panofsky or the artistic sociology of Francastel (which
is so similar to a visual semiology). This is the problem
which the "sociology" of the text encounters in its customary
undertaking. Is it possible to deduce the texts, and more
generally all the cultural forms, just like Kant deduced the
characteristic forms of the signification of the spirit from
the Aristotelian table of categories?

How do we break away from this constraint without condemning ourselves to the relativistic odyssey of the meaning;
and is it not necessary for the meaning, in order to be reproduced, to be enclosed by an interaction of constraints?
Must one then [p. 122] endlessly multiply the compositions
of the object to as many profiles as the careful reader would
draw, and which would refer to an ultimate perspective of
objectivity of this text, its "concrete universal"? This
superimposition or putting into perspective of the outlines
or partial structures produced and constructed between "reading" and "read" could be called the meaning of this text.
But such an hypothesis or "representation" of the analytic
task of reading would imply that the meaning may be ideally
composed, prior to every reading, as an innate "telos" and
that it would be necessary to attempt to connect the text
and its reading together again without ever hoping to make
one equivalent to the other. Can one save such a representation? The meaning is perhaps not the focal point of this
putting into perspective of the patterns of reading, even if
this focal point is a point of escape, but this putting into
perspective itself. Or if the expression with its metaphor
alludes too much to the *legitimate* construction of visible

space, the meaning is perhaps this profusion or infinite proliferation which is that a text is open at the very beginning to other texts and that it finds expression in itself, as we have often had the occasion to observe. There is a principle of non-limitation in this opening which does not exclude some rules and laws without which everything could then be read in anything at all. But don't we find then the difficulties which the "second constraint" poses? Unless the object or the biblical text itself implies the rules according to which it must be read and understood and by which it opens itself, not only to other texts of the biblical corpus, but to the very reading in which it is taken up and composed.

But this is not to make this text a privileged text and to transfer to it and into it what we have taken by choice from the transcendental. This is because the biblical text possesses its own norms of construction and production in itself. To this extent, one would be justified in reading the word of God as an outcropping of the transcendental. It is a spherical text without fissures which generates its own reading. The privilege of this text will only be able to be construed as a text provided that the reading is a part of the text. But then, isn't it rather *the opposite which is produced*? Fixed once and for all, the text becomes denser from all its readings and by a law which belongs to it. By endlessly obtaining meaning, it will be overshadowed for that very reason. It will be hidden in its meaning. The composition and contraction of the meaning will then be contemporaneous with the reading, and this is the way by which the living reader enters into his object by reading it. But does what is perceived so strongly in the biblical text—and in an "impure" way by the extreme overdetermination of this object for the western reader—not appear in every text?

The constraints of the text and the reader are contrary constraints. But they are combined in the space of the biblical text. The reader and readings are included in the text whose marks or signals one should find in the narrative which we are reading. Basically we find the first of the methodological decisions which we alluded to above: that a text *creates* some correlations between its elements and totality and that this creation reveals the rules for its reading with regard to each text. The self-composition of the text or its closure lies there. But its *infinitude*--and thereby we reject the second choice--defines what one could call the *principle of uncertainty* of the reading, which should not be confused [p. 123] with the relativism of subjectivity or the culture. As the reading adds to the signified by an articulation different from the signifier of the text that the text requires, so the text conceals the signified at another point of its surface. This uncertainty signifies the impossibility of stopping this movement between the signifier and signified. This is a movement which belongs to the reading and of which the gospel text gives us the exemplary form in the parable: "Why do you speak to them in parables? ... ... To you it has been given to know the secrets of the Kingdom of God. For to him who has, more will be given, but to him who has not, even what he has will be taken away. That is why I speak to them in parables, because seeing they do not see and hearing they do not hear, nor understand....Therefore every scribe who becomes a disciple of the Kingdom of Heaven is like an owner who draws something new and old from his treasure" (Mtt. 13:10-13 and 13:52).

II

Can we apply the methods and procedures of structural analysis (which have been scientifically proven on myths) to the biblical text and especially to the New Testament text? In other words, does the biblical text belong to the mythical category? This is the question dogmatically posed, because it presupposes a canonical definition of myth as a yardstick against which one can measure the biblical text. Perhaps it would be advisable to dismiss it or at least not to make it a preliminary question? It is no doubt because it was discarded as a preliminary question that exegetes and semioticians have been able to meet and work together on the biblical text. But to defer this question from now on is tantamount to specifying at the end of the research—impractically as an answer and not as a problem— a research which will apparently assume the problem to be resolved since it will apply (according to diverse modalities, which vary according to the researchers) the methods and procedures of structural analysis. We will quickly find, however, that the biblical text resists a mechanical application of models worked out in the greatest generality from narratives supplied by folk, classical, or scholarly literature. This is the reason for our *complexification* of the explanatory models, the construction of new strategic plans of use, the refinement of the transformational rules, etc. But has this method (which has been guided for a long time by the epistemology of the physical sciences) not led to that theoretical moment when the multiplication of the models with their increased complexity (by extremely fragmenting the epistemological field) requires either a change in the way of constructing the problematic or a

change in the level of its use. In short, it causes them to
question their very use and sets in motion a critical reflection of the practice about itself. The biblical text would
then be a privileged text since it would offer a concrete
epistemological test to the semiotician of the models of
explanation taken from somewhere else, and (as a repercus-
sion) a concrete test of the techniques of applying these
models to texts for which they are constructed.

What causes this resistance and in what perspective
must we [p. 124] study the specific characteristics of the
biblical text? If it resists the direct application of
models worked out for folktales, fables, or myths, this is
no doubt because of the importance which discourse receives
in the texts studied, especially those texts from the New
Testament. By discourse we mean the linguistic ensembles
which do not belong to the pure narrative, but are related
to the teaching, preaching, proclamation, and confession.
It is a discourse held by some characters of the narrative
with other characters whose presence demands that special
attention be given to the syntactic and semantic structures
of the dialogue or to the articulation of the "I-you" relationship within the narrative structure. But these discourses themselves are composed, on the one hand, from implicit or explicit quotations of another discourse held at
a moment prior to the narrative or even in another text.
They are quotations which are often used by the subjects
of statements in order to describe, characterize, or relate
the episode or the situation which is the very object of
the narrative which we are reading. Therefore it seems
that the narrative studied is divided or torn by a mode of
speech which does not belong to the narrative, although
this *parole* may belong to it. It refers to other *paroles*
or to other narratives where these *paroles* are enclosed,

but some of them were *already* in the process of stating this text which we are reading in a certain way. In other words, the biblical New Testament text poses the problem of articulation to the narrative in a systematic way. It also poses the problem of a discourse which to some extent goes along with it and to another extent goes against it, namely the *prophetic discourse*. Can one conduct the analytical study of this articulation with the powerful means which the linguistic models offer to an enlarged semiology which is more interested in what the underlying systems of the narrative would be (apparently, the diachronic combinative of the elements) than in the way in which the narrative manifestation is uttered in its successiveness? One will perceive the methodological angles of attack in the different studies of this collection, which are more complementary than opposing, from which this fundamental problem seems to me to be approached. But it was not worth the effort to do it by an abstract reflection about the methods and procedures as others will make use of them. It was worth the trouble to reject the division of scientific work for the moment in order to confront the texts directly with the presumption that the taste alone would justify endangering at the same time a perhaps decisive test for the structural method and the biblical text itself.

One research perspective (whose complexity and importance of which one only catches a glimpse) will be to perceive the ensemble of these texts as narratives intended for teaching, preaching, and proclamation. But one must perceive them as such neither from the outside because the tradition of the interpretive biblical commentary is one of the basic "native" traditions of western thought—nor because a certain knowledge of this tradition preexists in

the subconscious memories of the researchers even before their
research work begins. Certainly all this unconscious sedimen-
tation exists. He must not only forget it, but he must make
it reappear. If he does not, it will dangerously filter into
the interstices of a metalinguistic discourse (which will
want to be scientific) so as to split it and deny it every
scientific pretention. However, it is in the analysis of
the text itself and in the immanence of the [p. 125] careful
reader that it will be advisable to present, at the level of
what one calls the *narration*, the signs and traces of a transmission of the *parole* and a beginning of the message and the
signs and traces of its reception in the multiple hearing of
the meaning transmitted. That is precisely the diverse or
possible meaning which is formed in this distance covered
from mouth to ear, from text to text, from the written text
to the text read, or from the text in its discourse to the
discourse which takes place in the text during its reading.
It is therefore a matter of understanding the situations of
the *parole*, not by referring to a history or a tradition, nor
by a dubious return to an author (which/who is characterized
by a style or a literary form) but due to their inscription
in a textuality or what some will call the problem of codes,
decoding, and transcribing. No doubt the meaning is only
realized and grasped in, by, and through this mutual reflection of the codes. But this is more than an activity of
trans-position or of *trans-lation* [*tra-duction*] and more than
an intra-semiotic interaction, understood as a development
through a dictionary, even if it were multilingual. It is a
question of a *pro-duction* [Ed. note: Marin is here making a
wordplay between the words of pro*duction* and tra*duction*.] of
meaning, not only by a new combination discovered by the application of a new grid of decoding but by a real creation

of reading. Each reading puts the meaning into motion or
"sets it on its way" in a specified direction.

III

What justification can be given for the use in certain
studies of a vocabulary with a psychoanalytic connotation?
The question can only appear to be one of style, and the
answer demands that one accept this concession to a usage
or a way of speaking which is nothing else than the banaliza-
tion of a specialized lexicon. In fact, there is nothing to
it, and the justification demanded leads one to pose a problem which is fundamental to semiology and psychoanalysis with
respect to the biblical text and by it. We could formulate
it in the following way: Is the psychoanalytical model of
understanding and interpretation a model hierarchically
subordinate to the one which defines the *a priori* conditions
of possibility of the signification in their greatest generality and in their strictest formalism? Or does it provide
the concepts and operations necessary to every interpretation
in general and to an interpretation of the biblical text in
particular? But if this is true, what price must psychoanalysis pay for this methodological displacement--and should
it do so--and how is the latter articulated in the biblical
text, in a semantic, and in a conjunction which may not be a
foundation? The reading of the biblical text--and perhaps
that of every text--is simultaneously apparent to us as an
exhibition *and* withdrawal of the meaning in the interaction
of the signifier and signified along the narrative line. The
meaning appears to us in the text as always acquired to *excess*, an excess balanced by a breakdown of the meaning at one

point of the discourse—and a loss or a neutralization at
another point. This is the *infinitisation* of the reading
since the latter has never stopped controlling this loss of
meaning by the production of another meaning. The biblical
text, and more precisely the gospel text, presents this
process of production and loss of the meaning in the narrative in a privileged way as if the object about which it is
speaking could only be continually replaced and could henceforth only [p. 126] depict the appearance of meaning through
the narrative in the form of a *parole*. Basically the gospel
text, as a narrative, would show us the substitution of the
parole for this object. This would be the narrative which
it would present to us and which it would be a matter of
understanding. The long ceremony of putting to death the
Son of Man which *follows* in the narrative syntagm the establishment of the ritual by which this ceremony (or its
acme) is commemorated (which is therefore explicitly the
announcement of it and a running commentary on it) is in
some way the anamnesis of an event which has already taken
place at a moment of this ceremony which has never been
perceived as one of its moments. But at the same time, it
is the realization of it because this moment has been (at
the same time and inexplicably) event and *parole* or an event
of *parole*. In other words, everything takes place as if the
same event appears at several points in time in the narrative in order to reduce and reverse it. The prediction has
already taken place. The announcement has already occurred
and conversely—paradoxically—what now takes place is a
prediction from the past. And this can only be, to make it
comprehensible, a kind of decoding. This past was therefore
an event—the advent of the Word. This long ceremonial putting to death of the "hero" finds its conclusion (even before

its beginning) in the eucharistic meal in which what is eaten
is indeed the "hero". But it is not his flesh but his word
become flesh which is substituted as a body for the body.
Henceforth it is lost in every sense of the word. The
referent of the discourse has disappeared because the discourse itself has become its own referent as a message. It
is because there is this absence or this disappearance that
there is meaning which the discourse comes to display. It
takes itself as an object in order endlessly to fill in this
disappearance as its focal point which forms what it cannot
say about something else but only about itself because this
other has become a "body-discourse", that is a body absent
and present as a message. It is because there is this lack
that the endless movement of reading can begin. But we have
indeed understood it: *the object is lost in the discourse
in order not to be reunited with this lost object*. By being
uttered, the reading loses it at the same time that it finds
it, since it *incessantly repeats the message by which the
object is lost*, and since the discourse has seen it disappear
by entering into its immanence of language. The text in its
infinite reading is a production of the meaning as *significance* which is a withdrawal of the meaning as a reference.
But this is also precisely the event of the central word in
the Scripture by which the focal point as a *missing* object
is substituted as a message, message for message....It is
finally the death of the Son in a meal or in a judicial,
theological-political ceremony which is first an exchange
composed of words. It is a death which is established in a
verbal utterance where the word of an absence, which is re-
iterated and repeated, is given as a substitute for a departed body. The "religious", "textual", and "psychoanalytic" are thus the three poles of this methodological field

which opens a reflection on the analysis of the gospel text. This is because the religious pole exists only in a textuality, and this textuality in which the religious pole is produced is drawn from this lack of the object, from this disappearance of the referent, and from the Father in the Son substituted as a Message of the Spirit. That is to say, this lack becomes this text which is commented upon, decoded, and in one word, *read* from the beginning. These three poles are not at all identical. But where the same structure is shown to be a law of the exchange of the discourses which occur and which no [p. 127] doubt the end of scripture would define since it is a text, holy scripture, and outline and since it is only established as such in the three *moments* of the methodological triangle in a reading or a decoding. "The art of understanding has its focal point in the exegesis or interpretation *of the traces of human existence* contained *in the scripture.*"

It follows that one possible formalization of this law is the model of the elementary structure of signification or "representation" of the possible *a priori* conditions of the manifestation of the meaning. It controls the "semiological" exchange on the epistemological level or the "inter-production" of three (religious, literary, and psychoanalytic) discourses. These are three discourses whose intersection defines a unique object which they produce, each in their own way, but which never "exists" except in their intersection. No doubt it is the privilege of the biblical text--its specific characteristic--which displays this interaction more clearly than any other text. And it does so for two reasons. The first reason is that this text is, by itself alone, a tradition and one of the sources (but not original source) of every western textual production. Because it provides (as it were) a model to some extent, it is consequently not surprising that the analysis of texts in general more obviously goes back to it. The second reason is that the biblical text has this very interaction for an object. The generative text, author, "father" (who is substituted for the Father as Word), and the Message show themselves to be the transmitter in the commentary which it gives of itself.

Philosophical hypotheses of work and special hypotheses which are only accountable to their "author" but which it would be appropriate to note before starting with the analysis itself, the careful reading of the texts, because they specify one text (in the infinity of texts) where the reading will be immediately and necessarily semiological: the semiological readings would not result from a decision or a choice but from the most apparent structure itself of a particular text which thus occupies this exceptional position of being an object and model of reading at the same time. The most limited consequence of this methodological necessity will be the increased importance accorded to what one could call the "factual" structure of the text. It is on this plane and in this area that one can grasp the passage (which has perhaps always and already begun) from the referential object to the textual object where the syntagmatic structures link the signs into their ordinal position in the discourse and display the signs of the transmission and reception of the message. In short, they define it as a *parole*-event, a Word made flesh.

GLOSSARY OF FORMALIST-STRUCTURALIST TERMS

The American (or British) reader of this work (and structuralist literature in general) may feel that he is confronted with a formidable task. Not only is the vocabulary foreign to him because the discipline is new and the biblical scholar is more familiar with German rather than French hermeneutics, but the structuralists themselves seem to delight in coining neologisms which appear to defy translation into English. If that were not enough, they often use well-known terms with a meaning quite different from customary usage. Indeed the structuralist vocabulary may be described as a conglomeration of highly technical terms drawn from a wide variety of disciplines, countries, and time-periods. Its temporal range, for example, extends from the rhetoric and poetics of Aristotle, through the Russian Formalists, to the very latest terms of the American and French linguists, Noam Chomsky, Roman Jakobson, E. Benvéniste, Louis Hjelmslev, *et al.* One may also throw in many obscure and rare words drawn from psychologists, grammarians, and literary critics of every conceivable viewpoint.

However, I empathize with the reader learning this vast, perplexing, and foreign vocabulary for the first time, and I am going to try to remedy this problem by giving a list of some definitions which I have collected for my own use over the past three years. I would not have the reader think, however, that I have created these definitions myself.

I am merely compiling them here, and practically every one of them has been given by someone else. Although I have attempted to give credit in every case to the scholars who created them, there were a few cases where I paraphrased them to such an extent that I felt it best not to attribute them to their original source for fear of distorting that scholar's position. Moreover, each structuralist tends to use each of these terms in his own way, and therefore the reader cannot be certain that these definitions are universally valid for every structuralist writing he may encounter. This is also why I have attempted to give the reader the widest possible variety of definitions for each term.

In most cases the definitions are cited word for word from the source indicated (but only the scholar's last name is given). Moreover, I have attempted to cite these definitions from the "primary" sources for each term, but in many cases (for various reasons) they are drawn from (hopefully) reliable secondary sources, e.g. William O. Hendricks. I have *not* used M. Pei and F. Gaynor's *Dictionary of Linguistics* nor M. Pei's *Glossary of Linguistic Terminology* merely because most of the structuralist terms post-date these two dictionaries. Occasionally I have used Karl Beckson and Arthur Ganz's *Literary Terms*, rev. ed., New York: Farrar, 1975 (abbreviated here Beckson and Ganz) only because it had been recently revised and included a few terms which I could not find elsewhere. However, a really adequate and up-to-date linguistics dictionary appears to be as non-existent as it is needed. There is a structuralist dictionary (encyclopaedia is actually a better description) of technical terms in French by O. Ducrot and T. Todorov, *Dictionnaire Encyclopedique des*

Sciences du Langage, Paris: Seuil, 1972, 470 pp., but it
remains untranslated to date. My goal here has not been to
create anything comparable. Instead I have only attempted
to present an aid for the reader wishing to "digest" this
book. Thus I have *not* in any way tried to create a definitive, exhaustive, or authoritative structuralist vocabulary.

With this purpose in mind, I trust that the original
authors of these definitions will forgive me if I have
failed to give the complete citations for the books and
articles from which these definitions were taken. I also
hope that I have not paraphrased them to such an extent
that the definitions were over-simplified or distorted.
But in any case these risks seemed to be small in comparison to the benefits gained by the reader who hopefully will
now be encouraged to venture into those works whose vocabulary had previously intimidated him.

Finally, I would like to give my criteria for the terms
I have chosen to include and those which are omitted. The
reader will not find those terms here which can be found in
a "good" dictionary such as *Webster's Collegiate Dictionary*
(latest ed.)—when the definitions found therein seemed
useful for the literature. I have included some terms
which are not properly "structuralist" but are often found
in the literature and seemed unusual, obscure, or rare (to
me with a New Testament specialty). These latter terms can
be recognized by their source, *The Oxford English Dictionary*
(abbreviated O.E.D.). I have also given more extensive
definitions for those terms whose importance seemed to demand more explanation than others. No doubt some will
claim that I have omitted some important terms, and others
will say that I have included some that should be omitted.

Despite the fact that such judgments are dependent upon each reader's own knowledge or ignorance of the subject, I would probably agree with them in most cases. I am only claiming to present those terms which I felt compelled to record for my own usage during the past three years. In short, these are some of the terms which I have encountered and the definitions I have found for them. My rationale for sometimes presenting them in binary oppositions, i.e. with both the term itself and its complement or antonym appearing together by a slash mark, is that this is in agreement with the structuralists' own assertions that isolated words are meaningless. I should also add that I have purposively avoided defining some terms, e.g. Derrida's difference/differance dichotomy, because I have yet to find anyone willing to do so. I simply do not wish to venture where "others fear to tread", especially when Derrida himself claims that his terms are undefinable!

Alfred M. Johnson, Jr.

actant (and actantial) -- (see pp. 8-9 above).

affabulation -- (*L'affabulation*) -- the juxtaposition of events.

aleatory -- chosen at random.

algorithm -- "a series of sentences whose predicate-functions simulate linguistically an ensemble of oriented behavioral activities" (< Greimas).

allocution -- a formal, official, or authoritative exhortation or address.

allomotif -- those motifs which occur in any given motifemic context. Allomotifs bear the same relationship to motifemes as the allophones to phonemes and allomorphs to morphemes (< Dundes).

alterity -- a being otherwise; the state of being other or different; diversity; "otherness" (< O.E.D.).

"alternated" -- the first being interrupted by the second, the second by the first, etc.

alternation -- when two independent--or nearly independent--plots are developed simultaneously (and alternatively) within one text (< Aristotle and Todorov).

anacoluthon -- "A sentence which does not maintain a consistent grammatical sequence. In the following sentence, which contains an example of the fabled dangling participle, the subject is *water* when it should be Hotchkiss: 'Going down for the third time, the water closed over Hotchkiss's head.'" (< Beckson and Ganz); a violation of grammatical sequence, as for the sake of energy or to express strong emotion.

anagnorisis -- "a transition from a state of ignorance to a state of knowledge" (< Aristotle).

anagogical -- In a letter to his patron Can Grande della Scala, Dante explained the way in which *The Divine Comedy* should be read. The reader, he said, should be aware of four levels of meaning: (1) the *literal* or *historical*, that which actually occurs; (2) the *moral meaning*; (3) the *allegorical*, the symbolic significance which pertains to mankind; and (4) the *anagogical, the spiritual or mystical meaning stating an eternal truth*. Dante adds that all except the first level may be called "allegorical".

The technique of the fourfold interpretation was widespread in medieval criticism. Cassian (ca. 400) was perhaps the first to interpret the Scriptures according to the levels which Dante later refers to. In his Moralia on the Book of Job, Pope Gregory I likewise demonstrated how this device of exegesis could be employed. Later, secular poetry was also subjected to this method. (< Beckson and Ganz).

anamnesis -- a psychological term meaning: a reproducing in memory or a recollection.

anaphoric -- means "pointing backwards" or referring to some previously mentioned items.

anomie (sometimes spelled: *anomy*) -- "a state of society
in which the norms of conduct are disappearing and dis-
orientation prevails" (< Durkheim). Lévi-Strauss used the
term "entropy" to replace Durkheim's *anomie*.

antagonists -- agents with different, incompatible, or in-
consistent purposes.

anteposition -- (on p. 218).

antikeimena -- (see p. 24, n. 12 above).

aphorisms -- literary texts that consist of only one single
sentence.

aporia -- "A passage in speech or writing incorporating
or presenting a difficulty or doubt" (< *Webster's Third
New International Dictionary*).

applied science -- when the machinery of theoretical
science is applied to work out practical problems.

archetype -- "an invariable nucleus of meaning universally
present in man's unconscious" (< C. G. Jung). Lévi-Strauss
believes that Jung's conception of the archetype as possessing a certain signification is "comparable to the long
supported error that a sound may possess a certain affinity
with a particular meaning: for instance the 'liquid' semi-
vowels with water, the open vowels with things that are big,
large, loud, or heavy, etc." (< Lévi-Strauss).

armature -- a combination of properties that remain invariant
in two or several myths (< Lévi-Strauss); "that which refers
to the structural state of the myth as narration" (< Greimas,
def. by Hendricks).

ascendant movements (in a folktale) -- the procedures of
improvement in the situation of the hero (see also: "descendant" below).

association -- a rhetorical figure which refers to the use
of an inadequate person of the verb.

asymbolia -- "deafness to symbols" (< Barthes's).

asyndetic -- in rhetoric, the omission of conjunctions between parts of a sentence as in "I came, I saw, I conquered".
(The noun form is *asyndeton*.)

attributive statements -- (see p. 19 above).

author -- (to be differentiated from the "narrator") -- the
author is the ultimate designer of the narrative or fable.
He is the one who decides whether there *is* to be a narrator
and if so, how prominent his or her presence will be.

auto-reference -- preoccupation with itself.

axiology -- the text's static system of values (< Greimas).

"beyond the sentence" -- "The existence of grammatical
structures, within and beyond the unit of the sentence in

literary texts is undeniable, and their description and
classification are indispensable." The term "beyond the
sentence" is often used to refer to that linguistics which
explores the area "beyond" sentential grammatical structures, e.g. textual or narrative grammars (< Paul de Man).
(For further discussion see W. O. Hendricks, "On the Notion
'Beyond the Sentence'," *Linguistics* 37 [1967], 12-51.)

biographism (especially "causal biographism") -- the
theory which attempts to explain the individual literary
work by the circumstances of its creation, e.g. the *Sitz
im Leben*.

"bricks" -- a term from cybernetics which means sub-
programs as for a computer.

a byte -- a computer term which means a "basic or sub-
routine configuration in cybernetic language" (< Barthes).

cardinal functions -- These functions are parallel to
"kernels" (or the *charmières*, hinges, or turning points in
the narrative), i.e. it opens or closes an action or initi-
ates or resolves an uncertainty. Cardinal functions are
both consecutive and consequential (< Barthes). (See also
"catalysts" below.)

catalyst (or catalysts) -- catalysts are not as "important"
as the "cardinal functions". Their function is to fill in
the spaces or interstices which exist between the cardinal
functions or "hinges". They are only consecutive units.
The catalysts are indeed functional. Their discursive

function is to delay or quicken the discourse. Sometimes they even confuse the reader or purposively lead him astray. Catalysts presuppose the existence of cardinal functions but the opposite case is not true (< Barthes).

charnières (usually translated "hinges") -- according to F. Bovon, the "hinges" "show the place at which the story takes a chance by directing itself in one direction or another". The term appears to be synonymous with Propp's "functions".

cluster analysis -- to find out what goes with what and why.

code -- the pattern of functions ascribed by each myth to these properties (< Lévi-Strauss); "a formal structure which is (1) composed of a small number of semic categories and (2) whose combinatorics [or combinatives] can map out, in the form of sememes, the totality of 'content-fillings' belonging to a given dimension of the mythical universe"; also "a perspective of quotations, a mirage of structures" (< Greimas).

combinatives (or combinatorics) -- "that which has the faculty of combination, combining, or pertaining to the nature of combination; cumulative" (< O.E.D.).

competence -- an ideal grammatical knowledge or the abstract knowledge of the rules of language. Competence is parallel to Saussure's *langue* and is defined by Chomsky as "a system of rules that we can call the grammar of his [a speaker's] language". It takes the form of a finite set of rules or instructions of different types which lead to

the generation or the identification of a theoretically infinite set of correct sentences in the language in question
while also assigning a structural description to each sentence. W. G. Doty defines competence simply as "the ability
to generate utterances". Competence is often contrasted
with "performance" (see below).

comportment -- behavior or pattern of behavior.

compressions/expansions -- "compressions" = discourse-
time that is shorter than the story-time; "expansions" =
discourse-time that is longer than story-time.

concatenation -- chaining together (the term *enchainment*
also appears with this meaning).

condensation/displacement-- this binary pair originated
from Freud and corresponds respectively to the linguistic
terms: *metaphor/metonymy* (see both below).

configuration -- "the objective disposition of material
elements which are not immediately interpretable" (< G.
Genot).

connotation -- "Any determination or trait which is related
to anterior, ulterior, and exterior textual occurrences, to
other places in the text or other texts. Topically, connotations are meanings not found (provisionally) in the dictionary, nor in the grammar of the language in which the text
is written. Analytically, connotation works in two spaces--
the sequentially ordered space of the sentence and the ag-
glomerative space between the text and meanings exterior to

it. Topologically, connotation is responsible for a limited dispersion (*dissémination*) of meaning. Semiologically, connotation is the starting point of a particular code, or the articulation of a voice 'woven' into the text. Dynamically, it acts as a force by subjugating the text. Historically, connotation provides locatable meanings and institutes dated and datable meanings. Functionally, connotation introduces ambiguity into the purity of communication. Structurally, connotation and denotation form two systems allowing the text to function like a game as they refer one to another. Ideologically, this game grants the classical (readable) text a 'certain innocence' allowing denotation to appear to have a priority on meaning" (from F. Guenthner, "Review of R. Barthes', *S/Z*," *Poetics* 1 [1971], 114, on Barthes' use of the term "connotation").

consecutiveness (or sometimes *consecutivity*) -- what comes *after* (see also *propter hoc* below) (< Barthes).

consequence -- what is *caused-by* (see also *post hoc* below) (< Barthes).

context -- "The author's total consciousness. His total consciousness, therefore, must be the sum of its incarnations, or his total canon including every scrap of his writing, notwithstanding its form or genre, whether poetry or prose. The 'context' of literature is the autonomy of a writer's work, not the autonomy of any particular part of it" (< The Geneva School); "the specific social situation in which that particular item is actually employed. It is necessary to distinguish context and function. Function is essentially an abstraction made on the basis of a number of contexts. Usually, function is an analyst's statement of what (he thinks) the use or purpose of a given genre of folklore is....This is not the same as the actual social situation in which a particular myth or proverb is used" (< Dundes); "to place a text, an item of folklore in its context is not only to correlate it with one or more aspects of the community from which it came. Or if that is what 'context' means, then the new direction goes beyond a merely 'contextual' approach. It is not content to take folkloristic results on the one hand and results of other studies on the other, each independently arrived at, and then to try to relate the two after the fact. It wishes to study the relation between folkloristic materials and other aspects of social life *in situ*, as it were, where that relation actually obtains, the communicative events in which folklore is used. This concern is precisely parallel to the motivation of sociolinguistic research into the ethnology of speaking" (< Dell Hymes).

context (in relation to form) or *contextual function* -- "One cannot always tell from form alone what the associate contextual function is.....An item once removed from its social context...deprives the scientific folklorist of an opportunity to understand why the particular item was used in the particular situation to meet a particular need" (< Bascom).

contiguity (of meaning) is "a case of what is called the *cultural* as opposed to the 'linguistic' meaning of a word". "...within a limited amount of time and space, new meanings are attached to the original word. These [cultural] meanings come as a result of frequent associations between the linguistic meaning and the cultural context." In other words, words "mean the contexts in which they are usually used". These cultural meanings are called *implications* or *connotations* (< Todorov).

contraries/contradictories -- (see pp. 14-16, 24-26, n. 12 above). In brief, a "contrary" refers to a relationship of opposition (e.g. life is the "contrary" of death and vice versa) while a "contradictory" refers to a relationship of presence and absence, e.g. the "contradictory" of life is non-life (*not* death) and the "contradictory" of death is non-death (*not* life). It is of course possible to be in a state of non-life without being dead. Greimas uses these two terms in his well-known semiotic square where "contraries" are represented as horizontal axes and "contradictories" are represented by diagonal axes. (For a more extensive discussion of these terms see, A. J. Greimas, "The Interaction of Semiotic Constraints," *Yale French Studies* 41 [1969], 86-105.)

correlated content -- (see p. 11 and pp. 22-23, n. 9 above).

coupure epistémologiques -- (a French term sometimes translated "epistemological cut") -- the "cut" which marks the change of a prescientific problem into a scientific problematic.

culture/nature -- "Culture has been referred to as man's 'social heritage' and as 'the man-made part of the environment'. It consists essentially of any form of behavior which is acquired through learning, and which is patterned in conformity with certain approved norms. Under it anthropologists include all the customs, traditions, and institutions of a people together with their products and techniques of production" (< Bascom). The term culture is often used in opposition to the term nature, and it is Lévi-Strauss who elaborated this opposition. According to Greimas, "All human societies divide their semantic universes into two dimensions, culture and nature, the first [i.e. culture] defined by the contents they assume and with which they invest themselves, the second [i.e. nature] by those they reject." In other words, culture = permissable relationships, nature = unacceptable relationships.

cybernetics -- the theory of control and communication in machines and organisms.

deduction -- reasoning from the general to the particular.

deixis (adj. *deictic*) -- that which refers to the pointing role of the demonstrative pronouns (this, that) and certain adverbs (here, now--see *"hic et nunc"* below).

descendant movement (of a narrative) -- the procedures of degradation or diminution in the situation of the hero (see also *ascendant movement* above).

desis/lysis -- the terms respectively mean "complication" and "unravelling" of the plot (< Aristotle). "A *desis* is a situation which is set up with a constellation of characters which is followed by a *lysis* where a series of changes takes

place so that the final situation is the opposite of what it
was at the beginning" (< Peter Madsen).

diachronic/synchronic -- a diachronic order is an order
in which each moment can only be understood in terms of all
those which have preceded it, e.g. in a bridge game, the
meaning of any one trick depends on all the tricks before
it and cannot be understood without a knowledge of them.
The term diachronic is synonymous with the modern use of
the terms "history"·and "evolution" (< Saussure). (See
also the contrasting term "synchronic" and the compatible
term *parole* below.)

dialogue paragraph (symbol: DP) -- a textual grammatical
term which means the basic unit that can constitute a whole
dialogue or function as a constituent in a larger dialogue.

diathesis -- means simply "voice".

dictum/factum -- a "dictum" is "a saying or utterance
which is sometimes used with emphasis upon the fact that it
is a mere saying; but more often with the implication of a
formal pronouncement claiming or carrying some authority;
a thing that is generally said; a current saying; a maxim
in ancient logic, the statement in a modal proposition"
(< O.E.D.). On the other hand, a "factum" is "a person's
act or deed; anything stated or made certain; a statement
of facts or of the points in a case or controversy; a me-
morial" (< O.E.D.).

diegesis/mimesis -- According to Plato, *"diegesis"* is
"the poet speaking in his own name without trying to make

us believe that it is another who speaks"; on the other
hand, *mimesis* is "the poet speaking in the voice of the
character himself". The linguist Benveniste uses the
French terms *récit* (= narrative) for the first and *discours* (= discourse) for the second. In modern terminology
we would contrast the two as "telling vs. showing". (See
also Todorov's *story/discourse* below.)

discourse -- "the actual language in which the story is
presented to the reader (or listener)" (< Hendricks).
(See also *story/discourse* below.)

discourse-time -- the "outer-time" or the time that it
takes the audience to peruse the story.

distanciation -- "On the one hand, alienating distanciation is the attitude that makes the objectification which
reigns in the human sciences possible; on the other hand,
this distanciation...is the very condition which accounts
for the scientific status of the sciences [and] is at the
same time a break that destroys the fundamental and primor-
dial relation by which we belong to and participate in the
historical reality which we claim to construct as an object."
There are three kinds of distanciation: the distanciation
of the reader (1) from the author, (2) from the situation of
discourse, and (3) from the original audience. (For the
definition above and further discussion see Paul Ricoeur,
"The Hermeneutical Function of Distanciation," *Philosophy
Today* 17 [1973], 129-141.)

distributive functions/integrative functions --
According to Barthes, "distributional relations belong to

the same level while integrative relations straddle two levels". In Barthes' analyses, the "distributive functions" are roughly synonymous with Propp's functions (see below). These distributive functions imply metonymic relata and are functional in terms of action. Some narratives are primarily functional, e.g. folktales, while other narratives are primarily indicial, e.g. (see indexes below). On the other hand, *integrative functions* are synonymous with the "indices", "indexes", or "indicators", i.e. the personality traits of the characters, their identity, and the notations of "atmosphere", etc. Indices imply metaphoric relata and they are terms of being (not action) (< Barthes).

dominant -- "the focusing component of a work of art; it rules, determines, transforms the remaining components. It is the dominant which guarantees the integrity of the structure" (< Jakobson; for further discussion of this term see his article, "The Dominant" in *Readings in Russian Poetics*, 82-87).

dystaxy -- means "sign distortions" or the situation which occurs when the linear and logical order of a message is disturbed, e.g. when the predicate precedes the subject (< Barthes).

écriture -- French term meaning *both* "writing" *and* "scripture". For Roland Barthes, the term *écriture* means the written word or literary style in general. Unfortunately the English gerund "writing" inadequately reflects the combination of process and product which is conveyed by the French word *écriture*.

eidetic intuition -- the "seeing" or pinpointing of
general essences of the structures which are common to all
phenomena in a set.

eidons -- a plural noun which is synonymous with Propp's
"functions" (see below).

eikos -- means vraisemblance or probability and propriety.

elementary sequence -- is composed of three principle
elements:
1. a situation which opens the possibility or the
virtuality of a particular event.
2. the movement towards the realization of this
virtuality or an actuality of the virtuality.
3. the result or conclusion of this action which
ends the sequence with success or failure.
These three parts may be called: (1) initial, (2) procedur-
al, (3) terminal. Bremond's sequence is a larger unit than
Propp's function but it is a smaller term than a sequence of
functions (< Bremond).

embedding -- inserting one sequential pattern between the
narrative elements of another.

emics/etics -- (cf. the linguistic terms phonemics and
phonetics) -- "The emic approach [to folklore] is a mono-
contextual, structural one. An emic approach must deal with
particular events as parts of larger wholes to which they are
related and from which they obtain their ultimate significance,
whereas an etic approach may abstract events for particular
purposes from their contexts or local system of events, in

order to group them on a world-wide scale without essential reference to the structure of any one language or culture. *Emic* units within this theory are not absolutes in a vacuum, but rather are points in a system, and these points are defined *relative* to the system. A unit must be studied, not in isolation, but as a part of a total functioning componential system within a total culture. It is this problem which ultimately forms the basis for the necessity of handling *emics* as different from *etics*. There are three modes of *emics*: (1) *The feature mode* = Propp's function; (2) *The manifestation mode* = the elements that can fulfill a function; (3) *The distribution mode* = the positional characteristics of a particular function, i.e. where among Propp's 31 functions it appears." (< Dundes and Pike, see also *etic* below.)

emic motif (= motifeme) –– the minimum unit of the "feature mode" (see *emics/etics* above) (< Dundes).

enantia –– (see p. 24, n. 12 above).

enclave –– the pattern of embedding which transforms the paradigmatic binary relationship into a syntagmatic symmetrical relationship (< Bremond). (See also p. 70 above.)

Entfaltung –– (a German word) –– the specialized hermeneutical term for the temporal unfolding of a narrative.

enunciation –– enunciation (or *énonciation*) is often contrasted with statement (or *énoncé*) in the same way that the *parole* and *langue* or performance and competence are contrasted. Barthes also speaks of the difference between the *sujet de l'énoncé* as opposed to the *sujet de l'énonciation* (i.e. the grammatical *subject* of a statement, or the narrator, as opposed to the actual *subject* who is making the statement, or the author). (For further discussion see: Van Dijk, "On the Foundations of Poetics", *Poetics* 5 (1972), 89ff.

episteme -- "an epistemological unity [or field] that anchors and informs linguistic usage at any given time in history" (< E. W. Said).

esthetics (also spelled aesthetics) -- the science of beauty and taste.

etics/emics -- "The etic approach is *non-structural* but classificatory in that the analyst devises logical categories of systems, classes, and units without attempting to make them reflect actual structures in particular data. For Pike, etic units are created by the analyst as constructs for the handling of comparative cross-cultural data." (< Dundes. See also the term *emics* above.)

folk etymology -- (= Jakobson's "poetic etymology") -- the belief by ordinary people that similar sounds have similar meanings leading to the connection of words which are actually (linguistically) independent. Rhyme is a good example of this process when words that rhyme are thought to be related in meaning as well.

fable or fabula -- not to be confused with the genre "fable", the *fabula* (or fable) in structuralist thought is "the basic story stuff or the sum total of events to be related in the narrative or the material for narrative construction" (< S. Chatman); or "the set of events tied together which are communicated to us in the course of the work" or "what has in effect happened" (< Tomashevski).

factum/dictum -- (see *dictum/factum* above).

fictive -- This French word is ambiguous in many structuralist texts. Sometimes it means "non-referential or false, having no truth, value, etc." and sometimes it means *fictive* in the sense of a work of fiction, a narrative, or story (see the following definition).

fictive time (= French: *temporalité de l'histoire*) -- the time in the story, i.e. the actual time sequences mentioned in the narrative.

figuration -- the act or process of shaping something; also a type or symbol.

Finnish-American Historical-Geographical School (or method) -- the goal of this group was to delineate the "complete life history of a particular tale". It attempted to determine the paths of dissemination and the process of development of folkloristic materials. By assembling all the known versions of a particular tale, they sought to reconstruct the hypothetical original form of the tale. The most well-known member of this school is the American, Stith Thompson.

fixed-phrase genres -- genres in which the wording as well as the content is fairly constant.

"einfache Form" (a German term coined by A. Jolles and usually translated as "simple form") -- "an irreducible, genuine, archetypical form, an integral whole in both content and structure". There are nine so-called "simple forms": (1) *Legende* (legend), (2) *Sage* (saga), (3) *Mythe* (myth), (4) *Rätsel* (riddle), (5) *Spruch* (proverb), (6) *Kasus* (case), (7) *Memorabile* (memorabilia), (8) *Märchen* (fairy tale), (9) *Witz* (joke). Some form critics have appealed to this work (see A. Jolles, *Einfache Formen*, trans. by W. Templer and Eberhard Alsen, *Journal of the Folklore Institute* 4 [1967], 17-31). The German original was first published in 1929.

form (and content) -- "wherever there is unity or cohesion of content and form in folklore, content comes first: it gives itself its form and not the opposite. This priority is retained notwithstanding philosophical discussions as to the nature of form and content." (< V. Propp).

form and structure -- "Form is defined by opposition to a content which is exterior to it; but *structure* does not have content. It is the content itself, apprehended in a logical organization conceived as a property of reality." (For further discussion see Lévi-Strauss, "La Structure et la Forme", *Cahiers de l'institut des Sciences Economiques Appliquées* 99 [7, 1960], 3-36).

form (for the Russian Formalists) -- Form for the Russian Formalists "covers all aspects, all parts of the work, but it exists solely as a relation of the elements among themselves, of the elements to the entire work" (< Todorov).

Russian Formalism -- This school began in Russia shortly
before the Russian revolution. The Moscow linguistic circle
was created in 1915, and the St. Petersburg Society for the
Study of Poetic Language in 1916. The former group is often
called the Moscow group and the latter the *Opoyaz* group.
Roman Jakobson belonged to the first group which was primarily
composed of linguists. The second *Opoyaz* group was primarily
composed of literary critics. Both groups began a savage
polemical assault upon the orthodox Russian grammarians,
psychologists, sociologists, historians, literary critics,
etc. They drew many of their ideas from outside Russia,
especially from Saussure at Geneva and the phenomenologist
Husserl. After the revolution they formed the leading school
of grammatical and literary study in the U.S.S.R. (but only
for a short period of time). Some of the members of this
group were Eichenbaum, Shklovsky, Tomashevsky, and Tynyanov,
but presently the most famous members of this school are
Vladimir Propp and Roman Jakobson. In the early 1920's their
ideas came under attack by more orthodox Marxist writers. As
a result of this pressure, Jakobson and some others fled to
Prague, Czechoslovakia where they created what is now known
as "The Prague School". For a very brief statement of the
theses of the Russian Formalists see R. Jakobson and J.
Tynyanov's statement in *New Left Review* 37 (1966), 59-61
(these theses were originally written in 1928).

functemes -- means simply "functional semes".

functional analysis -- Propp's method in his *Morphology
of the Folktale*.

functions -- Perhaps the most important of all the structuralist terms, functions for Propp (who coined the term)

are the "recurrent constants of the [folk] tale". (For a discussion of them see pp. 5-6 above.) Quoting Propp: "First of all, [the] definition [of a function] should in no case depend on the personage [i.e. character] who carries out the function. Definition of a function will most often be given in the form of a noun expressing an action (interdiction, interrogation, flight, etc.). Secondly, an action [= function] cannot be defined apart from its place in the course of narration....*Function is understood as an act of a character defined from the point of view of its significance for the course of the action.*" Propp then summarizes his statements about the functions as follows: "1. *Functions of characters serve as stable, constant elements in a tale, independent of how and by whom they are fulfilled. They constitute the fundamental components of a tale. 2. The number of functions known to the fairy tale is limited. 3. The sequence of functions is always identical. 4. All fairy tales are of one type in regard to their structure*" (Propp, *Morphology of the Folktale*, 2nd ed., 20-23). There are 31 functions and each has a symbol: α - initial situation (this is not a function); (1) β - absentation; (2) γ - interdiction; (3) δ - violation; (4) ε - reconnaissance; (5) ζ - delivery; (6) η - trickery; (7) ϑ - complicity; (8) A - villainy; (9) B - mediation; (10) C - beginning counteraction; (11) ↑ - departure; (12) D - first function of the donor; (13) E - hero's reaction; (14) F - receipt of the magical agent; (15) G - spatial transference; (16) H - struggle; (17) J - branding or marking; (18) I - victory; (19) K - lack liquidated; (20) ↓ - return; (21) Pr - pursuit; (22) Rs - rescue; (23) o - unrecognized arrival; (24) L - unfounded claims; (25) M - difficult task; (26) N - solution; (27) Q - recognition;

(28) Ex - exposure; (29) T - transfiguration; (30) U - punishment; (31) W - wedding. Note also that Propp's function is more or less equivalent to Bremond's "sequence" (Bremond's sequence is intended to be an improvement of Propp's function), Todorov's "proposition", and Greimas's *énonce narratif simple* (= simple narrative statement), but in each of these cases there are some significant differences. E. Souriau (*Les deux cent mille situations dramatiques*) also uses the term "function" but with a different meaning, see Robert Scholes, *Structuralism in Literature*, pp. 52, 104ff.

generative grammar -- "the grammar of a language which generates all of the grammatical sentences of this language and none of the ungrammatical ones" (< Chomsky).

generative poetics -- E. Güttgemanns is attempting to create a "'generative poetics', which would be for the literary genres what a 'generative grammar' is to sentences, according to Chomsky. This generative poetics would have to show that the structures of a given 'genre' are rules of 'competence' which make possible the understanding of a text as a narrative, a parable, etc. The ultimate aim of this generative poetics would be to adjust the existential categories of Bultmann to the 'textemes', i.e. to the elementary structures which are to texts what lexemes are to elementary sentences" (< Ricoeur).

genetic (or historical) structuralism -- the sociological structuralism of Lucien Goldmann who attempts to understand literature in relation to its author and the relation between the work and the social group from which it originated, or the "equilibrium between the intellectual structures of the subject and his surroundings" (< Goldmann). Goldmann believes that there is a homological relationship between the literary structure of the narrative and the economic structure in which it was produced. Some however deny that Goldmann is a true "structuralist". (For a brief statement of Goldmann's views see "The Theatre of Genet: A Sociological Study", *The Drama Review* 12 [2, 1968], 51-61.)

The Geneva School -- Not to be confused with the linguistic school of Saussure, the Geneva School is the Swiss branch of French structuralism which "considers the literary work as dissolved in the author's consciousness whose impulse is articulation for its own sake", while the Parisian group of structuralists "takes language, and hence literature, exclusively as a system of inter-human communication" (< E. W. Said). Perhaps the best known members of the Geneva School are Jean Starobinsky and Georges Poulet. Others are Marcel Raymond, Albert Béguin, Jean Rousset, and Jean-Pierre Richard. There are other differences but this is the most important one. (For further discussion of this school see: J. H. Miller, "The Geneva School", *Critical Quarterly* 8 (4, 1966), 305-321.)

genre -- "the totality of creative works which share the same poetical system, purpose in daily life, performance forms, and musical structure" (< Propp, "Generic Structures in Russian Folklore", *Genre* 4 [3, 1971], 213). Genre can also be defined as a classificatory device invented by literary criticism to master the chaos of individual works. The term is not widely used by structuralists since Propp "showed that 'genres' cannot be used as [a] taxonomic principle because of internal inconsistencies" (< Maranda, *Structural Analysis and Oral Tradition*, xii). (See also *narrative structures* below.)

gnomic codes -- cultural codes or "references to a science or body of knowledge" (< Barthes).

grammar -- "a collection of certain linguistic forms or more precisely, of those forms of a language that do not enter into the lexicon of this language. Grammar includes the rules of formation and combination as a collection designed to describe and propogate the correct use of this language. Grammars answer the question: what does the speaker know about the phonological and syntactic structures of his language that enables him to use and understand any of its sentences, including those he has not previously heard? Grammars seek to describe the structure of a sentence in isolation from its possible settings in linguistic discourse (written or verbal) or in non-linguistic contexts (social or physical)."

grammatology -- "the science of the written sign" (< Derrida).

graphemic entities -- blank spaces between the written words or the boundaries which separate sound segments.

hermeneutical circle -- "this principle holds that the process of understanding is necessarily circular, since we cannot know a whole without knowing some of its constituent parts, yet we cannot know the parts as such without knowing the whole which determines their functions....By hermeneutical circle Romanticist thinkers meant that the understanding of a text cannot be an objective procedure in the sense of scientific objectivity, but necessarily involves a precomprehension which expresses the way in which the reader has already understood himself, his word. Therefore a kind of circularity occurs between understanding a text and understanding oneself" (< Heidegger; Ricoeur). (For an excellent discussion of this concept and its relationship to the structuralists, see W. Martin, "The Hermeneutical Circle and the Art of Interpretation", *Comparative Literature* 24 [2, 1972], 97-117.)

hermeneutics -- (see p. 31 above) -- "the art of discerning the discourse in a work" or "the theory of the operation of understanding in its relations to the interpretation of texts" (< Ricoeur).

heuresis -- the discovery of arguments.

hic et nunc -- "here and now".

history -- (two meanings) -- (1) the totality of past human actions; (2) the narrative or account which we construct of past human actions now.

homeostasis -- the maintenance and reproduction of structure or the exchange of one structure for another.

homology -- a proportional relationship involving four terms, e.g. A:B::C:D, which is read: A is to B as C is to D.

ideology -- sometimes used in its normal sense, but also as "the text's dynamic system of values" (< Greimas).

idiolect -- (adj. idiolectal) -- often contrasted with "dialect", the term idiolect is used "to represent the speech of one person talking on one subject to the same person for a short period of time" (< B. Bloch, "A Set of Postulates for Phonemic Analysis", *Language* 24 [1948], 3-46).

illocutionary acts -- "that which we do *in* speaking", i.e. ordering, questioning, denying, assuming, etc. or acts within language. As an example of an illocutionary act: "to say 'Close the door!' with the force of an order is an illocutionary act" (< Austin and Searle; example from Ricoeur). (See also *locutionary acts* and *perlocutionary acts* below.)

imbricated -- stacked one on top of another.

implication -- reasoning from the general to the general.

implicity (or "implicitness") -- entanglement, complication, or involution (< O.E.D.).

index (or indices or indicial elements) -- (see p. 61 above) -- "true semantic units. Unlike functions they refer to a signified not to an 'operation' (like the functions" (< Barthes). (For further discussion see A. W. Burks, "Icon, Index, and Symbol", *Philosophy and Phenomenological Research* 9 [4, 1949], 673-689.)

indicial analysis -- the analysis of indices (see *index* above).

induction -- reasoning from the particular to the general.

informants -- "bits of information used to identify or pinpoint certain elements of time and space. Informants, unlike indexes, do not signify implicitly. They provide pure, locally relevant data....The informant is there to authenticate the reality of the referent, to root fiction in the real world" (< Barthes).

inner story-time/outer discourse-time = the German contrast between *erzählter Zeit/Erzählzeit*. (See the contrast between story and discourse below.)

"instant of discourse" -- "the designation of the occurrence of discourse as an event" (< Benveniste).

integrative functions -- the "indices" or "indexes" or "indicators", e.g. personality traits of the characters, their identity, notations of "atmosphere", etc. (See *distributional functions* and *indexes* above.)

intertextuality -- a universe of texts in which every text is embedded, i.e. a textual context (< J. Kristeva) or "the network of relationships which links one text to other texts" (< J. M. Benoist).

inventio/dispositio -- these two terms from ancient rhetoric are roughly synonymous with Todorov's distinction between story/discourse (see below) and the Russian Formalists' distinction between fable/subject (< S. Chatman).

inversed content -- (see pp. 11; 22-23, n. 9 above).

isotopy -- "the redundant bundles of semic categories; a redundant set of semantic categories which make a uniform reading of the narrative possible: the unique reading is reached through the identification of isomorphic [i.e. comparable] levels" (< Greimas).

kernel -- a transformational linguistics term roughly equivalent to Propp's function (see *kernel sentence* below).

kernel sentence -- "basic patterns which can exist as independent tales" (< Robert A. Georges).

knot -- (especially of a story) -- that which closes, terminates or concludes the action in progress.

language (= French: *langage*) -- "an amalgam of the beliefs, customs, habits, social attitudes, and conventions that are current in the writer's milieu" (< M. Turnell). The French term *langage* includes *both langue and parole* and "the entire human potential for speech, both physical and mental" (< R. Scholes).

langue/parole -- It is best to leave these two French terms untranslated (except where *parole* has the meaning of "word" such as in the "*parole* of God"), because there is a significant difference between the terms *langue* and *langage* for the *langage = langue + parole*. The *langue* is that part of the linguistic phenomenon which is independent of any one individual utterance but which defines the general conditions which make them possible. The *langue* transcends any individual speech (or *parole*) and is not a function of the speaking subject. For Saussure, the *parole* is subordinate to the *langue* or in other words the latter controls the former. Using the chess game paradigm, the *langue* is the set of rules for the game and the *parole* is each move. Saussure's *langue/parole* dichotomy is roughly synonymous with Hjelmslev's schema/usage and Chomsky's competence/performance dichotomies. The *langue* belongs to reversible time. Its nature is *synchronic*; the *parole* is necessarily bound to non-reversible time, i.e. the diachronic (< Saussure--paraphrased); *langue* simply defined is "the language system which we use to create discourse understandable to others" (< R. Scholes).

Lansonianism -- a term coined by Roland Barthes from the name of one of his opponents, Gustave Lanson. This is the theory that "the details of a given work must resemble the author's life, the characters being the innermost being of the author, etc." (< Barthes).

legend -- the term "legend" is surprisingly of "church and Latin origin. Etymologically it signifies 'that which can be read'. In monastic usage it designated those pious texts which were read during meals or divine services." Today its meaning has radically changed so that it designates one of the *ethnic* (as opposed to analytical) genres. (See *genre* and *form* above.)

levels (linguistic and narrative) -- levels (in general) are defined in structuralist usage as "operations or a system of symbols, rules, etc. which must be used to represent expressions" (< E. Bach) or a "combinatory set of units considered as permutable with each other" (< G. Genot). There are two conceptions of *narrative levels* by Roland Barthes and A. J. Greimas respectively:

    1. *narrative levels for Barthes:* For Barthes there are three:

        (1) the level of the *functions*
            (= Propp's "functions").

        (2) the level of *actions*
            (= Greimas' "actants").

        (3) the level of *narration*
            (= Todorov's "discourse").

    2. *narrative and linguistic levels for Greimas:*
Greimas defines levels in general as "the combinatory set of units considered as permutable with each other". According to Greimas narrative and linguistic levels are related to one another and they are arranged in this way by him:

        (1) surface linguistic structures

        (2) deep linguistic structures

        (3) surface narrative structures

        (4) deep narrative structures.

Note that the narrative levels are separated from the linguistic levels and that the narrative levels are deeper than the deep linguistic structures.

lexeme -- an individual word.

lexia -- "a unit of reading; the lexia includes sometimes a few words, sometimes several sentences....All we require is that each lexia should have at most 3 or 4 meanings to be enumerated" (< Barthes, *S/Z*, 13-14).

lexis -- (not to be confused with *lexia* above or even with the plural form of that word, i.e. "lexias") -- *lexis* simply means "style".

linguistics -- "The scientific study of language. Descriptive linguistics is concerned with classifying the characteristics of a language, and comparative or historical linguistics with its development. Among the major divisions of the field of linguistics are etymology, the history of word forms; semantics, the study of the meanings of words; phonetics, the study of speech sounds; morphology, the study of the forms or inflections of words; syntax, the study of the groupings of words into sentences or units of meaning" (< Beckson and Ganz). (Hence a "linguist" is not merely someone with an aptitude for learning many different languages [don't laugh it is a common misconception], nor is linguistics to be confused with "philology", see below.)

linking and framing -- "linking" is a method of narrative construction which "presents the various deeds of a single hero", e.g. the N.T. gospels; while "framing" is a method of narrative construction which presents different stories about many different heroes, e.g. as in *One Thousand and One Nights*, *The Decameron*, and *The Canterbury Tales*.

literarity -- simply literary grammaticalness.

locutionary act -- (or a propositional act) -- "the act *of* speaking" or the act of uttering expressions. As an example of a locutionary act: "to say, 'Close the door!' *as a request* is a locutionary act" (< Austin and Searle; example from Ricoeur). (Cf. *illocutionary* and *perlocutionary acts* above and below.)

Aristotle's **logical square** — (see p. 24, n. 12 above).

logos — (not to be confused with the N.T. *logos*) — the *logos* is also a rhetorical term from Aristotle meaning "an argument".

meaning of words — "words derive meaning not from any intrinsic value a word carries inside itself, but from a double system of metaphor and metonymy that links words to each other, and gives the words fleeting intelligibility rather than detached permanence." Most "structuralists", e.g. Todorov and Barthes, claim that isolated words have no meaning at all when removed from their structural contexts. In the words of Saussure, "In language there are only differences". Hence it is only the *differences* between words that gives them meaning, with the assumption that these differences are orderly, consistent, and systematic. However, it is also true that every linguistic particle, every verbal emission, or every word conveys information of some kind. But these is never *one* meaning for a word or text, only meaning*s*.

meaning-effect — In the words of Daniel Patte, "A discourse does not *have* meaning; a discourse *is* meaningful." That is to say that the structures of the text produce what Greimas calls a "meaning-effect" on the reader, and this "meaning-effect" is different for every reader.

in medias res — means "to begin in the middle of events" or "if the normal order of the story is abc, the flashback will be acb and *in medias res* will be bc" (< Chatman).

metabasis -- means "reversal".

metafolklore -- "folkloristic statements about folklore,
e.g. proverbs about proverbs, folksongs about folksongs,
proverbs about myths, etc." An example of a metafolkloric
joke is: "Knock"--"Who's there?"--"Opportunity!" (< Dundes). *Metafolklore* is also defined as "the conception a
culture has of its own folkloric communication as it is
represented in the distinction of forms, the attribution of
names to them, and the sense of the social appropriateness
of their application in various cultural situations" (< Dan
Ben-Amos).

metalanguage -- simply "language about language" or "any
statement of a second-order language whose signified or
signifier is a sign of the first order system; a linguistic statement about language". Hence every grammar is a
metalanguage.

metalinguistics -- an area of linguistics concerned with
the interrelationship of the structure and meaning of the
language of a society and other aspects of its culture, such
as its social system.

metanarration -- (or meta-discourse) -- "the narrator's
commentary on the narrative" (< Hendricks).

metaphor -- in common usage it means the "substitution of
one signifier for another", but structuralists make a finer
distinction in that this substitution for them must be based
on a likeness or *analogy* between the original signifier and
its replacement, e.g. den or burrow for hut (see *metonymy*
below with which it is often contrasted).

metaphoric pole (or axis) -- the relations of similarity and substitution.

metonymic pole (or axis) -- the relations of contiguity and connection.

metonymy -- in common usage it means "the displacement of one signifier by another" but (as for *metaphor* above) structuralists again make a finer distinction. For them metonymy is a substitution based on a cause-effect, whole-part, or "things found together in the same context" relationship, e.g. poverty for hut, hut for thatch, or hut for peasant.

mimesis -- (μίμησις) -- this term from Aristotle usually means "the ability of discourse to state what it is". According to Ricoeur, however, mimesis does not mean the duplication of reality but *poesis* or "the fabrication, construction, and creation of reality" (< Ricoeur). (For a discussion see S. Morawski, "Mimesis", *Semiotica* 2 [1, 1970], 35-58).

modal statements -- (see p. 18 above).

mode -- the way in which the narrator reveals the story to the reader.

model -- not to be equated in any way with a structure, a model is an image (or representation) of a given object (or a common image of several objects), built or constructed to reproduce the relations between the parts of this object and to foresee transformational correlations (< G. Genot). It is perhaps not inaccurate to compare the structuralist's use of models with the use of models by the physical sciences, e.g. in organic chemistry or nuclear physics. Models are constructed whenever the analyst is dealing with an object or objects which the analyst cannot physically manipulate because of their size, complexity, etc. This does not mean that these objects do not have a real physical existence.

The Modistae -- a group of speculative grammarians who worked during the 13th and 14th centuries and are often cited by contemporary structuralists.

morpheme -- the smallest lexical unit of a language, such as a word, root, affix, or inflectional ending.

morphogenesis -- the ability of highly complex, goal-seeking adaptive systems, e.g. social systems, to change their structure and to elaborate new structures.

morphology -- "a description of the tale according to its component parts and the relationship of these components to each other and to the whole" (< Propp, *Morphology of the Folktale*, 2nd ed., 19). The paradigm for Propp's morphology is botany and not linguistics. (See also p. 5 above.)

motif -- "the smallest element in a tale having a power to persist in tradition" (< Stith Thompson). Structuralists rarely use this term (although Dundes [among others] modified and resurrected it) since Propp argued that like the genre it too was imprecise. According to Dundes, "the motif is used only as an etic unit like the phone or morph. The same motif may be used in different motifemes and different motifs may be used in the same motifeme."

motifeme -- this term from Dundes is roughly equivalent to Propp's "function".

move -- According to Propp, a "move" is the series of functions which begins with a villainy or lack, includes some intermediary functions, and concludes with a marriage. There may be more than one move in a narrative, i.e. Propp's functions are recursive (see below). That is to say, after a first resolution new complications can arise which are followed by positive or negative resolutions, etc. Each of these complications → resolutions constitutes one move. Narratives with more than one move are called complex or compound narratives. Lévi-Strauss, however, does not like the term "move" and prefers the French term *partie* with the sense of both a "part" and a "game of cards".

myth -- "a myth is a narrated story, but from the moment that it is perceived as a myth it is a story without an author. The audience listening to the telling of the myth is receiving a message that, properly speaking, comes from nowhere. This is why the myth will be said to have a supernatural origin" (< Lévi-Strauss). There are of course many different definitions for the term "myth". However, Lévi-Strauss is the foremost analyst of myths in structuralist thought, so his definition is given.

mythemes -- this term was coined by Lévi-Strauss for the large constituent units of myths which he discovered. Mythemes are composed of "bundles of relationships" which are paradigmatic and each of which concerns a specific subject. Daniel Patte defines mythemes as "binary oppositions of complex semantic units".

mythos (μῦθος) -- not to be confused with the genre "myth",
"mythos" as used in structuralist works most often refers
to Aristotle's rhetorical usage where mythos means "plot"
or more precisely the juxtaposition of events which is the
"basis" and "soul" of tragedy; or sometimes the *units* that
compose the plot.

narrative logic -- the narrative logic "is nothing else
but the development of the Aristotelian concept of the
probable, i.e. general opinion, and not scientific proof"
(< Barthes).

narrative statement -- this is *not* in any way to be considered a sentence since a sentence is *not* a narrative unit.
(The French word for "statement" in this case is *énoncé* and
there is a special symbol for a narrative statement: EN.)
The term "statement" is "a term quite independent of the
particular expressive medium (it includes dance statement,
linguistic statement, graphic statement, and so on)....
'Narrative statement' and 'to state narratively' are thus
meant as technical terms for any expression of a narrative
element independently of its manifesting substance. The
term is used in a broad discursive, not a grammatical sense;
for example, a narrative statement may be manifested by
questions or commands as well as by declarative constructions
in natural language" (< S. Chatman).

narrative structures -- these structures are not at all
to be confused with linguistic structures (although the two
are related, see the definition of *levels* above). Greimas
writes:

1. Narrative structures are translinguistic because they are common to cultures with different natural languages [i.e. French, German, Greek, Hebrew, etc., e.g. the narrative structures for Russian folktales are valid for American Indian folktales].

2. Narrative structures are distinct from linguistic structures because they can be revealed by languages other than the natural languages [e.g. in cinema, dreams, etc.].

3. *Narrative structures are not to be confused with the so-called 'literary genres'* [e.g. the same narrative structure can be used in a novel, play, myth, etc. Italics added.].

4. Narrative structures, although they serve as an organizing principle of a great number of discourses, do not account for the economy of these discourses....

   a) Narrative structures are located at a deeper level than deep linguistic structures.

   b) While they are verifiable and/or apprehendable at the level of the natural languages, narrative structures enjoy a certain autonomy with regard to linguistic structures and are not to be confused with them.

(From A. J. Greimas, "Narrative Grammar: Units and Levels", *MLN* 86 [1971], 793-794.)

In other words, "The narrative structure starts where the textual structure ends. It does not presuppose a particular language because it operates on units larger than the sentence and is not correlated to a verse or prose form of the texture. The narrative structure can be compared to a kind of 'syntax' according to which the plot elements--which can be compared to a vocabulary--are arranged into tales" (< Heda Jason).

narratology -- the science of narratives or the structural analysis of chains of events.

narrator -- not to be confused with the author, the narrator is the one currently telling the story or the *persona* telling the poem. He is a demonstrable, recognizable entity immanent in the narrative itself. The narrator may be: (1) a real character, (2) an intrusive outside party, or (3) he may be absent.

narremes -- simply "narrative text elements".

"natural" story-time -- the time which follows the normal rules of the physical universe as opposed to a "flashback" for example.

nets -- "The relation between the form of a word and its meaning has been aptly compared with that between a *net* and the dry sand it is spread out on. One language puts the net this way and includes within one of its meshes a piece of sand that in another language, which puts its net that way, falls partly or wholly within an adjoining mesh." For example:

Referent	The English net	The Dutch net
seat in a park	seat	*bank*
financial institution	bank	
the edge of a river		*oever*
the edge of the sea		

Thus, "There are no two languages that put their 'word nets' in the same position. That is why *words* can never be 'faithfully' translated by other words: between word meanings of different languages there is never more than partial correspondence" (from B. Siertsema, "Language and World View", *The Bible Translator* 20 [1969], 9).

the observer's paradox -- "the aim of linguistic research in the community must be to find out how people talk when they are not being systematically observed; yet we can only obtain this data by systematic observation" (< W. Labov).

oicotypes -- (especially "structural oicotypes") -- the models according to which the tales and songs of a culture are built.

onamastic code -- "the code of proper names" (< Barthes).

operant -- "one who or that which operates, works, or exerts a force or influence" (< O.E.D.).

organicism -- the theory that life and living processes are the manifestation of an activity possible only because of the autonomous organization of the system rather than because of its individual components.

organigram -- "a stemma (or diagram) that enables one to grasp visually the various kinds of relationships that bind together members of a complex, hierarchically structured organization" (< Lionel Duisit).

paradigm -- "the speculative or analytic reconstruction of the pattern underlying a performance" (< W. G. Doty).

paradigmatic axis -- the vertical or synchronic axis of selections or substitutions. In opposition to the syntagmatic axis, the paradigmatic axis does not follow the linear time sequence of events as they are unfolded in a narrative but it is a second dimension, so to speak, which exists in narrative structures, e.g. the meaning of a word in a sentence is not only determined by the words in that sentence but also by words or some groups of words *not* in that sentence or text, e.g. other words that are related to it such as synonyms or antonyms, words that sound the same, or even words that have the same grammatical functions. (See also p. 9 above.)

paramentrium or **parametrical element** -- "an element which remains constant throughout a musical piece, e.g. the tempo" (< Ruwet).

parole -- simply defined, paroles are "individual utterances" or statements made by individuals (< R. Scholes). (See also *langue* above.)

performance -- this term is parallel to Saussure's concept of *parole* and is defined as the effective use of language in concrete situations depending not only on competence but also on a whole series of other extralinguistic factors. If on the level of competence we speak correct or grammatical sentences, we find the concept of acceptability on the level of performance. The acceptability of a sentence not only depends on its grammaticality but also on the situation or context in which it is spoken. When one says, "But I was only joking", a violation of the laws of performance has occurred. Performance can also be defined as "the selection and execution of the rules [of language]" (< W. Labov) or simply the use of language. In brief, it is the effective use of lan-

guage in concrete situations. (For a more extensive discussion see *competence* above.)

perlocutionary act -- "that which we say *by* speaking" or
the consequences of an utterance. For example, "when fear
is created from the fact that an order is given by someone
such as 'Close the door!'" (< Austin and Searle; example
from Ricoeur).

peripeteia -- (also spelled peripety) -- "a transition to
the opposite of events" (< Aristotle); or in more modern
usage, "a sudden reversal of a situation in a narrative".

pertinence -- "a principled decision to describe facts
from only one point of view, even to the exclusion of all
others" (< Barthes).

phatic function -- that which affirms, maintains or halts
communication or signs whose "function is to establish, pro-
long or interrupt communication, to verify whether or not
the circuit is still in operation", e.g. "Can you still hear
me?" (when said on the telephone) (< Jakobson); also the
function performed by the catalysts, i.e. that of "maintaining contact between [the] narrator and audience" (< Barthes).

philology -- the study of written records in order to set
up accurate texts and to determine their meaning, primarily
by etymological studies and the methods of classical literary
scholarship.

phenomenology (and structuralism) -- contrary to present
opinion among many English-speaking scholars, phenomenology

and structuralism are not synonymous nor even compatible.
The following statement by Paul Ricoeur (who is a phenomenologist and not strictly speaking a "structuralist") makes
this quite clear:

> This type of [structural linguistic] model,
> which we need not hesitate to call semio-
> logical...presents such a radical challenge
> to phenomenology that it may justly be said
> that phenomenology will not survive unless
> it can properly reply to this challenge....
> Phenomenology sees before it another adver-
> sary, namely, a science of signs, already
> established on the same territory and dealing
> apparently, at any rate, with the same objects
> and the same problems. ("New Developments in
> Phenomenology in France: The Phenomenology
> of Language", *Social Research* 34 [1967], 14-
> 15.)

Hence it is no wonder that Ricoeur, while attempting to
argue a compatibility between semiology (and structuralism)
and phenomenology wishes to reduce structuralism to a "somewhat diminutive role: *his version* of its 'proper' role makes
of it little more than a prologomenon to the really important
task--the phenomenological one." (Robert Magliola, "Parisian
Structuralism Confronts Phenomenology: The Ongoing Debate",
Language and Style 6 [4, 1973], 242.)

phonemics -- "the study of speech from the point of view
of native speakers and hearers of the language to which it
belongs" (< Saussure).

phonetics -- "the study of speech as a set of physical-
psychological events with correlated psychic events: phona-
tion, sound-waves, audition" (< Saussure).

historical phonetics -- "the study of the sound-changes which a language undergoes in the course of time" (< Saussure). Hence phonemics, phonetics, and historical phonetics correspond respectively to Saussure's *langue, parole,* and *diachrony.*

phonology -- the study of the sound system of a language; the historical study of the sound-changes that have taken place in a language; the phonetic or phonemic pattern of a language.

plot -- the chain of events in a story and the principle which knits them together; "how the reader becomes aware of what happened" or basically "the order of the appearance (of the events) in the work itself" (< Tomashevski). This term was contrasted by the Russian Formalist Shklovsky with *fabula* (see above).

plurivocity -- the fact that a text is open to several readings, constructions, meanings, or interpretations as opposed to a work which is "univocal" (or possesses only one meaning).

poesis -- means "fabrication, construction, or creation".

poetic or aesthetic function -- "the relation between the message and itself" (< Jakobson).

poetics -- "This discipline seeks the general principles that manifest themselves in particular works. Poetics should not be confused with a desire to see in particular works mere instances of some general laws. The poetic study of any particular work should lead to conclusions which complete

or modify the initial premises of the study. A mere hunt
for archetypes or any preestablished structural pattern is
not an exercise in poetics but a parody of it" (< R. Scholes).
The discipline has "two mutually related tasks: (1) the task
of developing well-defined and verifiable *discovery procedures*
for analyzing and classifying literary texts and their units;
(2) the task of constructing and testing (in analysis and
experiment) formal models of literary structures and of their
particular aspects" (< L. Dolezel). Until twenty years ago,
poetics was primarily concerned with analyzing lyric poetry.
However, attention has now turned to the structural analysis
of narratives. This is the time therefore to emphasize that
poetics is in no way restricted to the genre poetry, despite
its name. Instead there is a poetics for every conceivable
genre. This is even more apparent in the next definition:
"Poetics is a discipline which has the purpose of a description of the properties of literary discourse" (< Todorov);
and finally, poetics "has a twofold aim: on the one hand it
attempts to understand and describe poetic communication in
structural terms; on the other hand, it must be capable of
doing justice to the structural essence of any individual
poetic object" (< Greimas).

points of view (or "narrative viewpoints") -- Todorov has
isolated three possible points of view (French: *aspects*)
which an author may choose to utilize in creating a narrative.
However, it is only the narrator who actually expresses these
viewpoints. They are as follows:

    1. "The view from behind" (*la vision par derrière*) --
the omniscient point of view or the point of view of the
deity, i.e. the narrator knows everything that *has* and *will*
take place in the future. This "view" is usually expressed

300

with the narrator speaking with the first personal pronouns,
"I" or "we".

    2. "The view with" (*la vision avec*) -- a limited point
of view, i.e. the narrator knows *only* what his characters
know. It too is usually expressed with the first personal
pronouns.

    3. "The view from outside" (*la vision du dehors*) --
a "sub-competent" point of view, i.e. the narrator knows
less than his characters know. This third *aspect* is usually
expressed with the third personal pronouns, "he, she, it" and
"they".

polysemy -- "the trait that our words have more than one
signification when they are considered outside of their use
in a determinate context" (< Ricoeur).

posited content -- (see pp. 11; 22-23, n. 9 above).

post hoc -- something which follows *from* something else
(see *propter hoc* below).

pratique/praxis -- these two terms are often contrasted in
structural usage. The first may simply be translated as
"practice" or something that is done as a matter of fact as
opposed to *praxis* which is used by Sartre to mean "man's in-
volvement in conscious and purposeful actions" (< S. Chatman).
Aristotle also used the term *praxis* to mean "the imitation of
actions in the real world" (< Aristotle). Granger defines
praxis as "activity considered with its complex context and
in particular the social conditions which give its signification in an effectively lived world". The term also has a
special grammatical meaning: "the practice or exercise of a

technical subject or art, as distinct from the theory of it"
(< O.E.D.). Finally, H. M. Davidson defines *praxis* as "an
activity designed to modify a situation". [Ed. note: The
reader may find *praxis* used with any one of these meanings.]

proaïresis -- the ability rationally to determine the result of an action or "the ability to deliberate in advance
the result of an act and to choose from two possibilities
the one to be developed".

proairetic code -- "the code of actions in a story. These
actions are syntagmatic, i.e. they begin and end at different
points. They interlock and overlap in a story but in classical texts they are all completed at the end" (< Scholes paraphrasing Barthes).

proairetism -- any narrative action involved in a coherent
and homogenous sequence.

problematic -- (in general) -- that which constitutes or
involves a problem, especially a philosophical problem; (of
a text) -- a special mode the text has of taking hold of its
subject.

projection (as a method of reading) -- "a way of reading
through literary texts in the direction of the author or of
society, or some other object of interest to the critic, e.g.
Freudian or Marxist interpretation" (< Todorov and Scholes).

propter hoc -- something which follows *after* something else
(see *post hoc* above).

protocol -- "the official formulas used at the beginning and end of a charter, papal bull, or other similar [literary] instrument, as distinct from the *text*, which contains its subject-matter." Its function is to tell the reader how it is to be read.

a "psychological" novel -- "a type of novel which is characterized by the fact that the characters 'exist' in it and absorb their actions with the slow-digestion of a boa-constrictor", e.g. *Les Liaisons dangereuses* (paraphrased from Todorov).

pure science -- a science restricted to abstract or theoretical problems.

rank -- (see p. 61 above).

reading (vs. projection) -- "Reading approaches the literary work as a system and seeks to clarify the relationships among its various parts. Reading differs from projection in two ways: it accepts the autonomy of the work as well as the particularity while projection accepts neither....Reading is a systematized commentary" (Scholes paraphrasing Todorov); also a *close reading* -- "a stylistic explanation of the text" (< Starobinsky).

reading-time -- (Fr. *temps de la lecture*) -- the time at which one reads the story as opposed to the time sequences within the story itself or the time when it was written.

receiver (of a narrative) -- "the real audience, e.g. a listener, reader, viewer, or whatever, *and the implied*

audience, even characters in the narrative may function as
its audience" (< Chatman).

recursive -- that which can be used over and over again,
especially "recursive rules which can be used over and over
again or an infinite number of times to produce sentences
or texts which are infinitely long, e.g. *One Thousand and
One Nights*" (< T. G. Pavel).

referent -- "an object which a sign refers back to" (< G.
Genot); "the relation between language and the reality
(whatever it may be) *about* which something is said in a
sequence of discourse" (< Ricoeur).

referential function -- that which defines the relations
between the message and the object to which it refers.

relations -- "properties of pairs, a relation is therefore
normally defined as a set of order pairs" (< Van Dijk).

relays (of language) -- the various alphabets of language
including both written alphabets and also morse, braille,
flag systems, deaf and dumb systems, even drum beats. It
also includes cryptographic codes of all kinds.

repetitive form -- "the consistent maintaining of a principle under new guises" or "the restatement of the same thing
in different ways" (< Burke).

rhetoric -- "In its most general meaning, the principles
governing the use of language for effective speaking and
writing. Classical theoreticians considered the study of

rhetoric essential for effective oratory. To this end, such writers as Aristotle, Quintilian, and Longinus codified the theories of rhetoric, which, along with logic and grammar, became, during the Middle Ages, one of the basic studies of the Trivium. (In the Middle Ages the seven liberal arts consisted of three studies--Latin grammar, logic, and rhetoric [including oratory]--called the Trivium, which led to the A.B. degree in four years; and the Quadrivium, consisting of four studies--arithmetic, geometry, astronomy, and music --which led to the M.A. degree in three years.)

The Greek Sophists at one time made rhetoric a tool for effective argumentation, regardless of the truth or validity of the viewpoint. Plato reported Socrates as saying that he thought rhetoric a superficial art, and in the dialogue *Protagoras* he reveals how the clever Sophist Protagorus argues with the aid of rhetorical devices. Because rhetoric may be used in such a manner, the term sometimes carries pejorative connotations" (< Beckson and Ganz).

Jewish and Christian scholars may be surprised to learn that both the Jewish rabbis and early Christians avidly practiced rhetoric (see G. M. Phillips, "The Practice of Rhetoric at the Talmudic Academies", *Speech Monographs* 26 [1959], 37-47 and W. A. Jennrich, "Classical Rhetoric in the New Testament", *The Classical Journal* 44 [1948/49], 30-32 for two brief introductions). In the past twenty years, interest in rhetoric has been revived when it was realized that research into linguistics "beyond-the-sentence" had not really progressed much beyond Aristotle! Aristotle had defined rhetoric as "the faculty of observing in any given case the available means of persuasion". However, the emphasis upon "persuasion" has now been abandoned and Roland Barthes now defines rhetoric simply as "the linguistics of discourse".

the **Saussurian Paradox** -- "the social aspect of language is studied by observing any one individual but the
individual aspect only by observing language in its social
context" (< W. Labov).

schema/usage -- this dichotomy is used by Louis Hjelmslev as parallel to Chomsky's competence/performance and
Saussure's *langue/parole*; schema also often bears the meaning "a chain of functions".

scientific explanation -- a scientific explanation
"consists not in moving from the complex to the simple but
in the replacement of a less intelligible complexity by one
which is more so" (< Lévi-Strauss).

semantic code -- "The semantic code makes possible the
linguistic creation of objects, atmosphere and character.
Here, for example, Barthes puts the proper name in historical perspective and compares it to a magnetic field, whereby
a configuration of semantic traits receives at the same time
a body and a history" (< Guenthner).

"the semantic aspect" and **semantics** -- the first of
these terms is peculiar to Todorov and means "the themes or
subjects presented". The second term has a more general
usage and is defined as the "study of significations, and
notably of signs or symbols in relation to their referents"
(< G. Genot) or "a set of functions determining the purpose
to which language is put".

semes -- "a unit of the signifier" (< Barthes); semantic
components which constitute a taxonomy of a given semantic

universe; "pertinent significant features" (< Greimas); "a minimum element of meaning" (< G. Genot); "semantic features or semantic connotations" (< Dan Patte).

sememes -- the term possesses two meanings. There is a narrow meaning--"the meaning of a morpheme" and a wider meaning--"a significant unit of meaning" (both from Bloom-field); the term is almost always plural (see the definition of meaning above) and is defined most simply as "the various meanings of a word", "the meanings of a morpheme", or "a significant unit of meaning" (the last three definitions are from Greimas).

semic -- "that which deals with semes, notably with their relations, without semantic consideration of their practical regrouping in symbols" (< G. Genot).

a **semiologist** or **semiologue** -- one who practices semiological analysis.

semiology -- "as opposed to semantics (see above), [semi-ology] is the science or study of signs as signifiers; it does not ask *what* words mean but *how* they mean" (< Paul de Man); hence semiology is "the science of the system of signs; the theory according to which any system of anthropological behaviour can be considered and analyzed as a system of signs" (< G. Genot).

semiosis -- "the process in which something functions as a sign." It has three (or four) factors:
    (1) *the sign vehicle* -- that which acts as a sign
                                 (or the "mediator")

(2) *the designatum* -- that which the sign refers to
(or what is taken account of)

(3) *the interpretant* -- that effect on some interpreter
in virtue of which the thing in
question is a sign to that interpreter

(4) *the interpreter* -- the agent of the process.

Finally, when "that which is referred to actually exists,
the object of reference is a *denotatum*" (< Charles Morris).

semiotics -- Greimas distinguishes semiotics and semiology
as follows: "One could reserve the term *semiotics* alone to
the sciences of expression [*sciences de l'expression*] and use
the remaining term *semiology* for the disciplines of the content" (*Du sens*, 33); hence semiotics can be defined as: "a
praxis inscribed inside semiological theory (e.g. literary
semiotics); as an adjective *semiotic* -- "having to do with
the production of a sense" (< G. Genot).

sender (of a narrative) -- is "a composite of the real
author, the implied author, and the narrator (if any)"
(< S. Chatman).

sense -- the functional value of an element in a system,
particularly that which it receives from its integration in
a unity of a higher level (theoretically defined).

sentence link -- "the part of a sentence which, in addition to having a function within the sentence, serves to
relate the sentence to another" (< Eugene E. Loos).

sequences -- (see *elementary sequences* and p. 48 above) --
"a syntagmatic pattern or an organized succession of clauses"
(< Todorov).

shifters -- "those parts of speech through which the individual accedes to language, the two best examples of this being proper nouns and personal pronouns" (< Barthes).

sign -- there are several meanings of which these may be the most important: "that which replaces something for someone" or a piece of experience referring back to another piece of experience; here considered as a purely transitive and unanalyzable entity (in which what dominates is reference and combinability) (< C. S. Pierce) or "a piece of experience referring back to another piece of experience" (< Granger); for Saussure *the "sign" is the signifier plus the signified* (see his *Course in General Linguistics* and *signifier/signified* below).

signa translata -- "transposed signs".

significations -- having a meaning; conventionally the word is always in the plural for structuralists since they dispute the notion that anything can have a single meaning. Signification is a reference back to what escapes a certain evident structuring, in an experience or the virtual sum of the senses that are possible for a symbol; a sum which is historically cumulative.

signifier/signified -- these two terms are theoretically inseparable. The signifier is a "concept", since Saussure is totally opposed to using the term "symbol" for the term concept because the relationship between the signifier/ signified is totally arbitrary, i.e. meaning is *not* determined by etymology. "One characteristic of the symbol is that it is never wholly arbitrary; it is not empty...., e.g.

the symbol of justice, a pair of scales, could not be replaced by just any other symbol, such as a chariot." The
signified is the "sound-image" created by the appearance
of the "concept". Signifier/signified may be compared to
two sides of the same coin, e.g. signifier: "tree"/
signified: 🌳 . These two terms are sometimes symbolized
--S/s. (The French terms are *signifiant/signifié* respectively.) What may be interesting to biblical scholars is
that these terms probably originated from St. Augustine's
signans/signatum! (For a more detailed discussion see
Saussure, *Course in General Linguistics*.)

simulacrum -- according to Derrida this term is undefinable,
which is not surprising since almost all of Derrida's terms
(according to him) are undefinable. However, it may perhaps
be defined as "a 'false' verbal, nominal, semantic property",
that "which no longer allows itself to be comprehended within the [binary] philosophical opposition and which, however,
inhabits it, resists it, disorganizes it but *without ever*
constituting a third term, without ever giving way to a
solution in the form of a speculative dialectic" (< Derrida).
With regards to texts, it seems to mean an "undecidable text",
a "false form". (For the only article [in English] in which
this term is discussed in detail and where Derrida himself
explains what it means, see Derrida, "Positions", *Diacritics*
2 [4, 1972], 35-43.)

situation -- "the body of nonassociated linguistic facts"
(< Halliday); "the body of facts known by the receiver at
the moment of the semic act and independently of this act"
(< Prieto); "the interrelationship at any given moment of
characters, either in terms of mutual interest or of opposition" (< Hendricks).

sociolinguistics -- "the ethnography of speaking" or another
term for that discipline which is based on the relationships
between the disciplines of sociology or anthropology and linguistics. For an extensive discussion see: Dell Hymes, "The
Ethnography of Speaking" in *Readings in the Sociology of
Language*, ed. Joshua A. Fischman. The Hague: Mouton and
Co., 1968. (See also the term *performance* above.)

spatial structure -- the paradigmatic relationship that
creates "a static array of characters who repeat their
identity throughout the story" (< Hendricks).

spatialization -- "the act of making spatial or investing
with spatial qualities" (< O.E.D.).

Sprachgefühl -- a German term synonymous with Chomsky's
competence, it means the authority and ability to judge the
correctness or incorrectness of linguistic forms.

stasis statements -- statements in the mode of "is" or
stated only as the existence of a set of things; in short,
statements which merely state the existence of something or
someone (most frequently with the verb "to be" or its synonyms) as opposed to process statements which express an
action taking place, e.g. someone who "does" something or
something which "happens".

a state -- a set of objects characterized by a certain
number of properties and relations.

a state change -- a binary relation over states or a
situation where a change intuitively takes place.

a state description -- the set of sentences or propositions
which are true in a particular possible world at some point of
time.

story/discourse -- this is a very important distinction
made by Todorov. A *story* is a logic of actions plus a "syntax" or characters, the content, chain of events (actions
and happenings or the *"existents"* (= characters and settings); the underlying narrative structure. This is opposed
to the *discourse* which is the tenses, aspects [i.e. "points
of view"] and modes pertaining to narration; the expression
or the means by which the content is communicated; the set
of actual narrative "statements"; the concatenation of events
and circumstances or simply the way in which the narrative
structure is presented to the reader. In other words, there
are two levels of the story: (1) the "logic of the actions"
and (2) "the characters and their relationships". There are
three methods of telling a narrative in a discourse: the
presentation of (1) time, (2) aspects, and (3) modes of
narration. These two levels of the *story* correspond to
Barthes' *functions* and *actions* and the three methods of
discourse correspond to Barthes' third level of narration
(< G. Wienold). But it is Dan O. Via, Jr. who best expresses the difference between *story* and *discourse* when he
writes:

> Narrative exists as two levels or dimensions.
> As *story* it is [an] objective statement creating
> a world of events and persons who are real from
> the viewpoint of that created world. *Story* is
> characterized by such as the use of the third
> person, and the aorist and pluperfect tenses.
> As *discourse* narrative is subjective articula-
> tion, a word spoken by a narrator to a hearer.
> Discourse is characterized by such as the use

of "I" and "you", adverbs like "today", the present and future tenses, and evaluative statements.
The narrative may be story and discourse at the
same time with the discourse level being signified in various ways along the story line. On
the other hand, either story or discourse may be
a fairly discrete enclave within the other.

story-time -- the inner time of the content (i.e. time as
represented *in* the story). Story-time distinguishes narrative from other discursive structures.

stratum -- the structure in which man finds himself and is
constituted.

stricto sensu -- "strictly speaking".

structural analysis -- in the simplest terms, structural
analysis is determining what follows what and why. However,
Todorov has given perhaps the best description of literary
structural analysis when he writes:

> If we contrast the internal approach to a
> literary work with the external one, structural
> analysis would represent an internal approach....
> For example, when Marxists or psychoanalysts deal
> with a work of literature, they are not interested
> in a knowledge of the work itself; but in the
> understanding of an abstract structure, social or
> psychic, which manifests itself through that work.
> This attitude is therefore...external. On the
> other hand, a New Critic...whose approach is ob-
> viously internal, will have no goal other than an
> understanding of the work itself; the result of
> his efforts will be a paraphrase of the work,
> which is supposed to reveal the meaning better
> than the work itself.
> Structural analysis differs from both of
> these attitudes. Here we can be satisfied
> neither by a pure description of the work nor

by its interpretation in terms that are psychological or sociological or, indeed, philosophical.
In other words, structural analysis coincides (in
its basic tenets) with theory, with poetics of
literature, literature that is virtual rather
than real. Such analysis seeks no longer to
articulate a paraphrase, a rational resumé of
the concrete work, but to propose a theory of
the structure and operation of the literary discourse, to present a spectrum of literary possibilities, in such a manner that the existing
works of literature appear as particular instances that have been realized.
    It must immediately be added that, in prac-
tice, structural analysis will also refer to
real works: the best stepping-stone toward
theory is that of precise, empirical knowledge.
But such analysis will discover in each work
what it has in common with others (study of
genres, of periods, for example), or even with
all other works (theory of literature); it would
be unable to state the individual specificity of
each work. In practice it is always a question
of going continually back and forth, from abstract literary properties to individual works
and vice versa. Poetics and description are in
fact two complementary activities.
(T. Todorov, "Structural Analysis of Narrative"
in *Modern Literary Criticism*, ed. Lipking and
Litz, 436-437 (also printed in *Novel: A Forum
on Fiction* 3 [1, 1969], 70-76.)

structural change -- (see p. 62 above).

structural description -- a determination of the component parts and especially the relation of the parts to one
another.

structural linguistics -- structural linguistics has two
common characteristics which differentiate it from other linguistic schools: there is a (1) "divergence from the Neo-
grammarian methods which tended to the psychologization and

atomization of linguistic reality; and (2) a tendency to establish linguistics, looked upon by the older school as a conglomerate of psychology, physiology, sociology and other disciplines, as an independent science based on the concept of linguistic sign." Presently there are three trends or "schools" of structural linguistics: (1) *functional linguistics*--or the linguistics of the Prague School; (2) *glossematics*--Hjelmslevian linguistics; (3) *descriptive linguistics*--the Bloomfieldian linguistics (< B. Trnka).

structuralism -- in simplest terms, structuralism is the application of principles derived from certain movements within linguistics to other means of discourse. Structuralism is definitely *not* a philosophy (see Ino Rossi, "Structuralism as Scientific Method" in his *The Unconscious in Culture*, pp. 60-100, esp. p. 63ff.). Some scholars primarily consider it to be a method, but others dispute this. Perhaps one of the best definitions is given as follows: "[Structuralism is] neither a theory nor a method; it is an epistemological point of view. It starts out from the observation that every concept in a given system is determined by all other concepts of that system and has no significance by itself alone; it does not become unequivocal [i.e. univocal] until it is integrated into the system, the structure, of which it forms a part and in which it has a definite place." (< Paul Garvin, [ed.], *A Prague School Reader on Esthetics, Literary Structure, and Style*, Washington: Georgetown Univ. Press, 1969, vi.) (See also the definitions of *structure* below.)

structuration -- that which is organized or incorporated into a structure.

.

structure -- each structuralist seems to have his own
preferred definition of the term "structure". We will give
four that appear to be the most popular: "the internal
arrangement of the units of a system" or "a whole formed
of mutually dependent elements such that each depends on
the others and can only be what it is by its relationship
with them" (< Benveniste); "It is scientifically permissable
to describe language as being essentially an independent entity consisting of internal dependencies in brief, a structure" (< Hjelmslev quoted by Benveniste); "those regulari-
ties which make it happen in a set that the transformation
of one element necessarily causes certain complementary
transformations of the other elements" (< L. Goldmann).
Here are two somewhat shorter ones: "what follows what and
why" (< Burke) and "systematicity of a system" (< G. Genot).

structure and form (similarities and differences) --
"Structure is a version of 'form' provided that 'form' is
not understood as an external shape or appearance but as an
order determining the meaning and position of its components.
Structure is a scheme of relations between components and
events" (< C. S. Pierce).

"structure of a system" -- the first usage of the term
"structure" was as the "structure of a system" in 1928. At
that time the term structure "designated an aspect of the
total system, the sum of articulatory and semantic combinations drawn from the possibilities inherent to the system"
(< Roger Lapointe).

style -- an (expressive, affective, or aesthetic) emphasis
added to the information conveyed by the linguistic structure,

without alteration of meaning; "the aspect of the [literary]
work that makes it a unique configuration" (< Ricoeur).

stylistics (or stylolinguistics) -- "a mediation on human
works...its task is to investigate the most general conditions
of the insertion of structures into an individual practice"
(< G. G. Granger); "the study of the relations or the covaria-
tion between language structure and literary structure (< Hendricks); "the theory devoted to the general conditions ruling
the insertion of structure into an individual practice (<
Ricoeur); "the study of all those relations among linguistic
entities which are statable, or may be statable, in terms of
wider spans than those which fall within the limits of the
sentence" (< A. A. Hill).

superposition -- "the way of locating and analyzing relationships between one text and another" (< Scholes paraphrasing
Todorov).

supra-sentential -- means simply "beyond-the-sentence"
(see above).

survivals -- an anthropological term which means the per-
sistence in a society of customs and beliefs originating under
circumstances not fully understood or no longer valid (a
"functionalist" would say they are no longer "functional");
or "the shadowy remnants of ancient religious rites still incorporated in the lives of illiterates and rustics or a lively
fossil which refuses to die". Almost all anthropologists today
(including Lévi-Strauss) deny that "survivals" exist, but Propp
thought otherwise.

syllogistic progression -- "given certain things, certain things must follow, the premises forcing the conclusions"
(< R. W. Stallmann). Propp's functions possess a certain
syllogistic progression or syllogism.

symbol -- some have erroneously equated this term with Saussure's signifier (see above). A symbol is a piece of experience or the objective counterpart of a piece of experience
which is capable of representing either another experience,
or a semic construction; it tends to conserve part of its in-
dividuality (in intransitivity, or opacity); its sense does
not entirely cancel out its significations. Each symbol is
analyzable into parts themselves capable of acceding to the
status of another symbol. The symbol "acts chiefly by im-
puted, learned contiguity between the signans [signifier]
and signatum [signified]", e.g. the letter "p" is a symbol
of the sound "p"; the word "cat" is a symbol of the animal.
(< Jakobson citing C. S. Pierce in "Quest for the Essence
of Language", *Diogenes* 51 [1965], 21-37.) Pierce's symbol
is approximately the same as the "conventional sign" of the
Scholastics.

symbolic field -- what is usually called "theme" in English literary criticism, i.e. "the idea or ideas around
which a work is constructed" (< Scholes citing Barthes).

synchronic order -- "an order in which the meaning of
any moment is inherent in the present: it is co-extensive
with the relationship of all the existing data to each
other. Thus, at any move, a game of chess is always comprehensible without reference to any of the previous moves"
(< Saussure, cf. *diachronic* above).

318

synonymy -- the identity of meanings.

synonymity (in language) -- "when two or more sentences which differ in their surface structures have the same under-lying deep structure" (< Hendricks).

the syntactic aspect -- "the logical, temporal, and spatial relations among the parts of a work" (< Todorov).

narrative syntagma -- "the isolated fragment of [a] text containing one or another action (and, therefore, the corre-sponding function)" (< E. Meletinsky).

syntagmatic axis -- (cf. *paradigmatic axis* above) -- the axis of combination or concatenations. The syntagmatic axis is equivalent to the horizontal, linear, temporal, or dia-chronic unfolding of events in the narrative. The method of Propp has been described as "syntagmatic" as opposed to that of Lévi-Strauss which is "paradigmatic". (Greimas and other structuralists use both axes.) (See also p. 9 above.)

syntagmatic indicator -- (see p. 61 above).

syntagmatic substitution -- "a substitution relation where one expression, a so-called 'substituendum' is refer-entially resumed by a--normally--subsequent expression termed a 'substituens'." The complementary term is "paradigmatic substitution" (< Roland Harweg).

syntagme -- the chronological sequence of elements in a performance.

syntax -- "the analysis of the sentence into its constituent relationships, e.g. subject-predicate, etc." (< B. Trnka).

system -- a collective assemblage constructed out of "units which are mutually conditioned" (mutual conditionment ≃ structure) (< Benveniste).

taxis -- one of the three main divisions of rhetoric (along with *heuresis*, the discovery of arguments, and *lexis*, diction and style) which means "composition".

temporal structure -- the syntagmatic relationship that creates "the dynamic aspect of a story" in which the characters interact in "conflictual situations which are built up and then resolved" (< Hendricks).

text -- "a production of significance and not at all...a philological object" (< Barthes). T. G. Pavel gives two definitions: (1) "any sequence of sentences having a certain coherence"; (2) "any unchangeable sequence of sentences which have a strong cohesion and the unchangeable character of which is related to a value system of some sort".

textemes -- elementary structures which are to texts what lexemes are to elementary sentences, or "a formal unit of meaning larger than a word which belongs to the...deep structure or competence which generates genres and texts" (< Dan O. Via, Jr.).

textual grammar -- (symbol: TG) -- the set of rules underlying the formation of *correct* texts (cf. *generative* *grammar* above); as the authority on answering the question of correctness, the linguistic competence, intuition, or *Sprachgefühl* of the ideal speaker decides. Therefore the task of a TG is the description of the intuition or *competence* of the ideal speaker to produce correct texts.

theologoumenon -- "a theological statement or utterance on theology as distinguished from an inspired doctrine or revelation" (< O.E.D.).

token -- the different objects of the class of objects forming a type (see below).

topical content -- (see pp. 22-23, n. 9 above).

topological -- the point of view according to which we consider the spatial relationships of the units in a system (e.g. succession, inversion, insertion, co-presence, etc.).

transduction -- reasoning from one particular to another particular.

transferential/referential -- transferential (as opposed to referential) "designates the construction of a text as the result of a system of internal rules, without any reference to an extra-text. Prepositions, conjunctions, shifters, etc. are to be considered as transferential morphemes" (< G. Genot).

transformation -- (see p. 62 above) -- a negation of the qualifications of the initial situation. The term is somewhat synonymous to our modern use of the term "evolution".

trope -- the definition of "trope" in ancient classical rhetoric differs from modern usage: *ancient usage*--a word used in a sense which it does not usually have; *modern usage*--a figure of speech, e.g. a metaphor, simile, hyperbole, personification, or metonymy.

type -- "a traditional tale that has an independent existence" (< Stith Thompson); "tales evidencing identical functions can be considered as belonging to one type" (< Propp). Van Dijk gives two definitions: (1) "an abstraction and as such related to a linguistic 'concept' denoting this abstraction. A type can be defined as a name of a class of objects that are considered 'identical' from a certain point of view"; (2) "a type is an abstraction from a class within a given universe of discourse and defined by the set of properties and/or a set of relations, which all members of the class satisfy" (< Van Dijk).

ungrammatical -- not acceptable to the intuition, the competence of the ideal speaker. (The noun form is ungrammaticality.)

unit -- "a utilitarian logical construct of measure which, though admittedly relativistic and arbitrary, permits greater facility in the examination and comparison of the materials studied in the natural and social sciences and abstractions of distinct entities which may be combined to form larger units or broken down into smaller units. There is an infinitude of units since they are man-made categorical attempts to describe the nature of objective reality. With a relativistic perspective, one can see that no matter

what unit one considers, other smaller sub-units may be
postulated" (< Dundes). Some of the most important units
that have been used in the past for structural analyses are
the following:

1. *type* (Aarne)
2. *function* (Propp)
3. *motif* (Thompson)
4. *mytheme* (Lévi-Strauss)
5. *motifeme* (Dundes).

a minimal unit -- the smallest unit useful for a given
analysis.

univocal (or the noun form "univocation") -- literally "one
voice", i.e. the reduction of meanings to a single meaning.

the verbal aspect -- "the style, or resonances of language
in the work" (< Todorov).

the writing-time -- the time at which the author wrote
(*temps de l'écriture*).

zeugma -- the use of a word to modify or govern two or more
words usually in such a manner that it applies to each in a
different sense or makes sense with only one.

Zussamenhänge -- the structure or "principle of solidarity"
between the parts (< Barthes).

SELECTED BIBLIOGRAPHY

We have only cited the fundamental (and still sparse)
works here which are devoted to the task of establishing a
semiology of the narrative structures (and not of the narrative itself). This choice is naturally inadequate and lacks
much of the research in process. Thus the works of those
semiologists in the U.S.S.R. (at the research center in
Tartu) are only beginning to become known, and they remain
difficult for us to obtain.

We thought it would be good to include some "actual"
works concerning the analysis of narrative structures which
poses the problem of its articulation with that of the discursive structures (the position of the narrator, enunciation, etc.).

Finally, the reader who is not a biblical scholar will
find some references here to the classical works on the
criticism of biblical texts which has been compiled by
Michel de Certeau.

Claude Chabrol

For the benefit of English readers of this translation,
I have attempted to find and cite as many of the available
English translations of these works as possible. Those de-

siring a more extensive bibliography should refer to my
earlier translation of R. Barthes *et al.*, *Structural Analysis and Biblical Exegesis* (Pittsburgh: Pickwick Press, 1974),
110-164, where they will find a quite extensive bibliography
of some 600 books and articles. This bibliography is now
somewhat out of date due to the flood of English books and
articles which have appeared since 1974. Therefore it would
be wise to combine this bibliography with one compiled by
John Dominic Crossan in volume I of the journal *Semeia*. In
a volume to follow (*Structuralism and Biblical Hermeneutics*),
I plan to expand and update my first bibliography giving
those works which I initially overlooked and those which have
subsequently appeared. The annotations which follow contain
Chabrol's and Certeau's comments as well as some of my own
concerning the English equivalents. My comments appear in
brackets to differentiate them from Chabrol's and Certeau's.

Alfred M. Johnson, Jr.
April 1, 1976

Claude Chabrol's Bibliography

1. Austin, J. L. *How to Think with Words*. New York: Oxford University Press, 1962. French trans.: *Quand dire, c'est faire*. Paris: Seuil, 1970.

2. Bakhtin, Mikhail. *Problems of Dostoevsky's Poetics*. Ann Arbor, Michigan: Ardis, 1973. French trans.: *La Poétique de Dostoïevski*. Paris: Seuil, 1970 (trans. from the Russian 1st ed., Moscow, 1929).

3. Barthes, Roland. "An Introduction to the Structural Analysis of Narrative." *New Literary History* 6 (2, 1975), 237-272. French original: "Introduction à l'analyse structurale des récits," *Communications* 8 (1966), 1-27.

4. _____. "L'analyse structurale du récit: Actes 10 et 11." *Recherches de Sciences religieuses* 58 (1970), 17-38. [An English translation of this article will appear in *Structuralism and Biblical Hermeneutics*, Pittsburgh: Pickwick Press, forthcoming.]

5. Bédier, J. *Les Fabliaux*. Paris: H. Champion, 1893.

6. Benveniste, Emile. *Problems in General Linguistics*. Coral Gables: University of Miami, 1971. French original: *Problèmes de linguistique générale*. Paris: Gallimard, 1966.

7. Booth, Wayne C. *The Rhetoric of Fiction*. Chicago: University of Chicago Press, 1961. New ed. 1966.

8. Bremond, Claude. "Le message narratif." *Communications* 4 (1964), 4-32. [An English translation of this article has been prepared by myself and is scheduled for publication in *Semeia* vol. 9 (or 10), forthcoming.]

9. _____. "La logique des possibles narratifs." *Communications* 8 (1966), 60-76.

10. _____. "Combinaisons syntaxiques entre fonctions et séquences narratives," in *Sign-Language-Culture*. Ed. A. J. Greimas *et al.* Janua Linguarum. Series Maior 1. The Hague: Mouton, 1970, 585-590. Originally presented at the international semiological conference at Kazimierz, Poland, 1966.

11. Chabrol, Claude. *Le Récit feminin*. The Hague: Mouton, 1971.

12. Dubois, J. "Énoncé et énonciation," *Langages* 13 (1969), 100-110.

13. Ducrot, O. "La notion de présupposition et la classification sémantique des énoncés Français," *L'Homme* 8 (1, 1968), 37-53.

14. _____. "Présupposés et sous-entendus." *Langue Française* 4 (1969), 30-43.

15. Dumézil, G. *Mythe et Épopée*. Paris: Gallimard, 1968.

16. Dundes, Alan. *The Morphology of North American Indian Folktales*. F F Communications No. 195. Helsinki: Suomalainen Tiedeakatemia, 1964.

17. _____. "The Binary Structure of 'Unsuccessful Repetition' in Lithuanian Folktales." *Western Folklore* 21 (1962), 165-174.

18. Dundes, A.; E. R. Leach; P. Maranda; D. Maybury-Lewis. "An Experiment" in *Structural Analysis of Oral Tradition*, eds. P. and E. Maranda. Philadelphia: University of Pennsylvania Press, 1971, 292-324.

19. _____. "Présupposés et sous-entendus." *Langue française* 4 (1969), [Erroneous?, see no. 14 above.]

20. Genette, Gérand. *Figures I*. Paris: Seuil, 1966.

21. _____. *Figures II* and *Figures III*. Paris: Seuil, 1969/1972.

22. Greimas, A. J. *Sémantique structurale*. Paris: Larousse, 1966. (See also, "Le conte populaire russe [analyse functionelle]." *International Journal of Slavic Linguistics and Poetics* 9 [1965], 152-175.)

23. _____. *Du sens*. Paris: Seuil, 1970. (See also *idem*, "Éléments d'une grammaire narrative." *L'Homme* 9 [3, 1969], 71-92 and *idem*, "Éléments pour une théorie de l'interprétation du récit mythique." *Communications* 8 [1966], 28-59. [Reprinted in French in W. A. Koch, *Strukturelle Textanalyse*, 115-146. An English trans. of the latter appears with the title: "The Interpretation of Myth: Theory and Practice," in *Structural Analysis of Oral Tradition*, eds. P. Maranda and E. K. Maranda. Philadelphia: University of Pennsylvania, 1971, 81-121.])

24. Harris, Z. S. *Discourse Analysis Reprints*. The Hague: Mouton, 1963. [The original articles were: *idem*, "Discourse Analysis," *Language* 28 (1952), 1-30 and "Discourse Analysis: A Sample Text," *Language* 28 (1952), 474-494. The first article has also been reprinted in *The Structure of Language: Studies in the Philosophy of Language*, eds. J. A. Fodor and J. J. Katz. Englewood Cliffs: Prentice Hall, 1964, 355-383.]

25. Jakobson, Roman. "On Russian Fairy Tales" in *Russian Fairy Tales*, ed. A. N. Afanas'ev. New York: Pantheon, 1945. Reprinted in *idem, Selected Writings*, IV. The Hague: Mouton, 1966, 90-91 [and Michael Lane, *Introduction to Structuralism*. New York: Basic Books, 1970, 184-201.]

26. Köngäs, E. K. and P. Maranda. "Structural Models in Folklore." *Midwest Folklore* 12 (1962), 133-192.

27. Leach, E. R. *Rethinking Anthropology*. London: Athlone Press, 1960. 2nd ed. 1966. French trans.: *Critique de l'anthropologie*. Paris: P.U.F., 1968.

28. _____. "Lévi-Strauss in the Garden of Eden." *Transactions of the New York Academy of Science* 23 (4, 1961), 386-396.

29. _____. *The Structural Study of Myth and Totemism*. London: Tavistock Publications, Ltd., 1967.

30. _____. "The Legitimacy of Solomon." *European Journal of Sociology* 7 (1966), 58-101. [Reprinted in his *Genesis as Myth*. London: Jonathan Cape, 1969, 25-83.]

31. Lévi-Strauss, Claude. "La structure et la forme, réflexions sur un ouvrage de Propp." *Cahiers de l'institute de science économique appliquée* 99 (7, 1960), 3-36. [The same article has been reprinted with the title: "L'Analyse morphologiques des contes russes". *International Journal of Slavic Linguistics and Poetics* 3 (1960), 122-149. An English translation of this article by the editor of this work is scheduled for publication in vol. 9 (or 10) of *Semeia*.]

32. _____. "The Structural Study of Myth." *Journal of American Folklore* 68 (1955), 428-444. Reprinted in his *Structural Anthropology*. Paperback ed. Garden City: Anchor Books, 1967, 202-228.

33. _____. *Mythologiques*. Vols. I-III. Paris: Plon, 1964-1968. [Vols. I and II of this series have been translated into English as follows: Vol. I: *The Raw and the Cooked*, trans. John and Doreen Weightman. New York: Harper Torchbooks, 1970; Vol. II: *From Honey to Ashes*. Trans. *idem*. New York: Harper & Row, 1973. A translation of vol. III is apparently forthcoming.]

34. *Théorie de la Littérature*, comp. T. Todorov. Paris: Seuil, 1965. [This work is one of the major primary sources for the writings of the Russian Formalists. Sections of it have been translated into English in a variety of sources. The two major English sources for these articles are: Lee T. Lemon and Marian J. Reis (eds. and trans.) *Russian Formalist Criticism: Four Essays*. Lincoln: Univ. of Nebraska Press, 1965. And Ladislav Matejka and Krystyna (eds.). *Readings in Russian Poetics: Formalist and Structuralist Views*. Cambridge, Mass.: M.I.T. Press, 1971.]

35. Maranda, E. *What Does a Myth Tell about Society?* Cambridge, Mass.: Radcliffe Institute Seminars, 1966.

36. Marin, Louis. "Essai d'analyse structurale d'Actes 10-1 à 11-18." *Recherches de sciences religieuses* 58 (1970), 39-62. [An English translation of this article will appear in *Structuralism and Biblical Hermeneutics*.]

37. Meletinski, E. M. "O strukturno-morfologicheskom analize skazki" in *Tezisy dokladov vo vtoroj letnej skole po vtoritchnym modelirujuchkim sistemam*, 37.

38. _____ and S. J. O. Nekliudov, E. S. Nobik, and O. M. Segal. "K postrojeniju modeli volchebnoy skazki." Tartu (U.S.S.R.), 1968, 165-177.

39. _____. "Problemy strukturno opisanija volchebnoy skazki" in *Trudy po Znakovym sisteman*, Tartu (U.S.S.R.), 1969, 86-135.

40. Nikiforov, A. I. "K voprosu o morfologicheskom izucheniju narodnoj skazki" in *sbornik statej tchest' akademika A. I. Sobolevskogo*. Leningrad, 1928, 172-178.

41. Pop, M. "Aspects actuels des recherches sur la structure des contes." *Fabula 9* (1967), 70-77.

42. _____. "Der formelhafte Charakter der Volksdichtung." *Deutsches Jahrbuch in Volkskunde* 14 (1968), 1-15.

43. Propp, Vladimir. *The Morphology of the Folktale*. Trans. Lawrence Scott, ed. Svatava Pirkova-Jakobson. Publication Ten, Oct. 1958 also Part III of *International Journal of American Linguistics* 24 (4, 1958). Bloomington: Indiana Univ. Research Center, 1958. 2nd ed. Austin: Univ. of Texas Press, 1968. Russian original: *Morfologija skazki*. Leningrad: Akedemia, 1928. 2nd ed. Leningrad: Nauka, 1969. French trans.: *Morphologie du conte*. Paris: Seuil, 1970. [An English translation is also available of the excellent introduction to the second Russian edition of Propp's book by Eleasar M. Meletinsky, "Structural-Typological Study of the Folktale," *Genre* 4 (1971), 249-279. It is perhaps the best brief introduction to structural analysis of the narrative now available to the English reader.]

44. _____. "Fairy Tale Transformations" in *Readings in Russian Poetics: Formalist and Structuralist Views*. Eds. L. Matejka and K. Pomorska. Cambridge, Mass.: M.I.T. Press, 1971, 94-115. [An abridged trans. entitled "Transformations in Fairy Tales" also appears in *Mythology*, ed. P. Maranda. Baltimore: Penguin Books, 1972, 139-150.] Russian original: *Poetika vremennik oidela slovesnykk iskusstv* IV (1928), 70-89. The French trans. appears in *Théorie de la littérature*. (comp.) T. Todorov. Paris: Seuil, 1966.

45. Sebeok, T. A. "Toward a Statistical Contingency Method in Folklore Research" in *Studies in Folklore*. Bloomington: Indiana Univ. Publications, 1957, 130-140.

46. _____.and P. J. Ingemann, "Structural and Content Analysis in Folklore Research" in *Studies in Cheremis: The Supernatural*, ed. T. A. Sebeok. New York: Viking Fund Publications, 1956, pp. 261-268.

47. Souriau, E. *Les Deux cent mille situations dramatiques*. Paris: Flammarion, 1950.

48. Todorov, T. *Grammaire du décaméron*. The Hague: Mouton & Co., 1969.

49. _____. "Les Catégories du récit littéraire." *Communications* 8 (1966), 125-151. [Reprinted with some changes in Todorov's *Littérature et signification*. Paris: Larousse, 1967 and unchanged in W. A. Koch (ed.), *Strukturelle Textanalyse/Discourse Analysis/Analyse du récit*. Hildesheim, N.Y.: Olms, 1972, 164-190.]

50. _____. *The Fantastic*. Trans. Richard Howard. Cleveland: Press of Case Western Reserve Univ., 1973. French original: *Introduction à la littérature fantastique*. Paris: Seuil, 1970.

51. _____. "Les transformations narratives." *Poétique* 3 (1970), 322-332.

52. V. Vjach, Ivanov and V. N. Toporov. "K rekonstrukcii praslavjanskogo teksta" in *Slavjanskoe jazykoznanie, V Mezdunarodnyj s'ezd slavistov. Doklady sovestskoj delegatsii*. Moscow; 1963, 88-158.

53. Voloshivo, V. "K istorii form vyskazyvanija v konstrukzijakh jazyka" in *Readings in Russian Poetics*. Michigan Slavic Materials 2 (1962), 67-98. [This should not be confused with the volume by the same title edited by L. Matejka and K. Pomorska.]

54. Vrabie, G. "Sur la technique de la narration dans le conte roumain" in *IV International Congress for Folk-Narrative Research in Athens*, 606-615.

55. Weinrich, V. *Tempus*. Stuttgart: W. Kohlkammer Verlag, 1964.

EXEGESIS AND NON-SEMIOLOGICAL NARRATIVE ANALYSIS

(Bibliography compiled by Michel de Certeau)

I. *Methodology:*

Barr, James. *The Semantics of Biblical Language.*
London: Oxford Univ. Press, 1961. French trans.:
Sémantique du langage biblique. Paris: Aubier,
1970. (In the name of a linguistic investigation,
J. Barr criticizes the theological presuppositions
which are based on an interpretation of the biblical language. By analyzing the semantic structures
of Hebrew and Greek, he attempts to state precisely
what the relationships are between language and
thought and what transformations of meaning are
created by the passage from one language to another.)

II. *"Formgeschichte"* and *"Redaktiongeschichte":*

Gunkel, Hermann. "Genesis" in *Handkommentar zum Alten
Testament.* Göttingen: Vandenhoeck & Ruprecht,
1901. 3rd ed., 1910. (The "Introduction" ["The
Legends of Genesis"] is the fundamental text of
Formgeschichte. It sets forth the analysis of the
narrative "structures" of Genesis by a comparison
with the *Sage* or the legend, i.e. "a narrative of
ancient folk and poetic tradition which deals with
characters or events of the past".) [The introduction has been translated into English with the
title: *The Legends of Genesis.* Trans. W. H.
Carruth. New York: Schocken, 1964.]

_____. "Die Grundprobleme der israelitischen
Literaturgeschichte." *Deutsche Literaturzeitung*
27 (1906), 1797-1800 and 1861-1866. (An expansion
of the problems and methods which are found in his
commentary on Genesis.)

Dibelius, M. *Die Formgeschichte des Evangeliums.*
Tübingen: J. C. B. Mohr, 1919. 2nd ed., 1933.
English trans.: *From Tradition to Gospel.* Trans.

B. L. Woolf. New York: Charles Scribner's Sons,
1934. (This study is supplemented by the article:
"Zur Formgeschichte der Evangelien." *Theologische
Rundschau* 1 (1929), 185-216. The former work is an
application of the method to the analysis of the
gospel narratives.)

Dupont, Jacques. *Les Béatitudes.* Vol. I. Paris, 1954.
2nd ed. 1969. (See the "Introduction", 9-40. This
is one of the rare French examples of the method.)

Muilenburg, J. "The Gains of Form Criticism in Old
Testament Studies." *Expository Times* 71 (1959-60),
229-233.

Koch, Klaus. *Was ist Formgeschichte?* Neukirchen-Vluyn:
Verlag des Erziehungsvereins, 1964. 2nd ed. 1967.
[The 1974 ed. of this work bears the title: *Was
ist Formgeschichte? Methoden der Bibelexegese.*
3rd ed. Neukirchen-Vluyn: Neukirchener, 1974.
This third edition has also added a 54 page epilogue
entitled "Linguistik und Formgeschichte" which attempts to defend form criticism against the German
"Generative Poetics School" under E. Güttgemanns.]
(The presentation by Koch is very clear and even
rather didactic.)

Rohde, Joachim. *Die Redaktiongeschichtliche Methode,
Einfuhrung und Sichtung der Forchingstandes.* Ham-
burg: Furche Verlag, 1966. (The book successively
analyzes the theories which have been worked out.)

Zimmermann, H. *Neutestamentliche Methodenlehre, Darstel-
lung der historisch. Kritisch. Methode.* Stuttgart, 1967. (This work is concerned more explicitly
with the New Testament and the relationship between
literary criticism and historical criticism.)

INDEX TO BIBLICAL REFERENCES

334

336

338